My Angel Leonora

Beethoven's Love for Antonie Brentano

By

Carter J. Gregory

authorHOUSE™

1663 LIBERTY DRIVE, SUITE 200
BLOOMINGTON, INDIANA 47403
(800) 839-8640
WWW.AUTHORHOUSE.COM

First published by AuthorHouse 07/14/05

ISBN: 1-4208-0232-1 (sc)
ISBN: 1-4208-0233-X (dj)

Library of Congress Control Number: 2004097341

Printed in the United States of America
Bloomington, Indiana

This book is printed on acid-free paper.

CREDITS

The author expresses his gratitude to Adrienne Ann Selle, who posed for the cover of this book.

Acknowledgment is made to Thomas Morgan, Photographer (front cover and author's cover).

For Adrienne

ACKNOWLEDGMENTS

To those of my friends who urged me to put down a fictional effort about the Chicago Cubs and Lupe the fortune teller (Lupe read in her cards that when the goatherd's curse expires in 2008, the Cubs will win the pennant and take on the Boston Red Sox in the World Series) and write about the great composer instead, I thank you and honor you for your wisdom and for prevailing against my stubborn nature. I am speaking of Roger Vernon, Harold Clay Piersall, Bob Hamlyn, "Happy" Surles, Carl Rossman, "Sooze" (Susan) Harrison, Walter vanDoren, Alicia Sabin, "Doc," Hunter Paulson, Vera Tomlinson, and Emily Kabrick. These kind friends read a chapter or two of the manuscript *Windswept: The Wind at Wrigley*, in which I indulged the fantasy that the Cubs and the Red Sox actually meet in the 2008 World Series—and they told me to forget it. I did. My interest revived when the Cubs came within five outs of going to the World Series in the 2003 season; but the notorious foul ball incident caused the Cubs to revert to type and brought me to my senses; I went on to finish the Beethoven manuscript. I am fortunate to have such friends. I thank them one and all.

I wish to thank Irene Shine, my eighth grade teacher at the Edgemont School in Rocky Mount, North Carolina, who one day showed up on my front porch with a gift—the Victor album DM640, in which the great Arturo Toscanini conducts the NBC Symphony Orchestra in Beethoven's Fifth Symphony. My head has been spinning since that day. I am reminded of the story about a man who, after hearing the Fifth Symphony at its premier in Vienna, said "I went to put on my hat, *and I couldn't find my head.*"

To my music theory instructor, the wondrous Beatrice Baumgarten, who labored after hours to play fugues so that I could understand them, I acknowledge a debt beyond my power of expression. Thank you, "Bea."

To Kay Sanderling, Raleigh Bascom, and Joy Weinhaur, who advised me about plot consistency in *My Angel Leonora*—a huge Thank You!

To Jim "Judge" Johnson and Rosemary, who welcomed me into their home and took me sailing in Boston Harbor in the summer of 2003, giving me just the boost I needed to work on several chapters of this book that just weren't coming easy at the time—Thank You!

To three little kiddies who brought out the 'inner child' in me and kept my spirits on high during a difficult period when the last pages of this manuscript eluded me—Thank You, Danny, Cassie, and Katie Tomlinson!

To Victoria Evangeline Parnell, who urged me to revise this manuscript and improve it—and she showed me how—Thank you!

To my own children, now grown, Mary Jeanine and Christopher— Thank you for making me so proud of you. (They still bring out the "inner child" in me.)

Finally I express gratitude to Adrienne Ann Selle, who a second time has inspired me to write what was in my heart, and who generously and graciously posed on the windswept headlands overlooking the Hudson River and again in an unheated mansion for hours with unflagging patience so that *My Angel Leonora* would have this beautiful cover. Adrienne, Thank You!

*

Now I pay tribute to a friend and comrade who did not read the Cubs manuscript because he was busy being a great healer, counselor, pastor, and friend to many. I will miss him, a friend of twenty years. In memory of Dr. Ian Reid, 1947-2004. May he rest in peace.

FOREWORD

Mysterious indeed, even after so much has been said and written, is the life and music of this great man. If he could compose his joyous Second Symphony and contemplate suicide at the same time, our predicament is this: we shall either understand the man but not the music; or we shall understand the music but not the man. And if both the man and the music are miracles, we may understand neither.

The poet Edna St. Vincent Millay, whose *On Hearing A Symphony By Beethoven* is printed in the front of this book, took the best approach to the mystery: the meaning of the music lies in its effect upon the soul of the listener. One who takes this music to heart has learned something about himself and mankind. Beethoven's "sweet sounds" make "mankind plausible, his purpose plain." The poet adds that the music is the "tranquil blossom on the tortured stem." This is a paradox: Beethoven, the "tortured stem" whose rages and passions and sufferings caused him to despair of life itself, composed music that confers the peace that surpasses all understanding.

This book, *My Angel Leonora,* is fiction. It proceeds from a sense of joy and rapture that Beethoven's music gave me even when I was a boy; and his music helps me as an adult search for the peace that others have found. In this novel I have probed into the great composer's own joys and raptures, and his search for the kind of peace he gave to others. I do not believe he ever found it. But he came close, I believe, when he met a woman whose identity has been unknown to us until recent times.

*

Shortly after Beethoven died, certain of his friends went through his writing desk and by chance came upon a secret drawer secured by a bent nail. In it they found a three part love letter addressed to "My angel, my all, my very self," a woman whom he calls his "immortal beloved." How the letter remained among his belongings, whether he made a copy of it, or he never sent it—or it was returned to him—is at the heart of the mystery of Beethoven's life. The letter is undated, and of course, it did not bear the name of the intended. (The intended did not need to be told her name!) Scholars rummaged through the composer's scattered and tattered notebooks looking for clues as to this woman's identity. They did find one entry of possible relevance: in 1813, Beethoven wrote that if he entered a relationship with a certain woman named "A," all things would go to ruin. The same person might also have been known as "T." Moreover, two portrait miniatures on ivory were found in his flat, one of which has been identified as Giulietta Guicciardi, the Countess Gallenburg. Who, then, is the other woman?

Anton Schindler, Beethoven's first biographer and his *factotum*, stated with a show of certainty that it was Guicciardi who goaded his Master's desire and that she was his true love. He has been proved wrong. Schindler also set back proper research by insisting that the letter was written in 1806: we now know better; Schindler is an unreliable, biased chronicler.

Numerous other names have been set forth as the recipient of the love letter and hence the object of Beethoven's true love: Amalie Sebald, Countess Josephine Deym, Bettina (Brentano) von Arnim, Therese Malfatti, Magdalena Willman, Marie Bigot, and others, but no agreement had ever been reached among the scholars who have burned much midnight oil over this subject; in 1977 however, a scholar named Maynard Solomon took a fresh look at things. Solomon was also a psychiatrist, and in this capacity he looked into the question why Beethoven never married. Beethoven feared the intimacies of the married life, Solomon concludes. He had a way of entering short-lived relationships, that may or may not have involved sexual intercourse. His offensive and boorish ways, and smelly chamberpots, contributed to his being rejected by women. He threw up barriers to intimacy. Once he considered a proposal of marriage to a teen-aged girl—he was forty at the time: a most unlikely prospect, as if he anticipated rejection. But there was one woman who loved him so much that she offered herself to him with a deathless, unconditional love. She is the one to whom he addressed the letter; she is the one whose image is contained in the second locket. Solomon's case for Antonie Brentano ("A," and, for short "T.") as the "immortal beloved" is so convincing that all other contenders are swept away.

My Angel Leonora takes an imaginative look into Beethoven's personal life. I have remained true in essence to the biographical facts, but I used Solomon's cues as I wrote about the intimacies that may have taken place when he met Antonie. I myself am a psychotherapist who has worked with persons with sexual inhibitions and fear of intimacy. None of my clients happen to be a genius of Beethoven's rank, but human nature does admit of some commonalities. I offer my work not as an hypothesis, however—that term is far too grand; call it a speculative premise, or simply an entertainment.

I struggled with the question of Beethoven's famous malady. Did he have syphilis? His symptoms were such that had he lived today, a doctor would have given him an immediate shot of penicillin. His deafness, for one thing, conjures up the suspicion: deafness often occurs in the syphilitic victim a year or two after the initial fever; it is caused by damage to the eighth cranial nerve, and the buzzing sound of which he complained is almost always present. Many of his numerous complaints, such as gastro-intestinal pains, mood changes, paranoia, suicidal thoughts, skin disorders, inflammation around the eyes, and fits of temper (He once threw a plate of stew at a waiter), lend substance to this diagnosis. It is possible too that he was given a prescription for tincture of mercury, which, along with arsenic, was the commonly prescribed treatment for this condition. And Beethoven cavorted with prostitutes, who may well have infected half of Vienna with the disease.

(In 1994, a sample of Beethoven's hair was tested for the presence of mercury or arsenic. Since the hair was taken from his deathbed, and mercury grows out with the hair, no conclusion could be drawn from the negative test report. However, Beethoven was full of lead—which could have come from dishes or from wine sealed in lead.)

Beethoven could have had syphilis *and* lead poisoning: he could also have had typhus—and childhood smallpox. I have attributed his early facial disfigurement to smallpox, which was rampant throughout Europe; it took the life of the Emperor Joseph II's young bride of twenty one years, and millions of others of all ages. And since smallpox sometimes causes ochitis, a condition affecting the genitals, I have taken this into consideration as I wrote of Beethoven's early childhood. I attribute his hearing impairment to beatings inflicted by his father Johann.

Something dark and twisted happened to the young Beethoven; it has to do with Johann, a tenor at the Bonn Imperial Court, who pushed his son to be a prodigy to astound the world like Mozart—and make money—and whose harsh demands and dissolute habits made an indelible impression. When Beethoven wrote his testament at Heiligenstadt he was unable to bring himself to use the word_____that was his father's name. Later in life, Beethoven once had a spat with a singer who was set to sing an aria that he had just written. When the tenor rushed into Beethoven's flat about to make more complaints, Beethoven lept from his desk, threw himself on the floor, and stated later to a friend that his deafness came upon him at the very moment—when the tenor rushed into his room. Solomon's comment on this bizarre incident is to suggest that Beethoven was reacting to a *primo tenore* he had known earlier in life and was the true cause of his deafness—Johann..

Of great interest to me is the "raptus" experience, which bears upon his health and his music. Beethoven would often stop in the middle of a hatless walk and, mindless of a downpour and strikes of lightening, stand immobilized, responding to no one; so much so that people thought he was mad. In medical terms, this mindlessness might be counted as *petit mal* epilepsy—although he never was reported to fall and foam at the mouth—or some neurological condition. (*Petit mal* is now called "Absence Seizure"—a temporary lapse in one's awareness of his environment.) Helene von Breuning, his "surrogate mother" in Bonn, knew of it, and was sympathetic. But those who are familiar with mystical literature may want to consider another possibility: that Beethoven, like Paul the Apostle, was caught up into the "Third Heaven," where he heard things not fit for mortal ears. Other ancient authors were familiar with the happening; they considered it a gift of the gods.

As a youth, Beethoven had an interest in attractive young women. The literature surrounding this is scant, but three names come to the fore: Jeannette d'Honrath, Maria Anna von Westerholt, and Barbara ("Babette") Koch, the daughter of the widow Koch who ran a tavern called the Zehrgarten in Bonn. I have chosen Babette for the role of Beethoven's first love, because she was called "The belle of Bonn," and he wrote her letters from Vienna.

This brings me around to the woman whom he met in 1812, Antonie Brentano. She figures hardly at all, as I said, in the standing literature. But quite a bit is known about her through her father, Johann Edler Melchior von Birkenstock of Vienna, who sent her to a convent school to be sheltered from life's realities. Shortly after she graduated from the convent school and still at an early age, she was coerced to marry Franz Brentano, a merchant from Frankfurt, and she lived there with him in the city until her death. When her father died, she returned to Vienna to assist in the auctioning of her father's estate.

There, thanks to her impetuous sister-in-law Bettina, she met Beethoven. At crucial times in her life, such as her many illnesses, Beethoven was an unannounced but welcome visitor in her home. He would play the piano to soothe her troubled soul, then leave suddenly as he had come, without a word. They fell in love. All that transpired between them from that meeting in 1812 to Beethoven's death in 1827 is not known—but it is the subject of this novel.

When Beethoven died Antonie was in Frankfurt with her husband. It must have grieved her that she was not among the few friends who were at his side when that moment came. That would not have been prudent. No doubt, however, those friends would have passed on to her the news that late that afternoon there was a flash of lightening and a single peal of thunder that awakened him—as if he had heard it! He opened his eyes, clenched and lifted his right hand, remained alert for several seconds—and fell back dead. Antonie must have felt a stab of pain that it was not she but another woman who closed his eyes for the last time. She alone, however, would have understood the meaning of the thunderclap.

Beethoven died March 26, 1827. At that time, Antonie began to enter into a journal the names and dates of death of significant persons she knew. It touches me to the quick that the first of a long series of names is

Beethoven. March 26, 1827

CARTER GREGORY

PINE PLAINS, NEW YORK

2005

ON HEARING A SYMPHONY BY BEETHOVEN

Sweet sounds, oh, beautiful music, do not cease!
Reject me not into the world again.
With you alone is excellence and peace,
Mankind made plausible, his purpose plain.
Enchanted in your air benign and shrewd,
With limbs a-sprawl and empty faces pale,
The spiteful and the stingy and the rude
Sleep like the scullions in the fairy-tale.
This moment is the best the world can give:
The tranquil blossom on the tortured stem.
Reject me not, sweet sounds! Oh, let me live,
Till doom espy my towers and scatter them,
A city spell-bound under the aging sun.
Music my rampart, and my only one.

Edna St. Vincent Millay

"He who truly understands my music must thereby go free of all the misery which others bear about with them."

Ludwig van Beethoven

"I am Bacchus who presses out the wine that intoxicates the world."

Ludwig van Beethoven

"So I endured this wretched existence—truly wretched for so susceptible a body, which can be thrown by a sudden change from the best condition to the very worst—Patience, they say, I must now take for my guide."

Ludwig van Beethoven

THE ANGEL VISION

"A," you portray before our eyes the angel vision,
a sacrament of Peace and Love immortal
that gave comfort to the soul who suffered derision
'till in death he passed through Heaven's open portal.

Carter J. Gregory

PROLOGUE

(March 29, 1827)

"The Dead Man's Secret."

The Requiem Mass was over. Anton Schindler, who had been Beethoven's secretary until the end, was on his feet and out of the Cathedral the moment the priest raised his hand to pronounce the dismissal. He forced his way through the crowd that stood in the courtyard between the Cathedral and the Schwarzpanier House until he found the Imperial horses that would draw the bier to Wahrig and the parish cemetery. A procession of royalty and noblemen would follow the bier to witness the priest's blessing and the lowering of the casket into the earth. His eye was fixed on the dignitaries as they filed out of the church. Rain stood in puddles between the cobblestones and splattered on the lids of barrels from which the horses drank. He took off his glasses to dry them with his handkerchief. If the King and the Archduke went to Wahrig, all was well. But if they returned to the dead man's flat, all was lost. He would have to hurry.

The rain began three days ago when a thunderclap split the ears of those on deathwatch in the flat—that much was true, he thought, because he heard it himself. But what fools they were to believe that God spoke to their great man through thunderclaps. The Master himself was a fool: he danced hatless in the streets during storms like this, and he did things even worse—unspeakable things. If he, Schindler, had done all of that, he would have been carted off to the asylum. Yet they worshipped him. Vienna was full of fools. For three days they have stood in the downpour to ogle the bier; they will not go until the earth covers it up. There!…the King, together with the Archduke and von Breuning, stepped into to a coach that set out for Wahrig… or did it? He wiped his glasses again. If he could find a coach…but the noblemen would have taken them all. He tightened his scarf around his neck and set out on spindle legs for the Master's flat. God forbid that Friedrich Wilhelm and that detestable von Breuning get there first.

Out of breath, he paused outside the flat. The key…where was the key? Yes, still in his greatcoat. The Master had trusted him with the key, but the Master could never have guessed at this…betrayal? No!—not betrayal: why should he not be allowed to make a few gulden in return for all the favors, all the errands, all the slights? He fingered the key and slipped it into the lock. At last he was inside the dead man's flat, where he had given so many hours of service to the ingrate. Now, where was the evidence?

In semi-dark he threaded his way past the trunks that held the pell-mell mess of the Master's wardrobe, three legless pianos, the wash basin on the inundated pine table, the night clothes strewn over the floor, the sack of straw on which he slept and bedded a certain woman. In a far corner near the sole window stood the broadwood piano where the Master had composed the Moonlight and Appassionata Sonatas, and near it the desk. With trembling hands he pulled out a drawer and reached deep into the back of the empty space, where a bent nail should hold in place the cover to a small compartment. The lockets should be inside, along with the letters. He pushed the nail aside; its sharp head drew blood from his fingers. He had studied the lockets many times, always when the Master was out. One in particular he admired: an exquisite feminine image on ivory. It bore no name, but he, Anton Schindler, knew whose image it was; and if the world should doubt it, the letters he now withdrew from the compartment would prove that his beloved Master, whom all the world worshipped, was immoral.

Of course, he would be paid well to hand over the lockets and letters to the King, who with his father had always favored the Master. How foolish of the man! And Grillparzer, too, who delivered the oration, was a fool. From the great marble pulpit Grillparzer spoke of the founding stone of the Florentine Cathedral and the words inscribed upon it, that the building was to represent "a heart expanded to much greatness," and he applied those fine words to the Master, so that all the world would believe that Ludwig van Beethoven was a man whose heart expanded to much greatness.

He knew the truth: Beethoven was a master of music but no master of his passions. He stuffed the lockets into a pouch, hid it inside his greatcoat, and turned to the door.

Suddenly he heard the stomping of booted feet on the lower landing, and voices—he recognized one, it was von Breuning—the others must be King Wilhelm and the Archduke.

There was no escape. He would have to face them.

PART ONE

BONN

(1770-1787)

Chapter One

"The Humiliation of Maria Magdalena."

Louis felt arms on his shoulders, shaking him, and he heard his mother's voice say "Wake up, go hide in the attic. Quick, before your father gets here."

The shuffling of unsteady feet on the stairs sent tremors through him. His father was drunk again—he didn't need to be told. He gripped his mother's hand as they hurried up the narrow steps to the cold room above, where even in summer warmth he could hardly bare to hide. It reeked of bat-dung; rodents were underfoot, and cobwebs caught in his tangled hair. He heard the door slam and his father's voice demanding Maria Magdalena. She let go his hand and hurried down to the parlor.

He huddled in a corner and cupped his hands over his ears to keep them warm and to muffle the sounds he knew would issue from the room below.

"No, Johann, no…"

"His father's voice was urgent. "Take it off, both of you."

A strange woman's voice interrupted. "Well, I don't have to be told that, dearie."

Who was this other woman? He pressed his hands over his ears harder, but he still heard most of the words, and scuffling, and what must be the bed being pushed across the floor.

The strange woman spoke a lot. She would laugh and say things like "Oh, she is so modest, your Maria Magdalena. But isn't she named for a whore, after all?"

"A saint, a saint of God…"

The woman sounded angry. "Hurry up, Johann, I can't stay here all night. Rip it off her."

"No, Johann, please—not so loud, the boy can hear," Maria cried. "He's only a boy."

After a time the voices were hushed.

Louis clasped his knees to keep them from trembling. It was cold, but he felt something worse than the cold: his body was running away from him, no longer his. His trousers were wet in front, his chest was tight, his breathing shallow; and he wanted his mother. But he knew she could not come to him. Something was being done to her. The last time it happened, his father slapped her and shoved her into the bedroom. Cold fear was in her eyes, and when she came out she was sobbing. He played the clavier that night. Perhaps, he thought, the music would please his father so that he would stop hurting his mother. His playing on the clavier or the violin was the only thing that pleased his father because, his father said, there was money in music. So he played on and on, until his father passed out and he could seek the peace of his bed.

But tonight was different: he was told to hide in the attic, where he had no clavier to play. And a strange woman was downstairs, a woman that his mother didn't like—he was sure of that.

He got up and tiptoed to the window where during the day he could look through one of the two telescopes that his grandfather had left there before he died. He missed his grandfather; it was good that his portrait hung downstairs, with his kindly face and a twinkle in his eye. He and his grandfather had this in common: they loved the Rhine.

By the river's edge stood the old toll-house ; and there was the bridge, and beyond rose the Seven Peaks Range. It was dark, but he kept a duty post by the window. What wonders lay beyond the great river? Would he ever know? He crumpled to the floor and fell asleep.

A door slammed below and woke him with a start. He heard Johann's cursing: "I earn the money; I'll spend it the way I want." Something was thrown against the wall, something that shattered. His father did that when he was angry or drunk. Not a word from Maria Magdalena. Was the strange woman still there? Maybe she left when the door slammed. He crept to another corner where the floorboards were split, and peered into the dimly lit room below.

His mother was directly below, pulling her gown over her head and down about her. The gown was dingy and it made her look old—he hated it. But he knew it was all she had. His father must be in the other room. When his father began to snore, it would be safe and his mother would come for him. He waited. Finally he heard the wheezing of his father's drunken sleep. Maria would wait until Johann was sound asleep before she dared to come for him. He prayed she would come soon. Again he fell asleep. Maria's tapping on his shoulder woke him after a time. She took him down to his bed without a word.

In the morning his mother's eyes were red. She looked down, as if to avoid his gaze. He knew she had some terrible secret, that she could never tell him what went on during those nights when she had to hold back her screams and lower her eyes. It was not meant for him to know the ways of fathers and mothers. Maria called up his two younger brothers from the cellar where they had been hiding. They rubbed their red eyes and sat

3

at the table where she served them milk and gruel. She said nothing. His father was snoring in the bedroom; he would remain in bed for the entire morning, then go out to give singing lessons to the children of English, French, and Imperial embassies, and add his voice to the chapel services. Louis knew his mother was relieved when his father left; but she also complained that he left her alone to manage things. This day she stared Louis in the eye and finally spoke to him: "Louis," she said, "Marriage is an ugly and terrible thing."

After they had eaten she cleared the table, washed the few dishes they had used, and got down on her knees to scrub the floor. She worked hard, but was never done. Had she sinned, that his father punished her so?

But, for all the cleaning, the house seemed dirty. She herself was dirty, it seemed. His father once called her a "filthy whore." What was a whore? Was dirt the cause of her punishment, the reason his father ripped off her clothes? That strange woman, was she a scrub woman who helped her father clean his mother? But why didn't his mother clean herself? He wondered what her skin must look like under that gown.

He himself was black. He knew this because the boys in the street called him "little black Spaniard," or "Spangy." And his hair was black and his eyes were black; once his mother sang to him and called him her "little black-eyed boy." She told him he looked just like his grandfather Ludwig, whose portrait hung on the parlor wall: the broad forehead, the thick neck, coal black hair and eyes. His father got mad once when his mother said Louis looked more like his grandfather than his father. Was that why his father beat him? Or was it because he was clumsy and knocked things over, even in the light? Once it was a lamp he bumped into, then a candelabra—his father was furious about that; he had picked it up for Maria as a gift, he said. But it really wasn't his fault he did that so much: it was because when his father beat him about the ears, his head spun around and he was dizzy for a time.

If he were bigger he would take care of his mother; he would hold out his hand for her to grip and would take her away from the dirt and from the punishment and from…whatever Johann and that other woman did to her. He would let her wash and bathe and be clean and pure, so that no one would touch her. Never again.

Chapter Two

"The Red Spot Disease."

Louis tumbled out of bed early Sunday morning and paid unusual attention to his grooming. At last his hours of practice and his mother's prayers accounted for something: today, at the age of thirteen, he would begin his new work as Deputy Court Organist at the Imperial Chapel and wear a splendid outfit—with a sword!— to signify his high status at court. When Maria assured him that he was perfectly attired, he scampered the seven blocks to the court chapel. The sword on his left side attached to his belt by a holster and silver strap and glinted in the light cast from the great Rose Window above the loft. He took the spiraling steps in stride and assumed his post at the great pipe organ. His feet groped for the pedals, his hands stretched to cover the three keyboards; yet he had proved his competence at the early mass, and this Sunday for the first time he would play the prelude before the Great Liturgical Service attended by the Elector himself and many of Austria's nobility.

As he settled into his seat, he glanced down upon the covered heads of the processing nobility as they entered and filed into their pews. Those people below should know his name, for he had composed already: a splendid variation upon a march by Dressler. No longer was he "the son of the drunken sot, Johann van Beethoven." He was Louis van Beethoven, composer. And he had also to his credit the title of "Cymbalist of the Imperial Orchestra."

He was not the son of a drunkard; he was a musician and composer and a child wonder—not a new Mozart, perhaps, but a wonder all the same here in Bonn. And he was bedecked in a manner fitting his pride: a sea-green frock coat, green knickers with silver buckles, silk stockings, black bowknots in his shoes, embroidered vest with pocket flaps, gold corded vest.

His mentor, the chief organist, Christian Neffe, smiled at him: "All very gala and proper for the occasion of your debut as my assistant," he said. "Ready now, here comes the cue."

The Master of Ceremonies in the sanctuary nodded at Neffe, who nodded to his new assistant. Louis took a deep breath, spread out his hands to cover, as best they could, the three keyboards of the great organ; his fingers moved and in a moment the sacred interior of the chapel was filled

5

with the divine art. A Bach Chorale Prelude *Ich Ruf' Zu Dir, Herr Jesu Christ* bestowed calm upon the people below and prepared them for what was to come. The Epistle Sonata would be a piece that he, Louis, had composed. True Royalty was present in the loft space above the heads of those below. He, Louis van Beethoven, would tell the world the meaning of royalty; it resided in his genius. van? No. He would be Louis von Beethoven: van was common; but von was royalty. With a name like that he could stake a higher claim; he could look down upon these nobles even as he stood among them.

The back of his father's head caught his eye and caused him to miss a beat. Johann sang in the electoral chapel choir; Louis knew he was there. But the sight of him in choir vestments—so out of character—caused him to suck in his breath. He flushed with shame—shame that he was Johann's son, shame that he had missed a beat. He glossed over the musical error with accomplished grace. But did the Elector notice? Neefe? Johann?

Christian Gottlob Neffe was the chief court organist and his music instructor, but it was his father's wrath that he feared. Already he was a better musician than his father. And, while his father was publicly boastful of his prodigy son, in private Louis sensed his jealousy, a jealousy that fumed and raged especially when drink addled his senses.

Not only was he a better musician, he was a better man. And that was a good thing for them all: Johann was in trouble over his drinking and the family fortunes were in decline—he overheard Maria talking about her fears. He himself heard the gossip at court. Worse: the Elector Minister Count Kaspar Anton von Belderbusch was sick, perhaps dying. The Count, for some reason neither he nor anyone else understood, favored Johann. Soon the Count's enemies would be Johann's enemies and his position at court would be in jeopardy. If Johann lost his position, what then? They were poor enough as it was; how would they make do? He understood these things. Someday, he knew, he would be his mother's provider and protector.

His day's work done, he returned home for his dinner. His step was heavy with the thought of Johann and the matter of his error in the loft. As he opened the ground floor door, he saw his father coming down the steps with a tall man. "I will deal with you later," Johann said, as he and the stranger brushed past him on their way out. The man was well dressed, an aristocrat; not the kind who would associate with the likes of his father. Neither was Belderbusch. It was odd. "Who was that man?" he asked his mother, as she ladled soup. Maria hesitated: her eyes were red. "He is George Cressener—a man of stature, the Ambassador from the English

Court." Louis had more questions, but Maria said only, "The man was kind enough to lend us money for our needs." She said no more.

After supper a sudden and unusual fatigue drove him to an early bed. Johann remained late, making his rounds of the taverns. Just after midnight Maria Magdalena was about to pull the bed sheets over her head when Johann reeled in, red-eyed and foul smelling. He tugged at Louis' feet and pulled him from his bed. Louis lay crumpled on the floor, his eyes still closed.

"You made an error today. You know what that means."

He shuddered. "Father, I must sleep."

"You will practice until I say stop." With that Johann pinched him on his ear and marched him to the piano. Maria Magdalena, under the bed sheets, turned over and said nothing. At least, she thought, this time he didn't bring the whore.

In the morning Maria went to wake her son, but Louis' eyes remained shut. His face was flushed and his forehead hot to the touch. She rushed to the kitchen and returned with wet towels. Carefully she pulled his nightshirt over his head—his body broke out in sweat. With the towels she bathed him head to toe. He whimpered and opened his eyes at last; his eyes were dull but love for his mother and her tender mercies shined through the glaze. When he was dry she wrapped him in clean sheets and let him fall back into deep sleep.

Two days later he was still in bed. Johann grumbled and swore but made no further moves to interfere with Maria's attentiveness to his son. Both parents began to realize that Louis had come down with the "red spot" disease that had felled many of their neighbors and their children and left them scarred—or dead. Even the Emperor Joseph's twenty one year old bride succumbed to it. Louis had indeed broken out in red blotches on his tongue and around his mouth. No doctor was summoned; Johann said money was too dear. Maria wanted to go to the church to pray, but she was afraid to leave Louis alone with Johann, who always had money for his whore.

The fever broke after three days, but red spots spread rapidly to cover the entire length of his body. A day later the spots hardened into ugly welts. There was little point to bathing him but Maria did so anyway, pouring water over his body until the bed and floor were soaked. Then the welts developed scabs. Maria expected this, because her neighbors told her that the scabs proved the plague was running its course. Louis endured the itching and the burning, and comforted himself by humming new tunes; his mouth was a wind instrument by which he could trumpet his assured recovery with martial airs and brisk marches.

But one morning in the second week he awoke screaming, "My balls, my balls!" Maria hurried to him and swept aside the bed sheets. Her son's hands clutched his private parts. It was not a mother's right to pull his hands away; her son was now thirteen, almost a young man—but she dared not summon Johann. "Louis, let me see, please—I'm your mother." He took his hands away. Both testicles were swollen, red with hideous black and blue wrinkles and veins. His penis was barely visible between the two masses of tissue, but she could see that a pustule erupted from the head. She turned and covered her face with her two hands: God forbid it should be scarred forever.

Louis however proved to have a sturdy constitution. After the third week most of the red was gone and he found the strength to play the piano for a few hours, then for a whole day. Sunday of the following week he rose early to walk the seven blocks to the court chapel where he would play the organ at the early mass. He walked with a forward sweep of gait, as if his head jutted forward and his feet had to scurry to keep up. Thinking ahead to the service, his mind was fixed on the prelude, a theme by Bach upon which he would improvise. Suddenly he found himself seated at the three keyboard console playing the very music that he had been humming in his head. Neffe gave him a nod; time to begin. How did he get here? Stunned, he moved his fingers over the keys and the Bach theme went through its paces. When the service was over he was ravenously hungry; he said a few polite words to the cantors and dashed home for breakfast. Somehow, he reasoned, his sickness and an empty stomach conspired to trick him.

At the great Solemn Mass he sat again at the console, under the benign eye of his beloved Neffe. His stomach happily full, he expected no more tricks. Again Neffe nodded. The Bach theme began as before; but Louis soon whipped the static theme into a high-stepping march to the heavens. Below, heads turned—what sorcerer was this who filled the sanctuary with such glories? Neffe tapped him on the shoulder: "Louis, you overwhelm them, keep it down." After the service, Neffe had to speak to his apprentice: "We are in Church, not the theater. Tranquility, Louis, tranquility."

That evening Louis returned to the chapel to play for an evening vespers service. One of the court choristers, Ferdinand Heller, was assigned to sing a solo during the service. When Heller ascended to the loft, Louis leaned over and whispered: "You sing so well, and I am so inexperienced, that if I make a mistake or two, you won't be harsh on me I pray."

"No, my child, I sing perfectly on pitch. You just do the best you can."

8

When it came Heller's turn to sing the piece, Louis wove a harmonic tapestry so elaborate that the singer was utterly lost during the final cadence. The singer fumed and reported the matter to the Elector, who in turn brought it to the attention of Neffe. Louis received a scolding, but the twinkle in Neffe's eye put matters to rest. Then Neffe broke out into a wide smile: "Wait, my dear boy—I shall soon have an idea for you."

A special choir practice had been called for Friday evening to rehearse new pieces for a service of thanksgiving. The Rhine had overflowed its banks and inundated large parts of the city. Maria Magdalena had helped in the rescue efforts, although she was still exhausted from caring for Louis during his suffering. Now the crisis was over, the city was recovering, and the Elector proclaimed a service to commemorate the rescue efforts.

Louis sat again at the console and accompanied the choir through the new music. When the rehearsal was over, Neffe took Louis aside: "Look at this," he said, holding up a printed score that bore the name of Mozart. "From Vienna, a new piano sonata by the divine Mozart."

Was this Neffe's ideal for him? He was all too familiar with Mozart. Johann held up Mozart as an idol to be worshipped; he wanted Louis to be a second Mozart, a wonder child whose father Leopold had paraded before all the nobility of Europe and who by age thirteen had completed two operas and several symphonies, among other wonders.

"You must go to Vienna," said Neffe, "and play for Mozart."

Louis was startled by his mentor's assurance. "But that would be expensive. My father…"

"Never mind your father," he said, with a wink and a knowing smile. "I will speak to the Elector. From this moment, Vienna is your goal."

With thoughts of Vienna tumbling in his head, he said goodnight to Neffe and stepped out into the late evening. A dense fog had set in, the air having absorbed much moisture from the high waters of the Rhine. He made his way through the streets, now unfamiliar in the dense vapors, and passed some building fronts that were of no interest by day; but in the gas-lit glow of one of the shabbier doorways he saw a man and a woman. They were talking in hushed tones. When he got close to the doorway he heard the woman say "Twenty gulden and I am yours dearie," as she urged her hand against the front of the man's trousers. Her voice—he knew it. Their eyes locked for a moment as he raced past.

Suddenly, with no thought of the passage of time, he was in the flat staring at his mother's dear face.

"Louis, why so pale?" Maria feared a relapse into the red-spot disease. She put her hand to his head.

He was able to utter only a few words: "Just tired, mother, that is all."

It must have been the night vapors that tricked his mind. In a few days he forgot the strange incident.

He did not want to worry his mother. He had no fever; he knew that; all that was left of his disease—all that showed—were the scars on his face, which hardly bothered him at all. But the red scab on that part of his body that Maria looked at and turned her head away from, that was still there. In fact, it played a mean trick on him. It shocked him a few days ago when he woke up and saw that his little penis was not so little. It had grown to almost twice its size, and the red scab was bigger, too, and ugly. It went down again when he peed into the pot. But the skin that hung under it had withered and looked like an empty sack. He was afraid the doctor might come and cut it off.

Now this other thing—something like it happened again. He was walking between the house and the court chapel, but he had no memory of walking the whole seven blocks. He remembered leaving the house in the morning…then suddenly there he was at the chapel. Then at night, he left the chapel and suddenly there he was at home looking into his mother's face. What else might he have forgotten? Well, he had not forgotten what Neffe told him. He was going to Vienna!

Neffe, however, quite before he realized it, was in trouble. Never skilled in anything but music, Neffe had not cultivated the dignitaries of the Imperial Hierarchy and was therefore unshielded from political winds. Maximillian Fredrich had protected him, but Fredrich died in his sleep and a new Elector, Maximillian Franz, took matters in hand. Immediately he ordered a thorough assessment of the government, including the musicians. Thirty seven musicians were reviewed, a few of them were declared expendable. Christian Neffe was one of them.

Louis was deemed competent, but his new ambition was untimely and without support. Vienna would have to wait.

Chapter Three

"Do it in the Dark, Dearie."

In keeping with Johann's ambition that his son succeed as a prodigy composer like Mozart, Louis again turned his prentice hand to composing new works. He had just finished three sonatas for piano which he dedicated to Elector Max Friedrich before the Elector died. Now he was working on a concerto for piano and orchestra—a difficult form even for a Mozart—and some quartets for piano and strings. The earliest works were published, thanks to Johann's efforts, who unfailingly called attention to the composer's tender age.

One of the songs, his first, was also published: "To an Infant."

"You still do not know whose child you are, you do not know who prepares the swaddling clothes. Soon you will be able to distinguish your mother; nevertheless there is some occult giver who cares for all of us—our thanks go to him—who provides us food and drink. My dim intelligence does not yet comprehend this; but after the years have gone by, if I am pious and a believer, even he will be revealed."

But he put it aside and never played it again.

"Why do you not play the infant song, Louis?" Maria asked one day when he was seated at the piano.

He gazed into her loving eyes: "Because it makes your eyes wet, mother."

She took him into her arms. "I cry for joy when I hear you sing and play," she said. They held to each other for a time. Then Louis spoke: "But if father heard this song, he would be angry."

"Louis, what are you saying?" Her hands flew to her face.

"I don't know, I don't know," he cried. He knew only that the song held a mystery, as if hidden voices had dictated to him but kept their secrets for a later time.

What was most important, however, was to go to Vienna. In order to do that, he had to please the new Elector. Max Franz, the brother of the Emperor Joseph, was a young man of twenty-eight, who had many appetites and passions: education was one; it was he who attracted intellectuals to

11

Bonn and set up the University. He approved of youth serving according to their abilities, and he appreciated the need for reforms and flexibility in government. And he loved music: not only the organ preludes before mass, or the liturgical music of the old masters, but also Bach's secular pieces, banquet music, lighthearted Italian stage works, the German singspiele; and he knew Haydn and Mozart personally from his Vienna days. His experience with the child prodigy inspired him to keep an eye open for another such gift from the heavens. Unfortunately, nothing in the court report suggested that anyone in official service sang, played, or composed in a way that recalled Mozart.

Louis' talent was noted by others, however. In 1784 Helene von Breuning, a young mother and widow, heard him play at the chapel and engaged him to teach piano to her young children. Helene did not wallow in widowhood; she took charge of her brood—there was pretty little Lorchen, and Christopher, and Lenz, and Stephan—and had many guests to her home on the Munsterplatz, including the intellectuals. Her husband, Emanuel, had been the Court Councilor and a man of high intellect. Helene, much like her husband, kept up the custom of inviting students and university faculty for stimulating evenings. Louis found himself caught up in this social life, an adopted child almost; he visited there often, lessons or no lessons; the home was full of energy and bustle and laughter, and sometimes he slept there in order to escape Johann in his worst moods. Aristocrats from Vienna were there too; Louis drank in their words as they spoke of the theater, the symphony, evenings of music in the homes of the great and wealthy. One of these aristocrats was Count Ferdinand Waldstein of Vienna, who came to Bonn at the behest of the new Elector. Waldstein listened to Louis at the piano and was impressed, so much so that he paid Louis to write a composition for him to pass off as his own—a ballet, the *Ritterballet*, that he intended to perform before the Elector during an annual Mardi Gras.

Helene, with an eye out for Louis' future, spoke to Waldstein about making his name known to the Elector. That time would come, the Count promised; but Louis was roguish and abrupt, he needed refinement. It would be good, he suggested, for Louis to mingle with the university students. Helene knew a respectable gathering place, the Zehrgarten, just off the Market Square. "You must meet the intellectuals whose ideas are sweeping Europe," she told Louis, "for if you expect to impress the Elector and mingle with the greats of Vienna, you must know their minds. And read Voltaire and Kant." Louis agreed to go to the tavern, but he had all but despaired of going to Vienna. He did however pick up a copy of Kant at the court library.

One evening after lessons at the von Breunings, Louis pushed open the wide swinging doors that served as street entrance to the Zehrgarten and looked about for a place to sit.

All the tables were filled with university students, as he expected: intellectuals and radicals, in whom he had little interest. But he did hope to see Frau Koch who, he was told, ran the tavern, and—if he was lucky—her daughter, the beautiful Babette. But dim lighting and smoke clouded his vision. Maybe tonight at last he would speak to her; he only saw her when she attended the court service with her mother; from the loft he would gaze down upon her pale face, her green eyes, and locks of blond hair under her bonnet. She stared at no one; this proved her innocence. If there was any consolation for being denied his journey to Vienna, it was Babette and her innocence; someday she would be his pure virgin bride.

"Over here, lad," called a voice from a nearby table. "Can you explain Kant's categorical imperative so that my friends here will understand it?" Louis sensed the fellow's intent: an older student with a tipsy grin on his face, he expected that Louis, too young to be a philosophy student, would stammer and beat a retreat through the swinging doors. Louis moved close to the table and said in calm tones, "According to Kant, one must act in such a way that one would want there to be a universal moral law that commands all men to act in just that way." He grabbed the student's tankard and poured ale over his head, his suit, and onto his lap. "I hereby declare a universal law," he said, "that all men must behave as I just did." The students gaped at Louis: "Do you ridicule the revolution?" one of them cried. But Louis was quickly gone; among the back tables he had spotted Babette.

The girl was helping her mother by serving tables. She carried a tray loaded with platters of food and tankards of ale. If only he could catch her eye, he thought, he would smile at her and she might smile back. He stood in a corner watching her; when she passed close by he took in her fragrance, her pert nose, the delicate curve of her bosom. If only he could say to her, "I am the music-maker who fills the sanctuary with divine music. That was not Bach you heard, that was Beethoven." But he had no money for a table; at most, on his court wages, he could order one beer and stand against a wall, far from her rounds.

In despair he left the tavern and wandered toward the river. The autumn night was cold and clouded. Dead leaves covered the slope that led to the old toll-house, the one he loved to look at from his attic. Lying on his back, he stared at the sky. A half-moon drifted among the clouds and beneath him the earth gave him rest. Was there, as a poet claimed, a loving father who dwelt above the vault of heaven? The philosophers thought not; but

13

the poets say Yes. Was he, Louis van Beethoven, a philosopher or a poet? He had no knowledge of a loving father, above or below; but when he composed music he was a poet. He imagined himself at the console of the imperial organ; he filled the night air with music.

Babette came into his thoughts; a new warmth rose in his loins, that did not come from the cold earth. He grasped himself by the front of his trousers as the warmth spread slowly through his body, and opened his trousers front; but the wind was swift and cold. Suddenly, at one moment, he was standing in the dark alley behind the Zehrgarten, staring into the bright kitchen. It was almost closing time; the help was washing and scrubbing. Frau Koch went darting about, telling the help to do this, do that...and there was Babette, her radiant face visible through the glass window, pure, like the angel's face in a stained glass window over his head as he played the organ at the court chapel. Then she appeared at the back door and emptied out a bucket of slop. She looked his way—did she see him? He pulled back into the shadows. At that moment he knew, he believed at once, without understanding why, that he could never touch her.

He scrambled to his feet and raced up the slope toward the street where the tavern should be. The street was dark. Two men staggered and swayed as they passed, mumbling bawdy songs like Johann often did. The tavern was closed; he was too late.

It was long after midnight when he arrived at the flat. Maria would be at a neighbor's home, with his brothers—a safe haven when Johann was at his worst; but he had to stay home where there was a piano. Johann, unless he was still out, would be in his bed or passed out on the floor. He made the five flights to the flat and listened at the door for his father's voice. It was quiet. He opened the door slowly. Johann's bedroom door was ajar; a shaft of light came from it. He made his way through the slanting light toward the room he shared with his brothers. Something on the floor clung to his foot. He picked it up and moved toward the candlelight that came from Johann's room. It was a woman's undergarment. His mother's?...no, not Maria's. He turned and started toward his room. The door behind him opened wide and the woman's voice called to him, "Over here, dearie."

She came up behind him and wrapped her arms around his waist, her fingers searching for his trousers buttons. "He paid me already, then passed out. So I'll give you his money's worth." Before he could think, she spun him around by the shoulders, then reached down again; in a second his trousers were at his ankles and he was exposed. She knelt and took his penis between her fingers: "Oh, what a cutie, so tiny. But I'll make a man out of you, dearie." In a second she wrapped her lips around it and began licking it with her tongue. He was afraid to back away—she might bite it off.

In the dim light from Johann's bedroom, he was able to see the woman's head as it bobbed up and down. Something like the smell of dead flowers congested in his nostrils.

She lifted her head: "Just let it happen, dearie, just let it happen."

Let what happen? Then he knew. His penis began to swell until it filled her mouth. A delicious sensation from his loins got stronger and became urgent—his buttocks tensed, his back arched, his head fell back, his eyes clouded over. He felt the moisture in her mouth become turgid, sticky. Then she turned her head, spit twice on the floor, and went down again to give him a parting lick on the fleshy scrotum. Suddenly she shot him an amazed stare. "What's the matter, kid—you only got one ball?" She looked more closely in the dim light. "God almighty, what's that rash?" She spit again on the floor. "God almighty, if you made me sick…I shoulda looked first."

In the kitchen she retched and cursed: "If you ever do it to a nice girl, do it in the dark."

He avoided Helene's home for almost a week, until it came time for Stephen's lessons. When the music-making was over, she asked him about his visit to the tavern. He looked down and stared at his feet. She was like a mother to him; he wanted to tell her everything; but how could he? For shame—his thing inside a woman's mouth, the spasms; the scarlet rash, the shrunken testicle. Blood rushed to his face; he turned from her and ran from the house. For once he thought it better to face Johann.

At supper he stared at his mother. She looked tired and sickly. Johann bolted down his food and left for the taverns. When his brothers were trundled off to bed, he faced her with a question:

"Mama, if I go to Vienna, who will take care of you?"

She reached for his hand and blessed it with her lips. "Dear child, I take care of myself. Now, you go to the piano and play. When the time comes you must be ready."

He wanted to tell her what Neffe had told him. Neffe was still at the court, on half salary. Louis was given an increment; in essence, to his embarrassment, Louis was taking home half of his mentor's pay. This was a sign of favor, and Neffe said so. But his mind was clouded by other thoughts.

That night he lay in bed; the lights were off, but he was not asleep. He listened for sounds from Johann's room, where he and Maria were sleeping…or were they? Did Johann ever stick his big thing into his mother's mouth? Such a terrible thought—his mother was pure and holy, like the Virgin Mary. But what happened those nights when Johann and his whore made her undress? Maybe they were trying somehow to make her belly swell up so she would have another baby. No!—no more babies; he, Louis, was his mother's one and only and when he grew up he would take care of her—she looked so tired—and it would not matter if Johann were dead.

Johann! It would be better if Johann were dead and his big thing in the grave with him, so he couldn't stick it in her mouth. It was ugly. Blue veins streaked the length of it, and the head covered it like a hat that was too big. Once when Johann and Maria and he were walking home from his grandfather's house and Johann had drunk too much, he pulled it out and peed in the street. And when he finished, he shook it. Later, Maria explained that in that part of the city, people couldn't afford chambers in their homes, so everybody did it in the street. It was true, what she said, he later learned; but at the time it was only Johann in the street, and Maria hid her face.

At the von Breunings on a Friday evening, Louis agreed to play for an impromptu gathering of students who had dropped by. His playing was greeted by great applause. Helene served coffee and cakes, and as Louis reached for his hat and coat, she took him by the shoulders. "Dear boy, must you run off? Stay—keep me company and meet my friends."

But Louis felt himself different from the student crowd and he was uncomfortable among them. His mind kept wandering off into chords and cadences. But he picked up his ears at some words among students in a corner.

"Socrates had a *daimon*," said one student. "He would stop in the middle of a conversation and stand still like a statue, while his mind flew off somewhere."

What is a *daimon*? Louis wondered. He moved closer to the students, but their talk digressed into other matters. When the house had cleared of guests, and he was alone with Helene, he gathered the courage to speak to her. He asked her about Socrates.

"Socrates was one of the first Greek philosophers, dear boy. People said he had a divine spirit that flew away to far places and left his body behind."

Tears came to his eyes. "There are things I must tell you."

"Louis, tell me, trust me…" She sat next to him and clasped his hands.

Twice…no, three times, he was in one place and suddenly he was in another, he told her. "How could that be?" he asked.

"You have the divine spark in you. Wise men call it the raptus, when you are called away from the earth and taken to be with the gods for a time, who have a gift for you. You are beloved of the gods, Louis."

"I don't feel beloved—not by anybody."

She held his head to her breast, then lifted his head in her two hands and kissed him softly on the forehead. It was a mother's kiss. "You are loved by me, Louis. By all of us." Her smile was all-consoling.

He looked up at her wise and loving face. First, he told her about Babette—his vision of her face as he lay upon his back by the toll-house and the warm feelings that made his trousers seem tight. In a cracking voice he told about Johann's drinking, the terrible woman he brought to the house, what he saw and heard from the attic. Then his face went white, his lips quivered.

She knew something was wrong. "Go on, dear Louis—I am listening."

In broken tones he told her. "One night when mother wasn't home, the woman was there—she came up behind me…I didn't know what to do… she pulled my trousers down…and she put it in her mouth. Then when it happened she washed out her mouth and cursed at me. She said something was wrong with me. And she said if I ever did it to a nice girl, I should do it in the dark."

Her eyes rested gently on the boy who had trusted her like a mother. "Louis," she said, "I am the mother of three boys. You must show me, or I cannot know." He stood and lowered his trousers and undergarment. There was the rash that encircled the small penis and the flap of loose skin visible beneath it. Her eyes, soft and moist, rested on his face. What could she say to this dear boy? Her gracious spirit spoke: "Louis, sometimes when the gods give, they take away. They have given you a great gift; I pray you will go to Vienna and play before the great Mozart. Now pull up your trousers and do not fear. The right woman will come into your life and what you have shown me will not matter."

When the Count Waldstein came to a musical evening the following week, Helene took him aside: "You must speak to the Elector about Louis. A leave of six months even, to play for Herr Mozart and sell his music, will do wonders for him."

The Count stroked his chin. "Yes, Louis is talented, I agree. But six months…? Even Neffe was never permitted to go, and Louis is his assistant."

"But surely if you speak to him…"

"Yes, when the time is right. The Elector is setting up a new court. Be patient."

The Count's logic was impeccable. The Elector didn't grant court employees money and leave unless for exceptional reasons. Louis, therefore, would need to convince the Elector that the reputation of the court and the Elector himself would be enhanced by a resident genius who was endorsed by none other than Herr Mozart. And Louis was not ready to convince the Elector—not yet.

Louis spent more and more time in the von Breuning home, sleeping in an upstairs guest room or, if he returned to the flat, he waited until he was sure that Johann would be done with that woman and asleep. But, whether at the flat or at the von Breunings, he worked to master his art. Counterpoint was a weakness, he knew. When he got to Vienna he needed to study with some master. But his improvising skills were miraculous; he knew it and connoisseurs confirmed it. He would be either a great performer or a great composer; possibly both.

The image of Babette stayed fast in his mind, however. At times he would stop playing, let his eyes stray from the keyboard, and think only about Babette. Again and again he pictured her passing the kitchen window, when he stood in the dark alley where he could not be seen; she moved about inside, her face and hair bathed in light. The image was sufficient; he need not return to the tavern. At the chapel of course, he could not help but see her when she came with her mother. He played to her; he played for her. But she never turned her head, she never knew.

Helene and the Count noted Louis' progress well and they marveled at his genius. Louis was creating more and more; new melodies and harmonies streamed into his head and found their way to his fingertips and the keyboard. Music lovers from the court and the university came now to the von Breunings not only to enjoy the company of Helene and their peers, but to gape at this sorcerer who was teaching them things more important than their politics and philosophy. They would see him on the street and introduce themselves to him; invariably he would reply, "I am Beethoven," as if the name were known the world around.

He was sixteen now, and Helene importuned the Count yet again. He nodded: "Perhaps you are right," he said. "We should not wait longer. I have heard that Herr Mozart is distracted more and more by his father's illness. And he is pressed to compose more opera—for Prague, for the Emperor. Yet, the Elector has never granted leave to a court musician."

Helene's answer came tripping off her tongue: "The only permission he needs is money."

The Count understood at once.

On a wet, soggy day late in March, Louis stepped into the public stagecoach bound for Munich. This first leg of the trip, under the best of circumstances, required ten days, but the coach would make slow progress over roads soaked in rain. It might take a day or two more, the driver warned. Little did that bother Louis, who leaned against the stiff- backed seat as he turned over the pages of a piano sonata he composed to impress Herr Mozart, and from time to time hummed and snapped his fingers to the beat of themes he would use to improvise. Fellow passengers were amazed, delighted and finally bored by the incessant humming and snapping that ceased only at the evening's halt for lodgings; and even then, from a table in the back of Munich's Black Eagle Inn, he sat tapping spoons against glasses.

After Munich, however, even he was worn down by the tedium of the journey. He rested his mind by taking in the delights of the countryside. Melting snow and rains had rinsed the hillocks and riverbeds and cut gullies across open fields; the world was freshly scrubbed and clean. When in Vienna, he thought, if the Emperor and Herr Mozart could spare him for a few hours, he would roam in the forests and wade in the streams that the Count described to him, near places like Heiligenstadt and Hutteldorf.

On April 7 around midday he looked out of the coach window and saw in the distance the tall spire of a church. "St. Stephen's Cathedral," the driver told them; "We will be there in an hour." Soon the coach passed through large iron gates and onto city streets that bustled with energy: merchants, hawkers, smartly dressed men and women, and rag-tag urchins. Music sounded from inside restaurants, and boys in the streets hummed tunes—Mozart's.

He had with him a letter of introduction from Max Franz, which he should present at court. But the Emperor Joseph was on his way to Russia, he learned. Never mind: the Emperor was a formality only; the true emperor was a musician, whom he would meet. It was Herr Mozart he had to win over, and that on the basis of his skill and invention. He was no longer a prodigy of eight or ten, or thirteen years even; he was a growing man of sixteen. He could no longer excite wonder on the basis of his youth; he must impress with his skill and his invention.

A large inn near the Cathedral served as quarters. The next morning, rested and well fed, he set forth to find Herr Mozart at the address that the Count gave him; but Herr Mozart no longer lived there, the landlady told him; she gave him a new address, which proved to be far from the center of the city. When he came upon it—Landstrasse No. 224—he saw at once that it was a cheaper place than the one he had left. He knocked, but no one answered.

Louis paced the street up and down, stopping to order a sausage from a cart vendor, and eating it as he went on pacing. At dusk, he saw three men approach the number 224. One was short, thin, and his speech was punctuated by nervous laughter. Louis waited for them to enter, and then knocked.

"Herr Mozart is very busy," said the man who answered.

"I am Beethoven. I have a letter from Count Waldstein."

The Count's name was magical. "You may enter, but be advised that Herr Mozart has much work to do," the man said. "What may I ask is the purpose of your visit?"

The man's high manners told Louis that he was no servant.

"I shall play for Herr Mozart."

The man gave a benign smile. "I am sure the master will be pleased. But would you be so good as to return later in the week, when the master will be available by appointment. Shall we say one week from today, at this time?"

Helene had warned him never to offend nobility. He thanked the man for the courtesy of an appointment, left the place hat in hand, and bought another sausage from the street vendor.

Having no piano, he thought it good to take long walks around the city and into the countryside. It rained three of the seven days, but that served only to make nature more alive for him. Each day he wandered in the open fields outside the city and ate among peasants in their taverns. At night, with no money in his pockets for theater and sophisticated entertainments, he walked the streets and discovered the high energy of the city's evening entertainments. A boy handed him a playbill: at the Hetz amphitheatre equestrians and acrobats served as curtain-raisers for the main event, a fur and gut combat between two wild animals. In other theaters jugglers and rope dancers held forth; or puppeteers and comedians; or slapstick farces. Other signs advised him of masked dancing in certain beer halls and cheap theaters.

One evening, a cold snap overtook the city and drove the population indoors. Louis too, lacking a winter coat, returned early to the inn that served as lodging. He did not want to catch a cold the day before his appointment with Herr Mozart. The innkeeper saw him at once and handed him a dispatch from Bonn that had just arrived on the afternoon post coach. It was a letter from Johann:

"You must come home at once. Your mother is on her deathbed."

Chapter Four

"Behind the Altar."

Johann Melchior Edler von Birkenstock had his daughter's best interests in mind. Antonie, at age four, charmed and delighted the visitors to his home; at eight, she was the subject of rapt discussion among aristocratic circles in Vienna. The question was: whose bride would she be? In regard to her eventual marriage, Johann had definite opinions: he sent her away to a cloistered school in Pressburg run by the Ursuline sisters. The sisters would see to it that when she married, Antonie would be a pure virgin.

A part of his concern had to do with his wife, Carolina, who was sickly. He feared that she might pass on while Antonie was still young and in his care and keeping, posing a task for which he had no inclination. It was destined, therefore, that when Antonie graduated from the convent school, she would do well to marry at once. When that time came, he would have a candidate in mind.

The Birkenstock reputation in Austria was considerable. Johann was a statesman in the service of Emperor Joseph and Maria Theresa, and a lover of the arts who made his home on the suburban Erdbeergasse as much a museum as a residence, and his family was musical to an accomplished degree. Chamber music was performed regularly and the finest musicians were honored to be invited to play in their salon. Connoisseurs and aristocrats, as well as men of wealth and power, came to these concerts. One of these was the Frankfurt merchant Franz Brentano. He was ten years Antonie's senior—an ideal age differential, in Johann's opinion.

Antonie was fifteen when she left the convent school. At first, her days were bright with girlish enthusiasm: Vienna was alive with people, music, theater. But soon she realized that these things were not always permitted to her; her father kept strict rule over her comings and goings. Moreover, her ailing mother required much care and attention. When her mother died, stringent mourning fell upon the house. Even after the mourning period, her life was limited to chamber concerts in the parlor and to church, which she was required to attend every day. Sometimes Herr Brentano, who had attended the funeral service, came and sat between her and her father.

One evening after dinner, Johann took his daughter into the parlor. "Antonie," he said, "you have no mother now. There is no need for you to stay in Vienna."

She knew without being told.

"Herr Brentano is a fine man," Johan added. "In time, when the ceremony is over, you may call him Franz."

She knew Herr Brentano only from his dinner table talk. At first she thought of him as simply a routine visitor to the home for dinner and an evening of music, but when she learned he came all the way from Frankfurt, and that he came increasingly and suspiciously often, she understood. Still, she knew little about him: he was a merchant—she knew that—and at table he spoke about business, commodities, currency, and trade. It was hard for her to take part in those talks; but then, it was not expected of her as a woman that she do so. Johann at times would nod in her direction and ask her about music, a subject that she understood; but soon, as if a courtesy had been rendered, the talk reverted to Frankfurt and the politics of Germany and Austria.

When Herr Brentano looked in her direction, she felt she was being appraised as a commodity. The man was polite, but his smile was smug, as if he knew more about her than she herself knew. And such proved to be the truth, when her father took her aside and gave her to know that she would be living in Frankfurt. On his subsequent visit, Herr Brentano, in her father's presence, formally declared his intent. She knew what was expected of her. She agreed to the marriage. A date was set for late summer.

When in the convent school she was instructed in Duties of State. When God brings a person into this world, the sisters said, He assigns that person to a certain place in society and He expects that person to be content with that place and honor the duties that pertain to it. Some are born to be scullery maids, they said; such ones must accept their place and work honestly and diligently to please those who have hired them. This is the will of God. Others are born to teach, others to be priests and nuns, still others to rule. Young women of aristocracy have a special duty: they are to marry and marry well, to reverence and obey their husbands, and to bear children and raise them in the faith of the Church. And young women must present themselves at the marriage altar in a spotless condition—as pure as the Virgin Mary. God punishes with a heavy hand those who stray from the path He sets for each of us. These things were said in chapel services and on other occasions in classrooms. But a sister was assigned to meet privately with each young woman and instruct her in certain things that they deemed best not uttered in chapel. Antonie was given to understand that between her legs she had a sacred portal that lead to an inner sanctuary. In time, when she was married, her husband will instruct her in the proper entry into that sanctuary—for it is his right to do so. She was not to desecrate this sanctuary or its portal by any sinful touching or brushing or fondling—except when she relieved herself on the toilet, and even then, she was not to linger over it.

One Sunday after the morning service at St. Stephen's when Johann and Franz were talking to some of their friends, she hurried down a side isle and peered into the several ancillary chapels. He was not there. Finally, behind one of the great columns, she found him—his eyes greeted her silently. She caught her breath; she had never seen him so close. His eyes were warm and deep. He was very handsome.

She broke the silence. "What is your name?"

"Phillipe. Every Sunday I see you with your family."

She lowered her eyes. "I am Antonie."

He took her by the hand. "Come with me, quickly," he said. Soon they were in a small chapel behind the high altar, partly concealed by a large three panel screen with icons in red, blue and gold, depicting the Baptism of Jesus and the descent of a dove. A baptismal font with a wooden canopy stood in the center. Blue trails of incense wafted past the screen and thickened the interior with a haze that made their tryst even more hidden from watchful eyes. Even so, they stood behind the font.

"We do not have much time," she said.

He reached for her hand. "Stay with me a few minutes. We must talk."

"I mean, I will not be in Vienna long."

His face fell. "Where will you go?"

"To Frankfurt. I am engaged to be married…." Her hands flew to her face.

He heard the thud of his heart. "No, you mustn't."

"He is a man I don't like…"

They stood silently facing each other. Slowly, he put an arm to her waist and drew her to him. Her bosom, against his chest, was soft and tender; her sweetness possessed his body and his soul. She raised her head and parted her lips. It was her first kiss.

The day of the wedding was clear and bright. Johann escorted his daughter to St. Stephen's in a four- horse drawn coach, followed by other coaches for the bridesmaids and guests of honor. The bells rang out a merry song of blissful union, but she heard nothing. In her hands she clasped a prayer book that contained the responses she must make when standing next to Franz and in front of the priest who would bind them together in the sight of man and God. God? She knew so little about the God in whose name she would be joined to this man body and soul. And less about the man himself.

She stood before the priest, Father Wolf, whom she had seen many times at mass. At mass his back was turned and he wore lengthy vestments that concealed him, but she knew his voice, crisp and precise, as he read the lessons for the service. Everything was in Latin, but the convent nuns had told her she was being bound to this man. Father Wolf's homily made it even more clear: "A man cleaves to his wife and they become one flesh."

One flesh? The nuns read that to the students to prepare them for this holy estate; but the words "one flesh" struck her as ominous—there must be something the nuns had not explained.

"Wives obey your husbands in all things," Wolf intoned, quoting the Apostle Paul, "for as Christ is the head of the church, the man is the head of the woman. She is to be his handmaid." This too she had heard, but understood only that something dim and dutiful was expected of her. The humidity in the church was like a cloak; her face beaded, her breath was shallow and forced.

Franz inched closer to her; his breath was warm and stale.

Was it like this for all women? For her mother? If only her mother were alive—her mother would have explained this mystery to her.

She had not felt this way or had these thoughts when she was with Phillipe. Only a few feet beyond Father Wolf, behind the altar, was the marble tiled ambulatory that led to the chapel with the font. Phillipe was different; she was not afraid when he touched her. His breath was sweet and it drew her to him. The lightest touch of his hand on the back of her neck, on her cheek—and the kiss, the one kiss—proved that she was wed to him, only to him.

There was an artist in the Kohlmarket who painted portraits. She would have a portrait made of herself, a miniature locket sized image of her tossled hair, and her almond eyes, and plenty of neck; and she vowed that someday when the heavens permitted she would find Phillipe and give it to him.

Eyes were upon her. Father Wolf lifted her hand to Franz, who covered it with his moist palm. Hardly aware of what she was saying, she whispered the responses; they were not her own words; they were the priest's words that she must repeat. "In the Name of God…" she said, looking at neither the priest nor Franz, "…I take you Franz to be my wedded husband, to honor and obey, until death us do part."

Father Wolf, his stole draped over their joined hands, intoned the words that pronounced them man and wife.

She quivered: the only escape, death? Silently she prayed that it be Franz whom death should overtake, and she knew her wish was a sin in the sight of God.

Behind the altar, near one of the great columns that supported the church, a young man wept bitter tears.

PART TWO

VIENNA

(1792-1827)

Chapter Five

"To Triumph over Mozart."

The coach had followed the route from Bonn that led along the Danube and finally, as it passed through the city gates, Louis strained to see the great spire of St. Stephen's Church that reached into the sky. The spire first met his eyes four years ago when he visited Vienna hoping to play for Herr Mozart, a visit that was cut short when he got word that Maria Magdalena was on her death-bed; he hastened back to Bonn to hold her hand and hear her blessed last words. Now he was back, at last, in the "Emperor City," the city of his hopes and dreams. This time he had subsidy; Count Waldstein had persuaded the Elector to issue funds for one year. With money in his pockets, he could stand in the busy Kohlmarket, where the famous Artaria had a publishing house and Haslinger ran a shop where music lovers could buy scores of great music to play in their homes; and he could attend the grand theaters, like the National Hof Theater; and he would play for the wealthy nobility in their parlors and to their acclaim. Yes, royalty lived here and aristocrats and patrons of the arts, and great men who sponsored young musicians—even though those musicians had to eat with the servants. That would change: he himself was royalty; he would be servant to no one.

He knew he would have to triumph over Haydn and Mozart, whose music captivated the whole city. Mozart was dead, but his melodies were heard everywhere. While still in Bonn, he was told that *Figaro* and *Cosi fan Tutti* were sung or whistled by lovers in the streets and parks, and by practically everyone in the barber shops and taverns; and his solemn music was sung in the churches. This too would change. Beethoven's melodies will fill the theaters, the princely palaces, the music halls. Beethoven's tunes will dance on the lips of lovers who hold hands as they stroll along the ramparts that surround the inner city, or as they sport among the wooded gardens and groves just outside the city gates.

His first task was to find lodging. He rented a cheap musty attic, then, though it was a cold day in November, he walked about the inner city and observed the people about their business. It was raining slightly but he hardly noticed. Soon, as he spoke to shopkeepers and others, he realized that his accent identified him as a lout from the Rhenish lowlands; but that did not prevent him from taking in the narrow Herrengasse where gentlemen and their ladies strutted.

A few weeks after he had settled in, he was in a coffee shop reading the Weiner Zeitung and came upon an obituary from Bonn. His father Johann was dead. He shrugged and finished his coffee. He took the paper with him to the attic flat and stuffed it into the cracks in the plaster, so as to keep out the howling November wind. A few days later word got to him that the Elector had commented on Johann's death: the revenues from the liquor excise would suffer, he joked, now that Johann was gone. Louis shrugged again.

Later in the week he chanced upon St. Stephen's and stepped into its interior, dark but for streaks of colored light that pierced the interior space from high clerestory windows of various hues, and blue trails of incense that hovered in the apse, the aftermath of a Solemn Mass. Banks of prayer candles lined one side of the nave, while columns of confessional boxes lined the other. Here and there in the pews people crouched in prayer. Not a votary of religion, he looked up at the great choir loft, higher and more imposing than the court chapel in Bonn. That was his home, up there, among the console and pipes. He was a man not of knee-bending, but of music-making. Music, not candles or incense, takes one to the heavens. This he would prove to the world. A black cassocked priest entered the sanctuary with a flaming taper and lit the tall candles on the altar. People began to fill the church, and there were stirrings in the loft above. Several coaches pulled up in front and pallbearers in military uniform lifted a finely draped casket and carried it down the center isle before the priest, who sprinkled holy water upon it. The organist, high above, shrouded the nave with dolorous tones. As the service progressed, the organ imitated a drum roll, while outside a cannon salute paid tribute to a fallen comrade.

What music would he have played at Johann's funeral? Certainly not sentimental tricks like drum rolls. Nor would he have played any of the fine music he had already composed, like the music for Cressener's funeral. Too good for Johann. What did Johann and Cressener have in common anyway? Drink? Or Belderbusch, for that matter? But the Dressler variations—a march to the grave—would have done well here in Vienna. Odd: he had written so much music fit for death. Many of the songs were about death—even the death of a poodle—and in his sketchbook he had ideas for a funeral march for a piano sonata he would soon finish. And a cantata on the death of the good Prince Joseph…yes, especially that. He grieved more over the death of a remote governor than over the death of his father.

The man at the organ above might be Albrecht Berger; if so, the man had bad taste. Or was he required to play such bad music, as poor Neffe had been? In any case, he needed to make appointments to see men like Albrecht Berger, and other great musicians of the city: Haydn, and the abbey Gelinek, and Salieri. These men could help him cut a path into inner circles of the city's music life. Practically, it remained for him to earn a living so that he would no longer need the subsidy from Bonn.

But it was the aristocracy that he needed more than the music-makers. His pockets were not too heavy with money, but he invested in a good address moving out of the dreary attic; he took lodging in a large house, number 30 Alserstrasse. Prince Karl Lichnowsky owned the house and he himself lived in it, just above Louis' small room on the ground floor. When the piano arrived, he sat down and improvised music fit for the ears of a prince.

Before long, a light tap on the door drew his attention. A beautiful woman with a flutter in her eyes stood before him. "I didn't realize our new tenant was so talented." Her voice was sweet as ripe berries plucked from the meadow.

Without waiting for a word from her tenant, she stepped into the room, followed by a tall man with noble bearing, a Roman nose, and thinning hair. The Prince sat himself at the piano and played from sight the score that Louis had placed on the stand. "Marvelous," he said. "You should teach composition to men like Haydn and Salieri."

The woman stood behind him while he played, her hands on his shoulders. Now she smiled at Louis. "I am Christiane," she said, holding out her hand for him to kiss it.

"I am Beethoven."

The Prince stepped in, took his wife's hand, and raised it to Louis' mouth, who had no choice but to kiss it.

"Your music…" asked the Prince, "…what more have you written? Trios? Quartets? A grand concerto? Will you try your hand at a symphony?"

Louis reached into a pile of scores under a desk and pulled out some scrawled notes on old, wet paper. "I jotted this down during the coach ride, when it rained," he said.

The Prince knew to read scores at sight and assess their value in seconds. His eyes bulged. "Marvelous," he said, "but what is this?"

"Some notes for my first symphony. In C Major."

"In C Major? If so, you begin in a foreign key." The Prince made a mock frown and wagged a finger at the young composer.

Louis stiffened. "Mozart would not have done that; Haydn would not have done that. Beethoven does that."

"Well then, is this the first theme of the allegro? It's very formal, much like Mozart's C Major."

"Not like Mozart. A comedy."

Christiane clapped her hands. "Wonderful, we need something light, what with all the talk about war."

The Prince kept on staring at Louis' scribbled notes, picking out chords and themes and playing them on the piano. "This here," he pointed to a two bar theme, "how does it fit into your lighthearted C Major symphony?"

Louis made a quick move toward the piano and grabbed the paper from the stand in front of him. "This? This is something old, I will throw it away."

"Oh, do not," Christiane rose and took the paper from his grip. "Here, Karl, you play this for us."

Karl took to the piano and played the theme; it was slow-paced and doleful. "Heavens," he exclaimed: "We are lowering someone into his grave."

"No—you are wrong." His anger rose, tense and tight in his chest. "It should be played fast, like this." He lept to the bench, forcing the Prince to one side, and he played his dirge as an allegro that burst into a major key and pranced about and rollicked like tipsy peasants at a wedding.

"Bravo," said Christiane, on her feet again: "You saved us from the reaper. Louis, you are a genius. You must meet our friends."

Later in the week Louis was at dinner with the Prince and his guests. Christiane's mother was present, the Countess Wilhelmine Thun. A few remarks had been made about an impending war. Wilhelmine shook her head: "Why all this talk about war? Austria is no great prize that the French should want us."

A general at the table corrected her: "I am afraid, Countess, that if Napoleon becomes Consul, he may well strike first at our Italian holdings, to set the peasants free—so he says…"

"Yes," said another military personage: "Then he will topple our blessed monarchy—all on the pretense of equality."

The general had deeper thoughts: "Napoleon is dangerous precisely because he rose up from peasant stock himself. Therefore, he has no respect for royalty, no right to rule. He has neither a *de* nor a *von* before his name…"

Louis bristled: "Napoleon is a great man," he thundered.

The room was silent.

Christiane threw up her hands: "No more talk about war at this table."

Another of the guests, the Countess Thurheim, agreed. "Let us talk instead about our amorous rounds. Our young lion here will want to hear about our social life."

The Prince, his senses addled by wine, concurred: "Yes, Louis—even though you are no nobility, your *van* not being a *von,* your status among us is assured. Your music is your crown."

Christiane and the others, not being so tipsy, blanched at the awkward remark.

Louis lept to his feet: "My name is Ludwig von Beethoven…"

"Louis, please; he meant no offense. You are one of us." Christiane cast warm eyes upon him.

"…and I am the god Bacchus who presses out the wine that intoxicates all men."

The Prince, somewhat abashed, atoned: "Dear Louis, I only meant to compliment you on your genius. There are many vons whom we do not accept. It is your genius that admits you to our little society."

Pacified, Louis took his seat.

The Countess Thurheim stared at Louis. "Dear boy, do you have a girlfriend?"

"I am too busy for that…"

The Countess Thurheim and the Princess Christiane glanced at each other.

After dinner the prince and a few of the male guests took Louis aside. "The amorous rounds, dear friend, is a game we play. We meet for dinner every so often; then when the lights are dimmed, we make sport."

The Prince read incomprehension on Louis' face. He put an arm around his shoulder and led him to the drawing room, where men were lighting pipes and cigars. Just as the Prince drew the heavy oak doors shut, Louis happened to notice the Princess Christiane standing outside in the vaulted hall; she smiled at him in a knowing way. The Prince witnessed the smile.

Louis was offered a smoke, but he declined. Brandy was served; he accepted.

The Prince took him to a soft lounge chair in a corner. "Louis, we like you. You are one of us. Now, my lad, let me first tell you about Christiane, my wife." He drew the aromatic smoke deeply into his lungs and leaned back in his chair. "I know she likes you…very much."

"I don't understand," he answered. In fact, he knew very well.

"She is an incorrigible flirt. She makes eyes at many men, many. But when the men drop their trousers, she drops her interest. Do you know what I mean?"

Louis gave him a blank stare.

"Christiane is cold like the dead of winter — an iceberg in bed. She teases a man into her bedroom and orders the fool to undress before her eyes. But then she laughs at his nudity and marches out; later she will whisper and titter among her friends about the spectacle of his inadequacy. So, my lad, instead of the ice-mistress, you may have your choice of many lovely beddings in this society of ours. I especially recommend the Countess Thurheim; she is a most generous person, and her bosom is equally generous—as you know, dear lad." He wrapped his arm around Louis' shoulder: "Oh, don't be shy; I saw you gaze at her."

The Prince heard a clutch in Louis' throat as he responded, "It is not the size of a woman's breasts..."

"Then you may prefer the petite Contessa who sat to her left; she too is of interest. A dainty bosom..."

"I prefer music—my music."

"Ah, very well, my friend." The Prince pounded him on the back. "When you discover—if you have not done so already—the deplorable appearance of the street women, you will return to our amorous rounds. By the way, there is one particular bordello that I can recommend..."

"I am a man of music."

"Well then, my friend," said the Prince, puffing on his pipe. "Let's talk about how you will conquer Vienna...with your music, I mean."

Sometimes the talk at the table or in the lounge preyed on his nerves and bored him. Even the sight of the Contessa's dark eyes and pert bosom failed to hold him fast. Often, he would slip away from the table and head for the solace of the blessed countryside. The Prince and his guests accepted his "eccentricity" and permitted him to leave table without the formality of begging leave.

In the mornings he rose early and worked on his compositions. The variations he had written were merely cute and ornamental; they would not do for his Opus One. His music would not be pretty like Mozart's. In time, he knew, he would assert himself. For now, the three trios would do for Opus One. Perhaps the Prince would underwrite the expense of printing them.

But how would his name appear on the engraved title page? Von Beethoven sounded right to his ears. Did not genius confer its own crown? But he dared not; his birth certificate would prove him a liar. He pounded on the keyboard—a dissonance sounded from some hollow place in his soul, where something remained unsettled.

It was not yet dark. He put on his hat and stepped out to the street, toward the gates that opened upon the wooded suburbs. Soldiers stood on duty there, their muskets loaded with ball. They warned him the gates would close at ten; he had best remain inside lest he be locked out. One of the soldiers, he noticed, had a girl. She was pressing herself close to his chest and wrapping her arms around his neck, and she seemed to whisper something into his ear—until he pulled away with a start. She stepped back and spat at him. Another soldier caught her fancy for a moment, but he proved disinterested. Then she saw Louis standing by the gate.

Flicking her tongue, she sauntered over to him. "Hello, dearie," she said, "those silly men don't know what I'm worth. But you do, don't you, dearie?" She pursed her lips and tugged at his belt. "I live close by." She led him through a maze of dark, narrow streets that reeked of urine, to a fourth floor flat that had no window.

First she wanted to see his money. "One ducat," she demanded. He had it.

The girl turned the gaslights low, but not too low. "Take off your trousers, dearie."

She began to remove her dress, but slowly. She wanted to inspect her customer first. She knew her business.

He turned his back to her and pulled down his trousers.

"Don't be shy, dearie. Oh, I see how young you are." A slow smile crossed her face. "Is this your first time?"

"Of course not."

She knew the scent of a lie. "No? Well, we shall see how experienced you are. Turn around."

It was supposed to grow big. But it didn't.

"You can't do much with that little thing." She perched on the edge of the bed and beckoned to him. "Come here boy. Let me see what I can do." She took it between her fingers and lifted it. "What's this…a red streak?"

"A scar, only a scar. It's healed."

Her eyes narrowed. "Two ducats. And nothing less because you got only one ball."

"I don't have two ducats."

"Then you don't have me, either, dearie. Put it away and go home."

During the week, his fingers trembled over the keyboard as he forced them to obey his will. Nothing came to him; inspiration flagged. At night sleep eluded him. He would lie on his back in bed and grasp his member. "Oh," he cried, as he stroked it. It rose, only to drop again.

From the Prince he asked for the loan of a ducat—the price of a fine wig, which he would need for his first public concert. The Prince gave him the ducat as a gift; it was the least he could do for his resident genius.

She was nowhere to be seen, although some older women ambled about the soldiers' pavilion. Finally he found the darkened street where she had taken him and he stood outside the house; he recognized its charred brick and stone façade, the shutters carved with hearts and leaves, the door loose on its hinges. The flat was on the fourth floor, he remembered. The hallway was dark, but he knew the way. Uncertain, he waited. He heard muffled voices, then the door opened; a man brushed past him on the way down. There was the girl, framed in the glow of the gas-light, naked and unashamed, her long hair flowing down her back. "Oh, its you. Two ducats."

That night he slept no better. The image of the woman's body lit his dark: her breasts were two hillocks and a valley, her ass a sloped landscape split by a fissure that ran the length of it. But she was faceless, and that troubled him. The breasts and ass belonged to no person at all. On the bed, their mouths had not met—her wish or his?

The face of Babette was haloed in his memory. He was standing outside the kitchen looking in: the widow Koch was darting about giving orders...there!...Babette, her arm raised under a platter of plates and pitchers, came into clear view. Pure and virginal, her face lingered in his dark night. Their mouths had never met, nor even their eyes; they were separated by a mystery that lay beyond his grasp.

He moved into the Prince's residence and was given a private room. But soon life at the Prince's palace grew tiresome. The routine was confining: dinner everyday at three, obligatory shave and dress. He noted how the guests were greeted: a porter rang a bell three times if a Prince entered; twice if a Count. Two servants, finely liveried, admitted each guest: one servant relieved the guest of his outer wraps, the other escorted him through vaulted halls to an inner parlor where the hostess, seated, acknowledged him with a slight nod; but to friends, a kiss was granted. Louis, as a resident of the palace, was exempt from the bells and the escort; but he wondered if he left and returned as a guest, how many bells would ring? He would demand three or more; the kiss he would scorn. One day he tested it; he went for an afternoon's walk and upon returning he got three bells. Then he mentioned the servants: he noted that the Prince and Princess rang bells to summon the servants. It was granted that if Louis rang at the same time as the Prince or Princess, the servant was to answer Louis first. But Louis spent more and more time roaming the streets and the woods, and took no pleasure in the bells, which to the Prince was a sign of discontent.

The Prince offered to pick up the subsidy when the stipend from Bonn ran its course—that would be 600 thalers a year—and to underwrite the expense of publishing his Opus One. With income, he could live wherever he liked. He found a flat near the Josephplatz. Now his afternoons were free: he could compose, or enjoy long walks outside the ramparts, seek the ecstasy of the woods, carouse with peasants, or drink beer or ale at the taverns as he spied on lovely wenches.

One day he received a letter from Bonn. It was Helene: Napoleon's troops now occupied the city and were a menace to women in the street. The children were growing fast, Stephan may go to Vienna soon...Oh, remember the widow Koch? Her daughter Babette is engaged to be married to an Austrian recruiting officer—and rumor has it she will deliver her first child shortly after the ceremony.

He took to an early bed, but he turned and thrashed about. Visions of Babette in the arms of another assailed him through the night: tender intimacies, her parted lips, her spread legs, came to him like unwanted specters.

The early morning sun woke him; ignoring his unmade bed, he sat himself at the piano—a new Concerto in B flat was gestating under his fast flying fingers. The sun meantime moved overhead and streamed down upon him through an overhead skylight. A steady pounding at the door finally startled him: it might be the Prince, he thought, who was wont to drop by unannounced. But it was a man-servant in rich livery, who announced the presence of his mistress the Contessa, who stepped into the room, nodded to her servant that he should leave them alone, and perched herself on the piano bench. She tapped the bench beside her: "Come, Louis, play for me."

He reached for his coat. "I must go out."

"They said you might be difficult." She placed herself between him and the door and pursed her lips. When he tried to pass her, she slipped her hand inside his trousers and forced her tongue deep into his mouth.

He grabbed her offending hand and threw it in her face. "No—you must come back tonight...tonight when it is dark."

"I look better to you in the dark? I am here now, Louis...now...do you understand?"

She tossed her head in the direction of the unmade bed and moved to loosen her bodice. As she bent over, her breasts were visible to Louis' gaze.

"This is my bed, I alone lie in it. I alone."

Her hand struck him across the side of his face. "You refuse the Contessa? May your balls boil in hell."

With a furious sweep of her skirts and with rage and fury flashing in her eyes, she turned and in an instant was gone. He heard her feet pounding on the stairs, and a final slam of the great oak door. At the window he stared at the sight of her as she stepped into the waiting coach. He threw himself upon his bed and thrashed about, holding his swollen member and pounding it uselessly until tears formed in his eyes and shrouded his vision.

After an hour he leapt from bed with a start and gaped at the window, where streaking rays of sun told him it was almost noon. And it was Friday. On Fridays the Prince held private concerts in the music room of his palace, mainly rehearsals of new works. He must not be late. Some clean trousers were draped over the back of a chair; he changed and dashed through the streets to get to the palace before the others; he needed to go over his piano part alone, in quiet. Today's concert was important: his three trios were to be played for the first time. Ignaz Schuppanzeigh would be there; he was a violinist who could be trusted with the difficult part; and Nicolaus Zmeskall the cellist would play along side of them. They had rehearsed the pieces several times already, but this would be different. Great men would be in the audience, possibly even the famous Franz Joseph Haydn. Sometimes he worried about Zmeskall, whose knees were wont to swell up and the pain would cause him to flinch—but he had never yet put forth a sour note. They were the finest in all Vienna, and friends of the Prince. He himself would play the piano part.

At noon a small group had assembled in the marbled and pillared music room of the Prince. Louis glanced about. Haydn was there! "Papa" Haydn, who had invented the forms that all composers used when writing serious music. He, Louis, would be entertaining the master who laid down the laws that in these three pieces of his, he both honored and flouted. A hush fell upon the group as the Prince stood before his guests. How honored he was, he said, to host such great and distinguished musicians. Haydn beamed with a satisfied countenance when the Prince spoke at length and in glowing terms about the miracles wrought by the revered master. At last the Prince nodded in the direction of Louis and spoke of the young prodigy who would astound the world with fresh, invigorating new music. "Well then," he said, "let us begin."

Louis and his two stringed fellows took up their instruments and the four movements of the E Flat Major Trio winged their way into the world. Zmeskall made a few slips, Louis noted, but not serious: the music had been honored. He was satisfied. But was Haydn?

The audience was stone still. The tense silence was broken as Haydn stood and stared directly at Louis. All eyes turned to the great master.

"Bravo," he said. "What an infectious melody at the very start. Wonderful harmony. A most promising work." The entire group of two dozen or more—artists and connoisseurs—rose as if in unison and applauded. And the great man had more to say, when the noisy acclaim had faded: "The sense of motion, the modulations, all within the accepted form… marvelous. Shall we hear the second piece?"

Louis and his two friends scrambled back to their places. The G Major Trio began with a somber adagio, intending to fool no one—it winked, as if letting on that this is mock *serioso*: then a merry *allegro vivace* burst forth. The second movement, *Largo con espressione*, was warm-blooded and romantic, a song without words. Louis knew it would touch them deeply. At the conclusion of the movement, he heard only the hushed breathing of the listeners. A brisk *allegro* and a breathless *presto* finished off the piece. Haydn again stood to lead the applause.

Over an hour had been given to the two trios. The Prince declared an intermission and snapped his fingers for servants to bring in coffee and hot pastries called Mehlspeise, and Palatschinken for those with hearty appetites. Louis took the opportunity to chat with the illustrious inventor of the string quartet and the perfector of the symphony. The elder composer was cordial and agreeable. Yet, Louis sensed a reserve; he knew that Papa Haydn, as he was called, always praised some new piece as a courtesy; his hand-clapping therefore was no assurance of enthusiasm. The third trio, however, would test his honesty. It was no trifle; nothing like it had ever been written, not by Haydn, not by Mozart, not by anyone.

Seated at the piano again, he nodded to his fellows and plunged into the somber tones of the C Minor Trio. The stately sonata form prevailed, but the writing contained forceful and abrupt modulations; its first theme was given in a plaintive minor, the second in contrasting major. The atmosphere of the piece was bold, assertive, passionate. When all four movements were concluded, Louis raised his hand to hold off the applause. "I wish to dedicate these three trios, my Opus One, to our host, and my friend and benefactor, Prince Karl von Lichnowsky." He bowed from the waist, to the clamor of excited applause.

Without a word to Louis, Haydn took his friend Antonio Salieri, the Court composer, outside the music room to a small parlor where the two men sat on a side-sofa, both dressed in the formal manner as befitted men of their stature and age: chignon, silk stockings, fitted waistcoats. Louis dared not interrupt. When finally Haydn rendered a cordial farewell to the Prince, nodded in Louis' direction, and took his leave, Louis turned to the Prince: "Did he say anything about the C Minor?"

"Never mind, Louis. I shall speak to Salieri during the week and find out."

A word or two from Haydn carried great weight in Vienna and beyond. He needed the elder composer's blessing if he were to be taken seriously by those who were not beholden to the Prince—the great public. And the time for his first public performance was set: March 29 and 30 at the Berg Theater, less than a month away.

The Prince came to him at his flat in the Josephplatz one morning. "Louis, I found out that two new works are to be performed on the 29th and 30th, before and after your Concerto. Both are by an aspiring composer named Cardellieri, an Italian."

"And a friend of Salieri?"

"I am afraid so."

"What did Haydn say about my trios?"

"He had nothing against the first two, but the third fell heavily upon his ears. In a word, he didn't like it."

"Well then, my fortunes in Vienna will ride upon the Concerto. It is a fluffy piece, designed to please."

When the Prince left, Louis ran out into the cutting March wind and rain, forgetting his hat and coat. Oblivious to all but his intent, he made his way to a row of narrow streets near the ramparts where the soldiers stood guard at the city gates. He found the house with no trouble: the one with the charred brick and stone façade, the shutters carved with hearts and leaves. The door that had hung loose on its hinges was now fallen off and stood leaning against an inside wall.

Chapter Six

"A Fainting Spell."

The house did not seem the same to Antonie. She was born here, it was her home, her father's residence on the Landgasse. But tonight would be different; she would not sleep alone tonight. No one had said that to her; but she had seen the maids preparing the guest chamber. She knew.

Franz reached for her hand as they stepped from the coach. "You look tired, my dear. Would you like to rest before the dinner?"

If only she could go to her old room, where her mother had given her comfort when she was little, before she went off to convent school. "Yes," she answered. "I must lie down."

Franz led her to the chamber. He sat in a divan and lit his pipe.

It was a hot, moist day; St. Stephen's was stuffy; the ceremony long and tedious; sweat rolled down the face of Father Ferdinand Wolf, who performed the ceremony and sang the nuptial mass. He was noted for having performed Mozart's wedding to Constanza; that was in August, she heard—did they sweat too? She wanted to loosen her bodice and step out of the dress. But she could not.

"Herr Brentano…"

"Come now, you must call me Franz. And you must step out of that dress."

She stood still, hardly taking a breath.

"Very well, I see you are modest. I shall leave you for a while. When I return, you will be rested and ready to greet the wedding guests and the rest of our evening."

She knew little what to expect. At dinner, she would be safe from him; but to entertain the wedding guests—people of prestige whom Johann had invited, to accept their gifts, to be polite—seemed beyond her. It would be good to lie down, to rest, to never awake.

When Franz returned, she was sitting weakly in the divan, dressed as before, rumpled and red-eyed.

"You cannot face our guests like this. I will send someone up to take care of you."

"Oh, send Sigrid, please. I like Sigrid."

Sigrid had helped her unpack when she came back from the convent, and she helped pack for this trip to Frankfurt. She was a merry person,

39

the youngest of the servant staff and they had chatted from time to time. And she was married. She felt she could trust Sigrid. Happily, after a few minutes Sigrid knocked on the door. Soon Sigrid had her out of the wedding gown. Antonie summoned her courage and turned to the girl: "Sigrid, you are married. Tell me what happens on a woman's wedding night."

The servant girl turned pale. "Madam, it is not for me…"

"Oh, you must tell me."

"You must do everything he wants…everything. It is a woman's duty…"

"But what does he want?"

Sigrid understood at last what her young mistress needed from her. She stared at the slender undressed figure before her. How innocent, how helpless…it tore at her heart. "Have you ever seen a man's organ?"

"Only when I saw some boys in the street—they had to relieve themselves as my carriage passed by."

"Well, a man's is bigger…" As she spoke, she pulled garments from the closet—a silk pattern dress, a blouse, kerchiefs… "and when he is ready for you, it gets hard…" The servant girl hesitated as she saw the blood drained from her mistress' face and dread in the whites of her eyes. "Mistress, have you…have you been punctured?"

Antonie looked up. "Punctured?"

Sigrid came over and sat beside her on the edge of the bed. "A girl has a strip of skin over her opening, called a hymen. Sometimes a girl, before she…gets married…has it removed. My mother did it for me. It bled a little, but that didn't matter, because I was ready for my husband."

Antonie stared blankly.

"Down there," Sigrid pointed to Antonie's crotch.

Music from below announced that guests were arriving. Soon Franz would come for her.

"No," she said. "No one did that for me. But sometimes it bleeds anyway."

"If only we had talked sooner…"

"Sigrid, when it happens, is it at night?"

"Why, usually, yes. Why?"

"It seems best that way. In the dark."

"Dear Mistress, I will tell you a few things…"

The music quickened its pace; the guests would be arriving in great numbers; soon there would be dinner, speeches, and dancing. Sigrid helped her pull a fresh dress over her head. Then steps were heard outside the door. And a knock. Franz at least had the courtesy to knock, she thought. She nodded to Sigrid, who opened the door for Franz to enter.

Franz looked splendid in his blue frock coat, carefully tied ascot, and white trousers. But Antonie noted the beads of sweat on his brow. The room was wretchedly hot, the air stale. She stood, but her head became light; she fell back into the chair.

"No more delay, my dear. Our guests are expecting to greet us as we descend the stairs."

Sigrid understood; she fanned Antonie and offered to fetch a glass of water.

"No more delay," insisted Franz. He reached for her hand and he pulled her to her feet.

Together they stood at the head of the stairs. A six piece orchestra began to play a serenade: she knew it—Mozart wrote it for the marriage of a famous person, she couldn't remember who, her head was not clear. The images at the foot of the stairs were swimming around in a haze. Now it came to her: Mozart wrote it for Marie Elspeth Haffner. The poor girl—how, she wondered, did she endure her wedding night?

She looked down the length of the spiraled stairs. At the foot of the stairs, in the alabaster columned vestibule, the guests had parted to allow space for the solemn procession that she and Franz had commenced. The sun's rays passed through the large windows on either side and slanted down the expanse of the vestibule and parlor with dovetailing shafts of light and shadow. Dust shimmered in paths of light flecking the air with all the colors of the mosaics and the paintings that hung from the walls. The floor below teemed with garlands, birds, tritons, fish, griffins, gargoyles, ancient Romans, all glowing with deep tints and hues.

The figure of her father was visible through the haze; he stood tall and straight at the foot of the stairs; she must not disappoint him. And she made out the figure of Father Wolf who would pronounce a blessing at the banquet; she must not embarrass him. Franz, on her left, led with his right foot. She began with her left, and bumped against his side. That was bad. And he was taller than she, much taller. In bed, how would they manage? She did not want to be clumsy in bed, for she should not fail her husband. She would do her duty, but she prayed that it be in the dark; she would beg him to turn out the gaslights.

The colors from the streaks of light ran together in her head. The faces were no longer distinct. Her head felt heavy; no longer could she hold it up. Her knees buckled beneath her. But for Franz's arm, she would have fallen the length of the stairs to the floor below.

✶✶✶✶✶

Frankfurt seemed an endless row of smokestacks, dirty shops, clogged gutters, and street odors that she had known only in a chamber room where such chores were done in private with a window thrown open for relief. Small boys chased after the coach and one of them threw a handful of pebbles at the horses: Franz shook his fist out the window: "Urchins... should be stripped and flayed." He turned to Antonie: "Do not fret, my dear, soon we will be out of this slum—the coach must come this way to avoid the Hessian troops, who are barracked near the boulevard. Soon we shall reach the boulevard from the far side—then home."

She felt a stab of pain at the word "home." Never would she call Frankfurt home. Her home was Vienna.

The coach passed the Romerbürgplatz and the Grand Municipal Playhouse. Franz pointed and said "Herr Mozart played certain of his Concertos here, my dear. You see, Frankfurt is not devoid of the arts. I suspect you will spend many delighted hours here." Antonie recalled hearing that Mozart's performance in Frankfurt was poorly attended, but she held her tongue.

When at last the coach lumbered through heavy gates, she saw the columned porch. The house struck her as too large, too cold.

In the bedroom, a canopied four-poster bed dominated; two hooded chairs stood on duty alongside. It was a southside room; the sun lit up every corner, but there were heavy drapes to pull. He summoned a maid to help unpack and organize her belongings. The sight of a stranger touching her intimate garments—she turned her head. It would be worse tonight, when the stranger whom she married would touch her in intimate places. She pondered her excuse. On the wedding day, her fainting spell served through the night. At the inns where they had stopped on the journey, she had pleaded—feigned—a woman's monthly flow of blood. That was Sigrid's advice. And she pleaded a urinary complaint. But tonight...? Perhaps a fever, a chill? What if he summoned a doctor? Well, she would lie to the doctor too.

But no: she could not deceive him forever.

At supper she stared at her plate. Servants came and went, bringing dishes, removing dishes; she ate little. "Come my little sparrow, you peck at your plate like a bird. Won't you try a morsel, just to please the cooks..."

She looked up when he commanded: never before had she looked directly at him long enough to take in his austere eyes, the thin lipped smile, the hanging lobes of his ears, the rigid back and square shoulders. He reminded her of a statue she saw in a public square: a military figure

42

standing tall and straight, equipped for battle, ready to mount his horse. Tonight Franz would mount her. The statue spoke:

"—you have hardly eaten since I have known you."

It was true. And she could never tell him why. "I am not hungry, may I be excused?"

"We shall be in bed soon enough, my dear."

After dinner there were entertainments in the parlor. A troupe of several musicians in festive attire and two singers were ready to sing some arias from *The Marriage of Figaro*. She had not seen the opera on stage—her father had not permitted—but she heard people singing the tunes on the street: lovers, she believed, for they were holding hands or gazing into each other's eyes. Franz explained the plot to her: Figaro and Suzanna are engaged to be married, but they are both in the employ of the Count Almaviva, who insists on his feudal privilege—the *jus primae noctis*. "Have you heard of it?"

She shook her head no.

"It is a custom that required the bride to spend the first night in the Count's bed."

"Oh."

"Here now, the fellow will sing Figaro's aria, *Si Vous Bellare, Signor Conte*. That means, 'If you wish to dance, Signor Conte, you must dance with me.' Figaro is clever; he outwits the count. The Emperor frowned on the plot, considered it revolutionary."

Antonie listened with half an ear to the music, her mind diverted by the thought that she had outwitted Franz so far, but she could do no more.

After the entertainment, Franz ordered Hilda to take her upstairs and help her with her needs. She mounted the stairs in silence, her head bowed in ascent, her frail shoulders curved as under a burden, her skirt girt tightly about her. She heard the thumping of her heart against her ribs.

When he came up, sooner than expected, the servant girl was helping her out of her dress. She was standing in her petticoat when Franz walked in: "You may leave now, Hilda." The girl understood; she picked up her things and was gone.

Franz turned to his bride: "Come to the light, my dear—no excuses now—remove it all."

"Can we not dim the light?"

"A man is entitled to see his wife in her natural state. I am waiting."

The flame of the gas lit up the rich bronze of her hair and exposed the pallor of her face and the tremor in her lips. She turned her back to him. But he came to her, held her by the shoulders and whipped her around to face him. With deft moves he rendered her nude before his gaze. She crossed her arms over her bosom.

"What I require of you is most appropriate," he said, his eyes fixed upon her. "You will find that in all things I am a considerate husband; I honor my obligations—you must honor yours."

She felt she was being lectured, warned.

He seemed to struggle with some hidden excitement. His breath became short and shallow, his face flushed. His eyes narrowed and searched the length of her body down to the small bushy mound that shielded her virginity. "Do not move," he said, in a voice that cracked with an emotion she could not fathom.

With slow, deliberate moves he shed his shoes, his coat, his shirt, his trousers, his undergarment. In a moment, he stood before her in the light of the gas lamp, his body in full display before virgin eyes. "Kneel," he said.

Is he a god that I must kneel before his shrine? she thought. But she had no cause to resist, no excuse. She obeyed.

The day's heat trapped in the room, the odor of his body, so close, jarred her senses. His member, which had been small and innocuous shrouded in dark hair now stood stiff and menacing. What did he want of her?

"In your mouth… all of it… no teeth, use tongue, lots of tongue." With hot and heavy hands he took her head and forced her to him.

Fainting, she soon discovered, worked. It was real the first time it happened, the afternoon of the wedding.

Chapter Seven

"Baptized in Rain."

As he poured the morning bath water over his head, Louis bristled at the old man's words. Haydn was a revered master, his name was known to aristocrats and peasants alike, and he had been invited to perform his new symphonies in London. The water was too cold—he cursed and stomped to the kitchen to heat water. He needed a servant—that would come in time. Yes, Haydn was famous; his judgment prevailed in all matters. But he had no ear for music that was not his own—except of course for some second rate Italian composer whose works would be played along side his new B Flat Concerto.

Haydn's words burned in his gullet: yes, he said the trios were formally perfect, but that was damning with faint praise. The old man said nothing about the robust, out-of-doors frolic that were the first two, and he condemned the third, which was the most daring of the three. How important were Haydn's words in Vienna? Too much so, he was afraid. Quickly he dabbed himself dry, dressed and headed for the Black Camel Tavern, where he often came across musicians who wanted passion and virility in their music.

It was mid-morning and the tavern was already packed. He made his way to the back, where an iron pot of stew simmered over an open flame attended by a cook who held a bottle of wine in one hand and a ladle in the other, as he filled the stew bowls that serving girls would take to waiting customers. He found a place at table with Moscheles and Dragonetti, who played contra-bass in the Prince's orchestra, and sat down. Since he had not had breakfast and the busy serving girl was slow in coming, he grew peevish. When the girl passed by, he grabbed her by the sleeve and pulled her to the table: "I want stew and ale," he demanded. After a time, the order had not come. He chased after the serving girl and demanded she bring the ale at once to calm the rage in his belly while he waited for the stew. The girl brought him a tankard, which he downed, then he ordered another, which he downed.

After his third ale, he looked about for the serving girl and his stew. When she happened to pass his table, her arms uplifted carrying a tray for a customer at another table, he sprang to his feet: "You are slow, wench," he said, and grabbed a bowl of stew from the tray. It was hot. He let go of it, spilling its contents over himself, Moscheles, Dragonetti, and the girl. "It was too hot," he screamed, pointing a damning finger at the cook: "that man... it's his fault, drinking like a country lout." He picked up the empty bowl and flung it at the cook, then dashed the man's wine bottle to the floor. "No drunkard shall serve Beethoven."

His two friends took him by the arm into the street and into a coach. The City of Trieste Inn had tables; they sat him down, whereupon he ordered another ale. Moscheles hurried into the kitchen and explained to the manager that a serving of cold beef at once would avert an uproar. The manager obliged. "You see," said Louis, "at this inn I am respected." As he ate and drank he cursed the Black Camel, the cook, and the serving girl. "My father Johann drank," he added, "but never so bad as that lout with the ladle."

By mid-afternoon he parted from his friends and took a coach to the edge of the city near the ramparts. He knew a small tavern near Modling, where field workers liked to dance, and drink, and pinch the behinds of serving girls. It was a cold day for a walk, but he didn't feel the cold as he waved his arms, and sang, and shouted themes from his Concerto. "I am the man who will console the world for the loss of Mozart," he called out. Turning from the path he scrambled through brush and brambles toward a brook that gurgled nearby. He stripped and, kneeling as if in prayer, he cupped his hands and drank deeply; tears ran down his face; then he lept to his feet and jumped in to splash and bathe. "Who will console me for the loss of my mother?" he cried. He looked down at his member, shrunken and bluish in the cold. The red scar was still there, the scar that his mother could not wash away, not even with her tears.

Finally he fell exhausted to the ground and slept until he was roused by the sounds of stomping feet and clapping hands and loud singing from beyond a hillock. It was the tavern he was looking for, The Sign of Three Ravens. When he came over the hillock he saw seven fiddlers. Some of them, their heads heavy with sleep and wine, nodded or dozed all the while the band played their simple tunes. He leaned against a tree and watched them: a melody took shape in his head: the oboe falls asleep and comes to his wits too late for his solo; he starts with a false accent, and takes four bars to catch up to the procession—a stunt that would make Herr Haydn break out in a rash. A country symphony was coming to birth in his brain: the first movement, joy and release upon escaping the confines of the city and entering upon the wild beauties of nature; the second, a sedate scene by the brook, where pure waters cleanse an overburdened soul; and a scherzo, merry tunes of peasants whose tipsy fiddles cannot keep pace with the dancer's feet.

They saw him in the lengthening shadows and they beckoned to him: "Come and join us," they called. He picked up a fallen fiddle and played their tunes until the dancers fell to the ground in heaps, only to pull one another to their feet and begin again. A girl brought him an ale and pointed to a grill over which a loin of pork was sizzling. He ate and drank under a tree and laughed and joked with the merrymakers until the sun had long set and the moon rose high in the sky. He noticed that from time to time a boy and a girl would slip away into the woods, linger a while, then return starry eyed. One of the girls just back from the woods playfully pulled off his trousers and lifted him to his feet; he did a few dance steps with her, and took her by the hand and tried to pull her into the woods, but she held back at the sight of her strapping boyfriend who was not too drunk to block their way. But Louis himself was drunk, and his lids had grown heavy as the night grew long. The girls made a sack of straw for him in the back of the inn and gave him the comfort of a bed for the night.

When he awoke in the morning the serving girls made him coffee and raved over his spirited fiddle playing. "Are you a musician?" one of them asked. "Ah," he said, "if only I had a piano, I would lift your spirits as high as those lumpkins lifted your petticoats last night." The girls giggled and smiled. "Oh," said one blue-bonneted lass, "we must not joke so, for the priest from the village church is coming for his breakfast. He does not approve of our dancing, and our drinking, and what we do in the woods." The priest entered and frowned at the sight of Louis on his straw bed surrounded by pretty girls. "O Father," a girl said, "pay no mind to this. Sit, and we will make your breakfast."

There was one clean table, so Louis and the priest were companions at breakfast. "Have you read Strum's Observations of the Works of God?" Louis asked.

"I have never heard of it. Is Strum a Catholic?"

"No, a Lutheran pastor. He writes about the joys of nature."

The priest looked down his spectacles at Louis. "I preach the joys of sobriety," he said, with a glance at the serving girls and a few men who had gathered to ogle them and pluck at their apron strings.

"I drink in the joys of nature."

"Are you a Catholic?"

Louis' brow furrowed: a pained memory, buried in some corner of his brain, still had the power to prick him. His baptism? His birth? "My parents, yes. As for me, I was baptized by rain, confirmed by thunder; I commune with angels and I confess to no man."

The priest stared at him. "You are a pantheist, which is to say, an atheist."

Louis wearied of the pedant. "I look to the starry skies and I see no father in heaven."

The words with the priest goaded him as he trod back to the city ramparts. The hidebound cleric was no inspiration except that, yes, he had been baptized in the court chapel in Bonn. He had never seen the registry, but Maria said he was born on December 16th, and baptized on the 17th. But in what year? When he composed *An Einen Saugling*, he sensed that some mystery clung to his birth. Maria and Johann gave differing answers to his questions: Johann, of course, lied about his prodigy's age.

Bonn! If he failed in Vienna, he would have to return to the service of the Elector. The first public concert was set for March 29, less than a week away. But the B flat Concerto was unfinished. If he could solve a few problems, it would be a success; it was a piece of fluff, a bon-bon with a touch of romance; those who applauded Haydn would applaud Beethoven—louder, even. But the balances were wrong: some orchestral passages might be so dense the soloist would be lost. It would help to hear the work in rehearsal. But that would not happen until the 28th or even the afternoon of the 29th.

It was his habit to rise early, dash down a simple breakfast—sometimes just pumpernickel, butter and coffee—and sit at the piano until mid or late afternoon, when he would go to a tavern for a meal, or a long walk in the country. The long walks were not distractions; he drew inspiration from the sights and sounds of nature in the wild.

On Friday of the week before the concert, he had been working from sun-up; without breakfast even, for he had forgotten to put in supplies. In the mid-afternoon he set forth in search of his meal and a new tavern. Braced against the wind, he wandered down the Karnerstrasse to the Neur Market. A graceful fountain stood there, whose figures represented the great rivers of Austria, and little nude putti played in the basin—harmless creatures of stone whose nudity had offended the prudish Maria Theresa, he heard, who tried to have them removed. In the summer the fountain flowed and the market teemed with Italiante foods, wines, and music; but in the winter the nobility used it for horse-drawn sleighing. Suddenly a man's loud call turned his head: "Babette! Babette!"

A young man was running to overtake a girl who had just stepped from a sleigh. Her back was to Louis, but he saw auburn locks of hair under her cap, and when she turned, her face was rosy cheeked and dimpled. She was too plump to be his Babette, but he followed the pair into a coffee house and studied her and the young man whose hand dropped to her knee. She must be nobility, Louis considered, for she was finely dressed and had been in an elegant sleigh. When the pair left, he spoke to the proprietor and asked if he knew the girl. He did: Barbara von Keglevics. *Von!* She was nobility. Not nearly as beautiful as his Babette of Bonn, but she was nobility, and her name was magic to his ears.

The Artaria publishing house was nearby, where his Opus One should be ready for sale. The two Babettes danced before his eyes. How could he set a pretty face to music? He wondered. No, not the face—but a beautiful spirit he could render in music, just as a portrait artist captures beauty in oils. Inside the store he addressed a clerk on the subject of his Opus One. "Not ready until May," the clerk told him.

"What name is to be engraved upon the face?" he asked.

The clerk went to the back room and returned with the answer: "Ludwig van Beethoven."

"Change the van to von," he demanded. "And I must know how many of the nobility have subscribed to the engraving, and I must have an advance." The clerk summoned the owner, who advised Louis that in time the names of all the subscribers would be published and no, it was not the policy of the house to give advances against sales.

"Dolt, ass! The House of Artaria shall be evermore ashamed." He spat, cursed, kicked over a music stand, and stormed out onto the street.

The concert was a charity on behalf of widows and children of the Society of Musicians, and he would receive no payment from ticket sales. It was good, however, that the concert was a charity, for no critic would make uncharitable remarks about a charity concert, and he needed good reviews to bring his name before the public. But the risk was, first, could he complete the work in time? And, second, the orchestra itself, which would have little time to rehearse. The program would begin and end with works by the Italian: a symphony first, then an oratorio on a biblical theme. The orchestra, limited in the number of rehearsals allowed to it, and no doubt influenced by Haydn and Salieri, would take up the Cardellieri first—and Beethoven's, perhaps not at all. He must hurry.

But the concert and the money were not all that occupied him. The image of Babette, the real Babette, was a lighthouse over dark waters. Her beauty, her mystery, consumed his soul, where she reigned like a goddess. The muse is a woman, he knew—Caecilia, the goddess of music: Handel had honored her by setting an ode to music. But no composer had captured her spirit in tones. Some of Mozart's harmonies were beautiful, in a dreamy sense. But Mozart had never rendered Constanza in music. A new music was needed, music that embraced a woman, or his need for her, his longing for her, his troubled heart. This had not been done: even his B Flat Concerto, with its tender middle movement, aspired to no such heights.

Sunday he rose early again and, undisturbed by tolling bells, he struggled with the opening and the ending of the B flat. The opening had a two-part theme, the kind that Mozart used in his last symphony: something stiff and formal, then soft and lyrical. The problem was to work the two elements structurally into the whole and to lighten the orchestration. By noon he was satisfied with the first movement: now for the rondo; it was simple enough, but seemed ragged in a few places. It would not do, to give Haydn or Salieri cause to carp.

But before noon he was on his knees over the chamber pot: it was the colic, with wretched gas and wind, and loss of nourishment. He was prone to it: an accursed affliction, it came and went at the worst times. In the anteroom, his copyists waited for sheet after sheet as he handed them out, as best he could, between his bouts with the pot. One of the copyists had a question: "Herr van Beethoven," he began… Louis, clasping his stomach with both hands, his trousers at his feet, corrected him: "Von Beethoven, Von—do you hear me?"

The musicians assembled at the Burgtheater shortly before six o'clock, and the concert began with Cardellieri's symphony. Louis listened from the back, his hands folded ceremoniously on his lap, his head bent forward as if in rapt admiration for the Cardellieri piece. He noticed that Haydn and Salieri were present, and the applause at the end of the symphony, he thought, was more in honor of them than love for their student's composition, which he considered imitative and insipid. There would be an intermission, when at last the musicians would set eyes on the music they were about to play.

As the audience settled down for the premier of the new Concerto, he whispered a few words to the Prince. In a moment the Prince had gathered the musicians in a backstage wing and began passing out the sheets that contained their parts. Louis took the stage and sat himself at the piano; Haydn, Salieri, and Cardellieri were not in sight. No matter. He spread his fingers over the keyboard and played the first theme from Cardellieri's symphony, exactly as the Italian wrote it.

Then he put the theme through its paces—as if Herr von Beethoven had written it. First he added trills by way of ornamentation, making it fit for a burlesque. Then he brought the theme back to earth with grave solemnity, almost a funeral march. Suddenly he gave it new life as a joyous allegro and let it sail off into boundless realms of fantasy. Finally he snatched up pieces of the theme, combined them with the theme's bass, and improvised a fugue that galloped along to a breathless finish. The audience listened with rapt attention and at the end rose to their feet with tumultuous applause at the miracle that had been wrought.

When the musicians returned to the stage, they had studied the B flat's orchestral parts for a quarter of an hour. Not enough, Louis knew; but better than nothing. They would need his precise directions—and this was his first experience conducting an orchestra. He would have to lead them from the piano bench as he played and maintain his posture all the while he did so—no yielding to pangs of the flesh. He would beat time with nods of his head, and signal entries with quick stabs and slices of his arms. How he was to accomplish all this he wasn't sure.

When they were seated he gave the nod. The twofold allegro theme danced to life off the strings—not in perfect unison, but acceptable. If they could get through to his solo entrance, he would carry it from there. But when the strings came upon the bridge to the second theme, they faltered. The music came to a wretched stop. He stood and spread his arms in exasperation. "From the beginning," he thundered. The musicians, exposed to public humiliation, were obliged to obey. "It goes like this," he bellowed. "Dum—da dum, da dum, da dum: ta te ta ta, ta te ta ta…" He pounded on the piano as he growled it. "Now do it!" They got past it, but at the coda that should have closed out the orchestral exposition, they faltered again. He lept to his feet: "That was simple—a child could have done better at sight."

He failed to see the Prince standing in the back, shaking his head; and the Princess next to him, her face a pale hue, her eyes shut. He failed to note the frowns and narrowed eyes of the audience. He failed to take in the taut and drawn faces of the musicians as they struggled with his barked commands.

It had been planned that he and the musicians would gather at the palace after the concert for a late repast and celebrations. He arrived in the coach along with Prince Karl and Christiane. Hardly a word was spoken during the ride; he assumed the silence was due to a spat between the Prince and Christiane, for he heard the rumor that she followed him into his favorite brothel and made a scene. It seemed best to say nothing until they got to the palace. His thoughts turned to Babette von Keglevics: how could he meet her? What if he dedicated a new piano sonata to her?—she would have to be grateful and submit to him. When they arrived at the palace, he saw the delicacies and coffee and brandies set out in the domed parlor, in anticipation of the fifty musicians who were invited. But they waited in vain for the musicians to come.

He took a brandy with him to the piano and began to play. "A new sonata in E-flat," he called out. "Here, listen to this largo." The music imitated the broken accents of longing and grief: dissolving sighs, short chords, tense pauses. "It will win many hearts."

When he returned to the serving board for another brandy, Christiane took him by the sleeve and turned him to face her. "Louis," she began, "can you imagine why no one has come?" Her eyes cast reproach upon him.

"They played badly, they cannot face me."

The Prince intervened: "Some of Vienna's finest musicians, and friends of mine—and yours, too—have been insulted. I shall have to find some means to atone. As for you, a profound apology will only begin to suffice."

"They played the Italian's music better than mine…they must apologize to me." He turned his back to the Prince and took his brandy.

Christiane knew they could not reason with him. Even when sober, he was stubborn; but liquor made him impossible. She went to her bedroom and left Karl to deal with him. Later in the evening Moscheles arrived. "The others will not come," he said, "but I will speak for them." He stared past the Prince and caught Louis's eye. "Herr Beethoven," he said, "I doubt that any of these fine musicians will ever play for you again, no matter how fine a piece you produce. Had you given us the music sheets in time, the outcome would have been different. You have only yourself to blame."

"Fine words from a fiddler. When all Vienna is at my feet, you shall repent your harsh words." He downed his last brandy, threw the glass at the wall, and stormed out.

The Prince, with a large gesture of his arm, invited Moscheles to the serving table. "Our friend may soon be friendless," he said.

Moscheles agreed. "He has strange habits: he makes scenes in public places, he walks down the street growling and swaying his arms. He goes stomping about in the countryside, where he stands out in the rain and sleeps in sacks of straw. Even in his flat, he makes messes—he pours his bathwater so clumsily that it spills and runs over into the flat below. I have seen him do it."

The Prince shook his head in despair. "And there is something odd about his taste for women. He refused the young Contessa, who went to his flat and offered herself to him."

"I had not heard that," said Moscheles, "but a rumor says he visits a big-assed whore down by the ramparts."

"He will not win many hearts like this."

Chapter Eight

"All the World Makes Love."

The word "du", with its implied intimacy, passed Antonie's lips only when social necessity required it, as in the presence of guests. Alone, she called him Franz. She had thought when she was pregnant, that she could use the word to her child, but the infant died in her arms—it broke her heart and sent her into mourning that lasted it seemed forever. The mourning, she hoped, would keep Franz at a respectful distance; but before long Franz asserted his husbandly rights.

Frankfurt was a bane to her and she believed that it was sapping her health. She took frequent carriage rides about the city; they gave her no cheer, but they served as respite from her duties as manager of the household and from the burden of entertaining company—who were Franz's friends, mostly—and allowed her mind to wander into fantasies. The doctor had recommended to Franz that she take the frequent rides—prompted by Antonie herself—for nothing had sufficed to relieve her melancholia. Terrible headaches would come upon her with no warning and she would take to bed. Or it was indigestion, or constipation, or some other complaint. And lately she had taken to a strange behavior.

Franz heard of it from one of the servants, who whispered that the lady of the house had taken to locking herself in the bedroom and refusing to come down to greet visitors or even to answer knocks at the door. He came home early one afternoon and burst into the room. She was sitting nude before a mirror; her face was rouged, her thighs were spread wide and her fingers were massaging her vagina. Franz roared, "Is my wife a whore that she paints herself, and touches herself like some vile street trash?" He made as if to strike her; he had never done that, and when she was assured he would not, she spoke: "Better my fingers inside me than your contemptible member," she said, as she rose and covered herself.

Franz was dumfounded. Never before had he known a woman to do such a thing; never before had she spoken back to him. "Get dressed," he said. "We will discuss this another time." But he did not say a word.

But Antonie discussed it with Franz's sister-in-law, Bettina, who in spite of being single seemed knowledgeable where she herself was ignorant.

"Franz says women don't massage themselves, does he? But we do," Bettina assured her. "I did, and still do. Men don't know this, although I happen to know they do something like it to themselves when they have no woman around." Then she added: "But I usually have a man who takes care of things for me."

Antonie knew Bettina was a flirt, but was shocked at this plain talk. During a carriage ride about the city, Bettina told her of her latest conquest, the poet Wolfgang von Goethe.

"I went to him because of his letters—like his poems, they are so ardent." Bettina glanced at Antonie to see if her words were understood. But Antonie's face was blank, as it so often was. Bettina wanted to inflame her sister, as she thought of her, with some passion, for she understood that she needed a lover in her life. She tapped her on the shoulder and with a wink she went on about the poet.

"He thinks of me as a child still, but I proved my twenty four years to him."

Antonie comprehended. She had assumed Bettina's virginity, but she was wrong. "But you are engaged to be married," she stammered.

"O sister mine, you are so staid. All the world makes love. Now, as for Wolfgang, he is a great man, and I collect great men in my net. I steal their hearts, then toss them away—just like that!" With a snap of her fingers, she made her point. "I have a lofty mission—Achim must not know—" she said, with a finger to her lips. "Wolfgang is a collector, too; he says I am but a blossom in his bouquet of loves."

"He is married, is he not? And much older?"

She nodded. "It matters not. I met him in Weimar two years ago. He spoke to me of his ardor, his passion for me. We went for long walks. I told him that no man had ever set eyes on my bosom. I lied, but my words inflamed him; he took me under a tree and unbuttoned the top of my blouse and admired my bare breasts. In a moment he was kissing them, first the one then the other, until his tears ran down the valley between them, so grateful he was—at his age—to have such a precious child offer herself as I did."

Antonie wondered what it might be like to be so admired by a lover.

She confided to Bettina that she could not bear for Franz to touch her. "I lied to him once, when I was pregnant. I said that the doctor advised him to leave me alone. But Franz caught me in the lie. He was very angry; that night he forced me to do things that I cannot bear to speak of. I beg him to turn down the gaslights, to spare me, but he likes to stare at me in the light."

"My sister, dear—you must take a lover. It makes marriage bearable."

Antonie cringed: "The church has declared that it is a sin…"

"… the Church declares it is a sin to be happy. Maybe Napoleon will save us from the Church as well as from the Emperor."

That night Franz made his demands upon her. As she endured his panting and grunting she thought of Vienna, and Phillipe. Never could she forget the pain in his eyes; had he forgotten her? Would she ever have a lover? Why could she not be like Bettina and claim lovers everywhere? The answer of course was bestride her. She longed to return to Vienna; it was the prayer of her heart.

Later that year, when she complained of morning sickness, her doctor told her she was expecting a child. "You must forego all thought of Vienna," he said. "Always obey Franz. He knows best."

Chapter Nine

"Land of childhood."

He had toiled all morning over the C Major Symphony. With his inner ear he heard the pizzicato chords of the strings. They would be harsh on delicate ears, but only for a few bars until the music moved into the dominant and gave the ear a spasm of relief. His own ear delighted in the mysterious, groping bars as it was led into the sunlit interior.

The second movement was cloudless and carefree; it pleased him. But the third movement pleased him even more: it was no stately minuet, such as Haydn or Pleyel or Mozart wrote for their symphonies. He called it a Menuetto, but its pace was *Allegro molto e vivace*. The dance of queens had been replaced by an impish, waggish piece with no aristocratic airs— just an out-of-doors affair. It was a scherzo, really.

For the Finale he composed a brief introduction, a springboard to release an energetic allegro theme that should have the listeners treading on air like children set free to play on a fine summer day. Mozart, in some of his concertos, wrote such finales, taking the soul back to the land of childhood, where innocence and simplicity win out over all that has gone before.

He returned to the opening: as music, it was fine; why then was he brooding over it? Finally, thrusting aside his doubts, he rushed out onto the street. No hat, no coat—it was a warm day. Cabs, coaches, strollers, went up and down the avenues and people gathered in public squares to listen to street music and gossip. He called a cab and gave orders to be taken to the Black Camel.

The two companions usually ate at the tavern in the early afternoon. He stood outside, waiting. When late afternoon shadows darkened the street, and they had not come, he walked back to his flat, opened a bottle of wine, and brooded over the dissonant opening until his eyes grew heavy and he tossed himself upon his bed of straw.

In the morning his mouth was dry and furry and his head throbbed, a reminder that he had emptied the bottle that now littered the floor by the bed. At the window he saw that a thunderstorm had driven people from the streets. He stared out the window until at noon the storm blew over and the city began to bustle with life, even though dark clouds to the east threatened another downpour. Risking the rain, he called a cab and stood again across from the Black Camel. After an hour he saw Moscheles and Dragonetti step from a coach. He rushed to Moscheles and grabbed him by the lapel of his coat and pinned him to the side of a building. Then he pressed two ducats into his pocket.

"One for the girl," he said, "the other for the cook."

Moscheles grasped his intent, but was still puzzled. "Why not give it to them yourself?"

"They must not know. Do you understand? They must not know."

Dragonetti came over. "Louis does not want to go inside himself," he said.

Louis shook his head: "No, no—not that. They must not know."

The two fiddle players stared at each other for a moment. "Very well," Moscheles said, "I will do it, without a word."

At that Louis was gone.

Rain began to fall again, but he was hardly aware of it. On foot he made his way to the Herrengasse where, he had discovered, lived the Count von Keglevics and his daughter Babette. With water pouring from the brim of his hat, he stood on the columned porch and pulled a cord to announce his presence. A man-servant soon appeared and asked his name. "Ludwig von Beethoven, to see the Count's daughter." Fresh scents of spring pervaded the house: jasmine, clove, lavender. Silken draperies, oil paintings in wide golden frames, chandeliers glowing with numerous candles, gave him a moment's panic—he was a commoner with his mind set on a nobleman's daughter.

Babette was as he remembered her from the coffee-house: innocent eyes, amber locks, a cheery blush on her cheeks.

"I will be your music teacher," he declared.

"But I have a teacher…"

"I shall teach you the love of music. Where is the piano?"

She hesitated. "What impertinence…who are you?"

He saw the piano at the end of a long hallway leading to a parlor. Before the startled Babette could summon help from her father or the man-servant, he was in the music room seated at a broadwood piano. "Largo, con gran espressione" he called out, as he sent soft tender tones down the length of the hall, tones that told of hidden passion.

The Count von Keglevics, summoned by the man-servant, came to the foot of the stairs. "Who is this man who burst in here like a gale of wind?"

"Father, I am not sure, but…" she put her finger to her lips, "…just listen to the music. It is divine."

They entered the music room and listened. The stunted form bent over the keys, shoulder hunched, groaning as if in pain, was the least likely of human forms to be the author of such tonal perfection. She moved to the side of the piano to get a better look at the brash young man who had invaded her home. His head rose up as if searching the heavens, then fell to his chest. His eyes were on fire.

He swung around to face her. "When it is finished, I will dedicate it to you."

The Count intervened: "I take it that you know my daughter?"

She shifted her wide-eyed gaze from Louis to her father. Her hands flew to cover her mouth, then dropped to cover her bosom. "Father, he is the man who stared at us…at me…in the coffee-house." Blood rushed to her face as she remembered the black eyes from across the room that fixed on her knee and the hand that fondled it.

"Young man, explain yourself!"

"I explain myself to no one." Turning to Babette, he said, "Here is my card. You must come to my flat and hear the entire sonata. I shall play it for you and for you alone."

The next day he rose early, made a simple breakfast of bread, milk, and coffee, and sat at the piano. For once his fingers did not move. The new sonata needed a finale: what was it to be? He thought of Mozart's last concerto, a paradise where children play in perfect innocence. But his childhood was not that of a child: Johann and his whore occupied his early years; and his mother's grieving and complaining; and his disfigurement. Yet, there had been a face that lightened his dark night—his Babette of the Zehrgarten, in his mind forever pure and untouched by a man's hand. The Count's daughter was not the magical presence of his first Babette: but she was sensual; her bosom rose and fell with each breath; her lips, when they parted, held the promise of words that were for him alone. Maria's bosom had been like that, and she had words for him alone to hear. He had fled to her for comfort many times, with tears that stung in his eyes.

A rough pounding on the door stirred him from his reverie. It was Moscheles and Dragonetti. "Louis, we did what you asked of us. Is there anything more?"

He understood their broad hint.

"I will dedicate great works to the Prince and Princess."

Moscheles nodded his agreement, but added, "The musicians whom you offended are in need of reparations as well."

"I shall make good on that when I have the time…"

"Time?" Moscheles threw up his hands. "When Napoleon has taken our Italian possessions—and that may be soon—he will march upon the

city. Many will leave: officials, musicians, the nobility—all who can afford
to. As for you, what will you do?"

"I shall compose a symphony in his honor."

The two men fell back in open-mouthed horror. "Napoleon is the anti-
Christ," Dragonetti said. "You as well should honor the devil himself."

"He will rid the world of tyrants and scoundrels."

Moscheles told how his coach had passed by the General Hospital near
the Alserstrasse: soldiers on litters were being unloaded from carriages,
many with bloodied bandages around their heads, their chests, their legs—
except when their legs were stumps only. "War comes closer every day,
Louis. The anti-Christ will encamp outside our gates and you will hear
shelling as his cannons take down our walls and houses and hospitals,
and our music halls. You admire him? Very well, ask him if he will spare
you—and us, and our wives and our children—from the rapists that he
calls a noble army."

Thoughts of war and death weighed upon him through the afternoon
and into the night. He pondered the abrupt contrast between immanent
armies and the tinseled gaiety of the Viennese beer halls and cheap theaters:
the city will go on singing and playing and whoring even when doom
espies its towers. The contrast was not unlike the modulations and mood
changes that ran wild in his Concerto and the Symphony and the sonatas:
most of his works were tender-hearted romances with pleasing finales; yet
there were diversions into the minor keys and unexpected dissonances.
And always a mysterious drumbeat dogged his steps—the *march funebre*.

When the city was at its darkest, he could neither work nor rest. A
needling in his loins and the need for a woman's breasts urged him into
the street and down the avenue and alleys to the house with the unhinged
door. He pounded at the door of her flat until at last it flew open. A man in a
soldier's uniform stared down at him: "Keep it wrapped, young fellow," he
said. "When you are my age, you too will take your time." Louis brushed
past the man and slammed the door. A thought passed through his head:
had the soldier betrayed a wife or a lover in the arms of this whore who
stood before him bare naked? She put out her hands for the ducats. In a
moment he was standing at the duty-post by the city gates. The guard called
to him: "The gates will close at ten—you will be locked out." Heedless of
the warning, he stumbled into the dark and through the forest until his foot
struck a root and he fell headlong against the trunk of a tree. Panting, he
turned on his back and looked up. The sky was black, except when lit by
slashes of lightening in the east that foretold more rain. Above, no stars;
no heavenly father in a celestial vault.

Father Johann! The memory came to him like a flash of lightening in the deep ignorance of the night. He was a small boy who woke up thirsty. Rubbing his eyes he found the door to the big bedroom. It was unlocked. He pushed it open and asked for a drink of water. Johann cursed: he sprang from the bed; he had no clothes on; his sweaty, unwashed body smelled bad; his arm sliced through the air and struck him on one ear then on the other, and he went sprawling against the wall and onto the floor. In the glow of two candles he saw Johann's thing—the thing little boys have— but it was like a big thumb that was in the wrong place. Behind him, Maria was perched on the side of the bed; she had no clothes on; she rolled over and reached for a cover, her arm across her bosom; the other arm flew down between her legs as if to hide something; her mouth opened wide, like when she screamed, but he heard nothing. A strange woman was on the bed: she had nothing on; her legs were bent at the knees and spread apart, showing a small black bush in the middle; the sides of her mouth were pulled back in a hideous grin, bearing teeth, gums and tongue; her lips moved as if she was trying to speak, but he heard only a ringing in his ears.

He felt dirty. Rain beat down on him but he didn't mind. It was like a baptism from heaven. But the dirt didn't wash away. He lay on the wet earth, not sleeping, not resting—but thinking, remembering.

Not only dirt but an odor was lodged in his memory. Both came from Johann. Every time he got up from the whore's bed, he had to go wash his member and scrub it until it bled. That is where the odor came from. The woman was always annoyed: "Hey, don't use all my water, I got another gentleman to take care of," she would say. The Prince told him that at his fine bordello the women are not like that; they will wash it for you. But he was not drawn to those finer type whores.

The dirt, the smell, the silence—memories from the big bedroom— overwhelmed him. Johann's dirt was a part of him, and so was the smell, sticky sweet, that came from Johann's body. Johann lived in him. When Johann boxed his ears, his head would spin and he would hear a ringing sound. The ringing stopped when he left Bonn, but here it was again—it began when he struck his head against the tree. He thrashed about on the ground to shake it off, but it clung like the dirt and the smell.

The sun struck him directly in the face as he stood outside the soldier's duty station. Two guards emerged and pulled back the wrought iron gates. As he passed through, they stared at his disheveled clothes and mangled hair, his eyes puffy from lack of sleep. "You have been outside all night? Good thing Boney wasn't there—he'd have stripped you to your socks and put you to work scrubbing his stables." The ringing and the buzzing were gone. Coaches and cab drivers were beginning their day's work; he called to one, but realized he had given his money to the whore; he shook his head and the man drove away. But he still had his notebook. It was wet but intact. On the last page, in his scrawled hand, were the first bars of the *march funebre*.

At his desk he shoved the music scores to the floor and penned a letter to Helene von Breuning.

Dearest mother of mine (for so you have been to me even before Maria died). I have had another raptus, as you called it. They come when I am lost or frightened. Last night I was in the room of a woman—I grieve to tell you this, but to whom else can I bare my heart? A woman of the kind that Johann shamed himself with. I have been to her often, but this time my raptus-angel rescued me and took me to a dark forest outside the gates, where rain washed over me all through the night. The angel came again during the night and gave me a memory I didn't know I had.

I was a little boy again, and I wandered into the big bed-room where Johann and Maria slept, but they were awake and they were naked, and that woman was there, the one I told you about. Johann boxed my ears and they stung. Maria and the strange woman opened their mouths to speak, but I heard nothing. I rubbed my ears, but a shrill ringing sound then a buzzing set in. But in the forest last night, when the angel left, the sounds came back. They are gone now; I pray they never return.

When I looked in my notebook I saw eight bars of music that I wrote long ago—a funeral march. Did the angel do that during my raptus? Why?

Worse—the stench of Johann lives in me. I drink, like he did. I yell at people like he did. I disgrace myself with a whore like he did. That dreadful woman! Why do I do it, when there are fine women who would be right for me, even as wife? But I feel wrong about them—except one, but she is above my station in life.

I must kill Johann, if I have to kill myself to do it.

The following day as he scored the last pages of the Symphony, a knock on the door startled him; lately knocks on doors and the grinding of wheels on granite streets made his hands fly to his ears. A liveried man handed him an envelope containing a letter sealed with the name Anna Louisa Barbara von Keglevics. He tore it open and read: "Dear Herr Beethoven, How kind of you to treat me and my father to a private recital of your music. Your sonata is most beautiful. However, we must ask you to refrain from any further uninvited visits to our home."

He put a match to it and stomped on its ashes. When his fury was spent, he took to his desk and wrote a note: "If the hand that snatches at your knee moves you more than my music that moves the gods, you are not fit for my bed." Other, more vengeful, thoughts burned in him the length of the day. But in the evening he repented: if he dedicated the sonata to her, she might leave the knee-snatcher and beg to come to him. And he had another thought: he took to the piano where he worked on the sonata through the night.

Later in the week he dropped in on the Prince and Christiane. "My hat is in my hand," he said. Christiane smiled; she understood his meaning.

"Sit down, my friend," said the Prince, with a royal wave of his hand.

Louis began: "Even friends can have their spats." It was a shrewd remark, for he sensed that the Prince and Christiane were still fighting over the bordello incident. The Prince looked distressed: Christiane would not part her legs for him, but she spewed her anger at him when she caught him at his amorous rounds. He was married to a jealous bitch.

"I was thinking about the soldiers," he continued. "If the war gets worse, there will be many more wounded. Where are the funds for their care?"

The Prince looked puzzled: This was not what he expected. He stroked his chin and remained silent.

"We should give a benefit concert. Not for the musicians, but for the hospitals, which must care for the wounded," Louis went on.

Christiane threw her arms around his shoulders. "Louis, I believe you have come here to make peace with us."

He stood, leaving her arms to dangle by her side. "Moscheles says many will flee the city if Napoleon attacks us. Will you go?"

The Prince and Christiane exchanged glances. "Yes," the Prince responded, "I expect we will seek refuge in Croatia."

"Why do you ask, Louis?" Christiane asked. "Do you wish to come with us?"

"Never will I leave this city."

The Prince had the benefit concert on his mind. "The Redoutensaal is the place for the concert," he said. "I will get word to Haydn; we cannot leave him out, Louis, for the musicians will not play for you alone. Are you still interested?"

"Yes, provided some of my works will be played."

The Prince smiled. "Agreed. I will speak to Herr Peter Frank, the hospital's director. Now, my unrepentant friend, would you like a brandy?"

Later in the evening, the Prince's coach took Louis to his flat. He was tired, but could not sleep. The note from Babette: he regretted he had destroyed it. But he remembered its few words. She acknowledged that she admired his music. Perhaps she would attend the benefit concert and hear his Symphony. What else had she said? It seemed that her father was behind her words: something transpired between the two in the music room. Yes, that was it—she was forced to write the letter against her will. His heart bursting with hope, he worked through the night. He would finish his masterpiece by sun up. But the music faltered. He bent over and pounded the keys until his hands were sore and bruised; but the tones faded into the gloom of night.

Later in the week he spoke to Herr Doctor Schmidt. He described the periods when the world grew silent, and the ringing that began when he struck his head against the tree.

"You must try tepid baths in the Danube," the doctor said.

"How will bathing help my condition?"

Schmidt shrugged. "It is to relieve your bowels. You tell me you suffer from colic. The gas from below rises and gets into the cavities of your ears."

Louis was not adverse to long walks in the country and bathing in streams and pools. Why not the Danube? He stripped and plunged into its waters every day until the weather drove him indoors.

The colic improved; the deafness grew worse.

Chapter Ten

"Take a Lover."

The little one was slow coming into the world, and she caused Antonie almost to despair of life. It was a long painful childbirth, but when she took the infant into her arms and placed her upon her breasts, she felt life's joy at last. The little one was healthy; she snuggled and gurgled at the breasts, and slept peacefully. But Antonie was fatigued from the long hours of delivery; she had lost much blood and was weak. A woman was brought in to relieve her of domestic duties while she recovered. It was a long recovery that served the purpose of keeping Franz at bay.

Antonie had prayed that her child be a daughter. The thought that she might bring a man-child into the world who might be like his father was repugnant. Happily, a girl-child, Maximilliane, came into the world and she could begin to prepare her for what must lie ahead of her. If Franz insisted on sending her to a convent school, as she herself had been, she would resist him with all her might. And if Maximilliane wanted to marry the man of her choice—if she could find a decent one like Phillipe—that would be her right, and if Franz objected, she would take her daughter and her lover away in the coach to some far place—she knew not where—and let them make love under her watchful eye to their hearts content. Franz be hanged.

When she felt up to it, she received a few visitors. Bettina was the first. She burst in singing the praises of her Wolfgang. When she had near exhausted Antonie with her exploits, she began to rave about a new musician in Vienna.

"His name is Ludwig von Beethoven. The critics and old men with shrunken balls hate his music," she said, "because it is fresh and new. And he breaks the rules…"

Antonie looked up. "He is nobility and he breaks rules? And in Vienna at that. I am amazed they have not put him in jail."

Bettina caught the humor in her sister's tone. "He may yet be thrown in jail, but not for his music. They say he stands on street corners and howls like a madman, throws temper fits in restaurants, drinks too much, visits whores, dresses shabbily, forgets to bathe…and it is whispered he swims and dances naked with peasant girls outside the city gates."

That was too much for Antonie. "I am not sure I want to hear music by a man like that. Have you heard it?"

"No, but I will soon—and so will you, if you want. A pianist is in town who knows Beethoven and has some of his piano scores."

Antonie turned her pale face to the wall. "Bettina, dear, I am too tired to get out. I must rest. Besides, if Franz sees me up and about, he will..."

Bettina clapped her hands: "I will take care of that. Leave it to me."

One evening the following week, a young pianist from Vienna, Ferdinand Reis, who described himself as a pupil and admirer of Beethoven, played at the home of Bettina's fiancé, Achim von Arnim. Antonie arrived with Franz, her first night out of the house since the birth; she was pale and a bit unsteady, but she believed music would lift her spirits. At the convent-school she had been instructed in piano and, while not an accomplished player, she knew the rewards of learned listening. Bach's fugues were no terror to her; and she enjoyed arias from the operas of Handel and Mozart, particularly the tunes from *Figaro*, even though Franz's remark about the *jus primae noctis* caused her an unsteady moment. Tonight, Bettina said, the young Reis would play some of Mozart's lighter music: the sonata with the march *alla turka*, a perpetual favorite. Then he would introduce the new work: the young master's Sonata in E-Flat.

The Mozart piece went by swiftly and the small gathering applauded. Refreshments were served and the pianist mingled affably among the host and his guests, answering questions about the composer whose work he was about to introduce. "He is a genius whose music will change the world," he said. Eyebrows were raised: the words sounded too political, too much like the intent of Napoleon, whose name was on the lips of a frightened populace. The citizens of Frankfurt, like most of Germany, were entrenched in their secure past and had no stomach for change and novelty. Some of the guests left before Reis could return to the piano.

"It is the Sonata in E-Flat, Number Four, Opus 7," Reis announced. "It is in four movements: *Allegro molto e con brio; Largo, con gran espressione; Allegro; and Rondo: poco allegretto e grazioso*. It is dedicated to the Countess Babette von Keglevics."

Antonie however had only half an ear for the new music; the evening was wearing on her. It would be rude to leave during the performance, but she would leave soon after.

The first movement struck her as bright, but too loosely structured with its bold part-writing; it was as if the composer couldn't settle down. From what she had heard of the man, that was no surprise.

The *Largo, con gran espressione* began. It was lyrical, songful—the man had perhaps a better side to him. In the middle section, however, when the trained ear expected a change of key or new development, the music seemed to dissolve into short chords, broken accents of grief; it sighed and swooned, then erupted in passionate fortissimos before the music subsided and returned gracefully to its lyrical beginning. The coda seemed to hover in the air amidst still clouds, unwilling to take its last breath.

She had come to refresh her spirits, but the Beethoven piece pressed against her and threatened to crush her—such emotion. Those who left early did well.

The following day Franz announced that he had to leave the city for business. Antonie's heart lept at the words: she suspected at once that Bettina was behind the scenes—in fact Bettina had spoken to her brother Clemens Brentano and persuaded him to take Franz away on some business venture.

Leaving little Maximilliane in the hands of a care-taker, Antonie stepped into the coach that was waiting, and gave the driver instructions to pick up Bettina from her brother's home.

"What do you think of Beethoven's sonata?" asked Bettina.

"It was written by a member of royalty, dedicated to a royalty; but parts of it seemed too untamed, too emotional—in a word, unrefined."

Bettina's cheeks turned red, her eyes blazed. "The heart-stopping largo—I thought I would expire, if the music did not. He is to music what Goethe is to poetry."

Antonie took interest in the remark about Goethe. "What has transpired between you and him?" she asked.

Bettina put a finger to her lips. "Beware the ears of Hans," she whispered.

"Hans? Our coach-driver?"

"He spies on you—and me, too—for Franz. Every word gets back to him. Here, ask him to take us to a park that I know. It has a pavilion where we can sit and talk while he waits at the curb."

Antonie issued the order and Hans did her bidding although, it seemed, with a puzzled furrow in his brow.

"There now, we can talk all we want," Bettina said, as the two women sheltered themselves from the ears of Franz's spy. "As for Wolfgang, I had mentioned I would be at the baths in Baden during the summer. Somehow he found my lodging, and walked up three flights of stairs to surprise me late at night. But the effort of the stairs puckered him out. He clasped me to him under his cloak and spoke passionate words to me, but he was unable to carry out his desires."

"You are fortunate for that," Antonie responded, with a broad smile the likes of which Bettina rarely saw on her face.

Bettina relished the thought: "A child born of my lust and Wolfgang's brains. The child would be a prodigy!"

Antonie studied her friend as if for the first time: Bettina was a petite beauty, with flashing black eyes and a bulging bosom that trapped and held men's eyes. She was bright and witty and charming; no wonder the poet lost his senses in her presence. She relished her seductions of men, especially those with brains and power. Who would be next? Of course— the man who is to music as Goethe is to poetry. How would she manage it?

Chapter Eleven

"A Rightful End."

In the spring of 1802 Louis took new lodging in the Petersplatz near the center of the city where every day the bells of St. Peter's rang out from one side and the bells of St. Stephen's sounded down upon him on the other. His friends wondered if perhaps the bells would disturb him at work, but he made no comment that such was the case.

Hardly had he moved in, when it came time for him to leave the city, as was his habit, for a summer in the country. He rented a four-horse wagon and driver, freighted it down with furniture and belongings, and set out for Heiligenstadt, a peaceful environ of Vienna, a place that offered relief from the heat and noise of the city.

As they passed through the city gates into the country side, he marched ahead of the wagon, singing and swaying as ideas come to him from the azure blue. Soon they came upon a meadow full of wild flowers, honey-colored corn, and sweet smelling berries. He strayed off into the meadow where he stood stock still for several minutes, then opened his notebook and scribbled furiously. The driver observed all this and began to suspect that the trip, usually an hour and a half, might take much longer.

"Hey there, I haven't got all day," he shouted. Louis kept on scribbling.

Finally Louis folded his notebook and resumed his place at the head of the march. But after a few minutes his attention was drawn to a copse of small trees and golden flowers, which he explored until he came to a hidden brook that delighted his soul. He lay down beside it and contemplated how to finish his Second Symphony. When he returned to the road, the sun was much lower in the sky and the wagon was gone.

At dusk, filthy, hungry, thirsty, and drenched in sweat, he came to the village. There, heaped up in the center of the marketplace, near a row of horse-drawn hacks, were his belongings—boxes, crates, chairs, his desk, and numerous scores of music, some of it bound, some loose. A half-dozen street boys were gawking at the sight; one of them was parading around the square with a bound book of scores, hawking them to passersby. Louis charged into the midst of the scene, scattering the boys and the scores.

"Thieves, urchins, maggots," he snorted.

Then he broke out in riotous laughter, bending forward and backward at the waist, holding his sides and heaving. "Come back," he called to the boys, "I have work for you." Reaching into his coat pocket, he called out, "A kruetzer to each if you will help." The boys clamored for their pay as they took up the pile of belongings and followed Louis up a hill toward a solitary dwelling, a simple peasant house that was unfurnished except for a piano.

The house had large rooms and an unbroken view of the Danube and the Marchfeld; further in the distance, faintly traced against the horizon, rose the Carpathian Mountains. Louis had looked for a house just like this, isolated, close to nature, far from society, on the advice of his doctor, Professor Schmidt: Louis had reported that the bathing had not helped his ears; moments of silence came more often and the ringing and buzzing droned in the back of his head night and day. He would stay in this quiet haven the entire summer, even into the fall if need be, to get rid of the nuisance. His time would not be wasted, for he had to finish the Second Symphony and he had stirring ideas for another symphony, his Third.

That very evening, after he had paid the urchins, he went to the piano and began to work. He had forgotten to eat, so eager was he to compose a coda to conclude the Second; it would be something loud and boisterous, so that the critics who complained that his music was too loud will flee from the theater, their ears a-buzzing and a-ringing. Then he will begin his Third, something even louder—something new and monumental.

The Second was completed easily: a joyous work, it was as sunlit as the meadows and streams through which he roamed and waded everyday after lunch, even when it rained. But in time the summer began to weigh him down. Work progressed; but his thoughts were dim; he brooded. One of his piano students, Ferdinand Reis—one of a very few who knew his whereabouts, and that was the equivalent of an invitation to visit—arrived one Sunday morning to find the master in an agitated state. "Come with me," said Louis. They hiked through a long field and down into the valley near the riverbed, where he pointed to a small band of shepherds who were amusing themselves with songs and jokes. One of them stood up and piped a tune on a wooden flute. "A charming tune," said Reis, "wouldn't that sound fine in a merry scherzo?" Louis' face darkened. Without a word, he turned and climbed back to the house. When Ferdinand caught up, Louis was seated at the piano. He was not playing the shepherd's tune or anything like it. It sounded like a funeral march.

Near the end of the summer, when normally he would return to the city, he made no effort to pack. One rain-drenched night he sat brooding at the piano, then he plucked at the strings of an old violin. Inspiration flagged. Finally he picked up a quill and began to write a letter to his two brothers:

> *How humiliated I have felt if somebody standing beside me heard the sound of a flute in the distance and I heard nothing, or if somebody heard a shepherd sing and again I heard nothing-such experiences almost make me despair.*

He put the letter aside, unfinished, and turned again to his music. Again, he played the funeral march—he called it *adagio assai, marche funebre.* Where, he wondered, had the theme come from? It was so intimate, so familiar. He pounded on the keys, he twisted the theme this way and that, until it came to him; it was the allegro theme in disguise—the vigorous allegro theme that was the basis of the first movement. Sometimes these things happened when he composed; he knew not how. Did it matter? More important: who died, that he was being taken to his grave? He sprang to his feet, knocking over the piano stool and scattering pages of music, and hurtled through the valley toward a flooded stream in a gorge. In a torrent of rain, he stripped and spread his arms wide to face the full fury of a passing storm; sometimes answers came when he submitted to the gods who sent the wind and the rain. But the gods were silent.

Years ago in Bonn, as he lay on the ground by the toll house, a vision of Babette's pure face framed in light smiled upon him. But that vision lied: Babette was impure. And so too was he. He let the wind sweep over him and the rain rinse away his impurities, and the ache in his loins that made him run to the house with the unhinged door. But no: that ache, and the joy of it, was life itself.

And his music, that too was joy. For the sake of his art, he must live. Music did not lie; it was a truth that contained within itself the reason for its own being and his own being.

Music raised no questions, demanded no answers...or did it? Much of his music had the rot of death about it, from the day he learned to hate his father and wish him dead. Johann was dead in fact. That march by Dressler—that was a march to the grave. Then he composed a "Funeral Cantata" for someone...whose death was that? Cressener, yes, Cressener the British Ambassador to Bonn and a friend of Johann. And more about death: the "Joseph Cantata" memorialized the life and death of a good prince. There were some songs, too, about death: "Opferleid," and "Klage," and "Von Tode" and "In questa tomba oscura." And his reading of Shakespeare spilled over into the first Opus 18 Quartet, which put him in mind of Romeo and Juliet in the burial vault. Even that wasn't enough;

he wrote a funeral march for the Piano Sonata in A flat. And he had just finished an oratorio about the death of Christ. Now he was at it again, with this *marche funebre*. Why?

Johann put him up to writing that cantata for Cressner's death. He hadn't wanted to, but he had to please his father. Even Christ had to suffer to please his father—so said the priests during the Holy Week homilies and readings in the Bonn chapel, and he had read for himself the passion story from the New Testament. He was shaken by the story. The Father of Jesus was a cruel god, that He demanded suffering of even His son. If God's own son suffered, what about the son of Johann?—no hope for such a one as he. The text of the oratorio struck his ears like the lament of a man cursed by a father: *O my father, oh see, I suffer greatly; have mercy on me...Father, deeply bowed and weeping, Thy son prays to Thee...He is ready to die the martyr's death so that man, man, whom He loves, may be resurrected from death and live eternally...*

Why had he not returned to Bonn for Johann's funeral?

In spite of his agitation his work progressed steadily. Over the summer he had completed the first two movements of the new symphony: the opening *Allegro con brio* and the second, *marche funebre*. He had converted suffering into the substance of beauty. It remained to ponder what themes would follow the *marche funebre* and bring the symphony to its rightful close.

He could compose, but could he hear? The summer's rest had done nothing to help his ears; if anything, the malady was worse, for at times he could bang on the piano keys and hear the tones only as if from a great distance. Once more he picked up the letter to his brothers, sat at the desk, and read it from the beginning to be sure his words were well chosen.

For my brothers Carl and _____,
to be read and executed after my death...

The name of his other brother, the one who worked as a pharmacist—the one who bore that name Johann!—was missing. There, and twice again, he left blank the space where the name Nicholas Johann should have appeared.

He read what he had written so far:

Oh you men who think or say that I am malevolent, stubborn, misanthropic, how greatly do you wrong me. You do not know the secret cause which makes me seem that way to you.

71

Again he is shocked. His message is not for the two brothers alone; it is for the world. He wants all men to understand his loss:

Ah how could I possibly admit an infirmity in the one sense which ought to be more perfect in me than in others, a sense which I once possessed in the highest perfection...

So I endured this wretched existence—truly wretched for so susceptible a body, which can be thrown by a sudden change from the best condition to the very worst—patience, they say, I must now take for my guide.

I am prepared—already in my twenty-eighth year—forced to turn philosopher...

Thus I bid thee farewell. As autumn leaves wither, so does my hope. Let providence grant me one day of joy...when O God, can I feel it once again in the temple of Nature or Humanity?

Through October he had made no move to return to the city, nor did he work at the piano; instead he roamed the blessed fields and bathed in the flowing streams near the gorge. Late in the month a bolt of lightening struck a tree near his house; he gaped at its stunted shape and thought of himself. At dusk he lay down beside the stunted tree and stared at the sky. Philosophers ridiculed the notion that a loving father dwelt on high. But poets loved to sign the praises of such a One. Who was right? The bolt was his answer. What loving father would make a tree, then consume it in a moment of wrath? What loving father would make a son, then cripple him in body and spirit? The poets—they were fools. No father would send fiery bolts from a starry sky.

From a starry sky? The storm that sent the bolt had cleared the air and revealed a thousand lamps. He knew a poet, Schiller, who must have looked up on such a night as this, when he wrote about a starry sky and heros who marched among those stars. And, yes, a loving father who lived beyond the starry vault, and a mankind on earth who will live in joyous unison. *Ode to Joy,* that was the name of the poem. Ach!... utopian speculation, fancy oratory and words on paper. No more. Unless the truth of it could be proved in tones.

At the piano, the bolt became a stroke of fate in the shape of a four note motive repeated. During the long night he labored over the phrase and its sequel until his alchemy transmuted it into a theme fit for a new kind of symphony: here is destiny—stand fast! Resist, persevere—do so and you will rise to shout and march among the stars. But he swept the sketches aside: their time had not yet come. First he needed to march back to Vienna like a hero and startle them with his new Symphony, the one with the *marche funebre*. The critics will howl and hurl their insults, but let them—he won't hear a word.

He picked up the paper he had written the day before and studied it, his lips moving silently as he pondered its meaning. How sad, he thought, to wither as an autumn leaf when he was in the springtime of his life; to say farewell at age twenty eight. Twenty eight? He was thirty two.

Farewell? Farewell to whom? His brothers? Mankind? No—he had underscored the words to joy. Farewell to joy. Why those words? When had he known joy? Yes, while wandering in the fields and bathing in the streams, worshiping in nature's temple, there he knew joy. But he knew no joy in the house of Johann, Johann who made money off him as a child prodigy like Mozart and lied about his age to make him younger than he truly was. Now he caught himself in the same lie. He was thirty two.

Should he say farewell to joy, or should he stand fast? The answer was before him. The four note theme. But even before that, the third symphony with its *marche funebre*. In it he had said farewell to Johann. He had in fact buried him.

73

Chapter Twelve

"Sunk in Abstraction."

A year after Maximilliane was born, Antonie urged Franz to let her visit her home in Vienna, even if for a short visit only. But he refused: the child was too small, he said, and besides, her health was poor. It was true about her health: it sank with the passing of each year. The headaches grew more intense and frequent so that she spent her days reclining in bed or taking aimless carriage rides about the city, while at night she lingered over Maximilliane until her time for bed, then she wrote letters or read books so as to avoid her own bed. Franz's doctor attributed her illnesses and eccentricities to the malaise that followed childbirth. But she knew better.

Bettina, her only solace, was a loyal confidant, even though she expressed concern to her brother Clemens, writing to him that Antonie had taken to using rouge and painting herself during certain times of the day—he was never to let on to Franz—"like a stage-set, as though impersonating a haughty ruin overlooking the Rhine toward which a variety of romantic scenes advance while she remains wholly sunk in loneliness and abstraction."

Antonie's plight was revealed in her many letters; her one sunshine other than her children was the brief excursions from the city, when she could find peace; but true peace could be hers, she would say, only if she were free from the need to deceive—and that could be only when she returned to the city of her birth.

When Franz took her from Vienna, he had agreed that once in two years she could return to visit her father for a week or ten days. The visit would have to be brief, because the journey consumed ten days and he could not be expected to neglect his affairs for any length of time. A first visit was delayed by Antonie's pregnancy and the need to care for her newborn daughter. But in the early spring of 1803 Johann wrote that he would like to see his granddaughter, so Franz agreed that she could go; he of course would go with her and the child.

Her father greeted her warmly and took to Maximilliane with an idolatrous eye. A dinner party was held in Antonie's honor; it consisted, she noted, of a small number of persons who had not attended the wedding dinner. Her father, no doubt, wanted to give her a fresh social slate. But the conversation was all about the war and the despicable Napoleon. Things had gone bad since the battle of Marengo, when "Boney" slaughtered their army and moved even closer to the city. As for the Second Coalition, it was deemed incompetent to thwart his plans to take all of Europe. Fugitives were pouring into the city from the Provinces and housing was scarce; the cheapest backroom now cost fifteen florins a month. The cost of butter had gone up to thirty kreuzer, they complained, because the armies were tramping over the fields and raiding the farms to feed themselves. Antonie listened and said little. She noticed, however, that these guests at her father's house seemed to suffer little from the inflation: the cost of black bread may have risen to famine prices, but those of the Herrengasse were well fed and perfumed.

One afternoon, following early showers, a bright sun inspired her to take a coach into the countryside and around the city to refresh her memory of its beauties: the Prater, the Glacis—an open space that, her father told her, had once been a moat that surrounded the city and protected it from invaders—the Graben, the Herrengasse, the Belvedere palace with its terraced garden, even the sounds of vendors and hawkers and music-makers in the streets, all lifted her spirits. Finally she ordered her driver to take her past the gates into the Weinerwald, the green and gracious forest where city-dwellers seeking relief went to splash and swim in gurgling streams, doze on the cool grass, and eat and drink in country taverns. She called to the driver to stop. In bare feet she stepped from the coach and walked upon the cool grass. In the near distance she heard the gurgling of a brook and the voices of merrymakers who must have come upon a tavern just beyond a small hill. She lifted her skirts to wade across little streams of water that the morning rain had left and began to follow the voices; but she was startled by the voice of the coach driver. Franz must have tipped the man well.

In the coach she asked him to take her to St. Stephen's church: "That is where I was married," she told the man. There!... let him report that to Franz; it should relieve his mind. On the way to the church she passed the new Theater-an-die-Wein and noticed a large billboard: Herr L. von Beethoven will conduct the orchestra in premiers of his two Symphonies, in C and D, a Sacred Oratorio, and a new Concerto for Piano and Orchestra.

Remembering the E Flat Sonata that had burdened her with emotion, she shuddered.

The church was as she remembered. Behind the high altar was the three paneled screen, the marble font with its suspended mahogany canopy, and the sweet air that lingered in her memory of that day. But now the emptiness of the place afflicted her spirit. A thought that she had nurtured in silence for years almost passed her lips: "Do I have the courage to do what I must do?"

A mass was being sung at one of the altars. She knelt before a bench and meditated on her standing in the sight of God. Every child was born with some kind of love, she believed; they took it with milk at the breast; as they grew older they took it from parents and friends. Then comes the love between a man and a woman, of which she knew little, but she was taught in her catechism that it was the saving kind or it was the damning kind. The church said that Franz's lustful entries into her body were the saving kind because they were blessed by the church. But to her they were the damning kind.

The church forbade divorce and consigned offenders to a fiery hell. But then there were those who braved it; and there were those who stayed married but took lovers, as Bettina had said. When the mass was over she followed the priest to the door of his sacristy and tapped upon it until it opened and the black-cassocked priest stepped out. He saw the face lined with pain—tragic in one so young. "Can I help you, my child?"

She looked up at eyes of kindness. "Father, do you remember a young man who used to attend mass here almost every day, about four years ago—perhaps he still does. His name is Phillipe Baumer."

The priest stroked his chin. "No, but perhaps if I look at the registers I may come upon his name for some reason. Was he baptized here?"

Phillipe had given her his name and told her he was born in Vienna and his family always attended mass at St. Stephen's. "Yes, I believe so."

He led her to an office where he turned pages in a heavy bound volume. Finally he looked up and asked, "Was he a good friend of yours, my child?"

"Why…yes," she stammered.

He hesitated a moment, then spoke: "In the register I read that Phillipe Baumer was married last spring. He married a girl from this parish, right here at the altar. Do you wish to know the girl's name?"

Friday evening Johann had invited guests for an evening of music, which he announced as an occasion to honor his daughter and granddaughter. Antonie felt the obligation to attend, though she had eaten and slept poorly since her visit to St. Stephen's. And she worried that, if she proved difficult, her father may not issue an invitation for her to visit in 1805. She steadied herself and took a seat among the guests in the salon, smiling and chatting as if she had no care beyond the interests of her father's guests.

The pianist arrived: he was Daniel Steibelt from Paris; Johann heard of him through the government and issued the invitation to play for his guests. As Steibelt approached the piano, he announced his selections: a few bagatelles by Clementi and Haydn; some contradances by Mozart; and finally a new piece, *Sonata Pathetique in C minor* by Ludwig von Beethoven.

Before Steibelt could set himself, Johann stood up and addressed his guests: "I had not realized that our friend from Paris would select a piece by the upstart Beethoven. The man is rude, uncouth, and he admires Napoleon." With a nod and half-smile at Steibelt, he joked, "Perhaps our friend from Paris chose this piece precisely for that reason. However, we are generous here in our home, and we will do our friend the courtesy of letting him play his selections."

She stiffened at those words, words that took her back to the day he told her she would marry Franz—she saw him again, looming over her from the foot of the stairs—and how like the words of Father Wolf, who spread his stole over joined hands and pronounced her and Franz one flesh. How unctious, how ingenuous did those words seem to her. Now those tongues were set against this upstart musician.

The first three pieces were light entertainment and were greeted with applause. Some nervousness hung over the parlor, however, when the pianist resumed his place and opened the score of the *Pathetique*. He paused, took in his breath, and began the first movement.

She was shaken by the opening: was this the same composer whose E-flat Sonata lacerated her heart in Frankfurt? Chromatic shifting chords, sultry phrases, and plaintive falling intervals told her of a troubled heart that searched for refuge and release. The heart was stricken but willed to live, though life would be grim and lived on the barest terms. The minor-keyed music was almost too much for her to bear; she closed her eyes: but what other thoughts could she turn to? Franz? Phillipe? She would brave the Beethoven, if the softer second movement would offer consolation. The second was a major keyed *adagio cantabile*, but its grave tread offered little hope. The third movement set out at a brisk pace but it was no celebration; it was a twilight dance that went on and on because it knew not what else to do.

"We shall have no more Beethoven in this house," Johann said, when the piece was done.

She saw her father as if for the first time: Johann was rude to Steibelt, an embarrassment to his guests...and...he was altogether like the man he picked for her to marry—arrogant, rude...he called Beethoven rude!...if the government of Austria was like her father and her husband, maybe Beethoven was right to speak well of Napoleon. After a sleepless night, Antonie approached Franz about the concert at the new Theater-an-die-

Wein. "I hear the building is beautiful," she said. "I must see for myself. And they have talented management. Oh, shall we?"

"We shall see," he said. But later in the day he had said nothing. She found him at her father's desk writing letters; she interrupted and reminded him of the concert. Franz continued to write and spoke from the side of his mouth. "Johann says that the concert is nothing but Beethoven. And the egotistical composer has upped the cost of tickets from four florins to twelve ducats."

"Can we not afford it?"

He turned to face her with a squinted eye: "That is not the question…"

"…What then is the question?"

In a second he was on his feet. "Do not turn a sharp tongue upon me, or you shall regret it instantly."

"I shall go by myself."

He pointed to a chair: "Sit there…"

She turned and left the room.

After dinner, during which conversation was desultory and strained, Franz and Johann cornered her as she was bathing Maximilliane. With the wet child in her arms, she could make no escape.

Johann began: "That man whose music you have taken a strange liking to is worse than rude. There is more you must know."

She did not look up. She wrapped Maximilliane in a towel and took her into the bedroom. "Give us some privacy if you please," she said.

Ignoring her request, they followed her into the room. "Very well, we shall talk in here," said Johann. "That man is immoral. You shall hear it from me here and now. Not only is he suspect in the political sense, he is the object of scorn among decent people. He has been seen down by the ramparts where he visits street-women, women who paint themselves— whores, to be precise, lest you fail to get my meaning. And other things: Reliable witnesses report that he will strip himself naked in public places, like taverns and beaches where he exposes himself to women. Complaints have been made to the police; if they catch him at it, he will be arrested and sent to jail."

"Yes," Franz added, "and he is filthy. While you left the dinner party to tend to Maximilliane, some of the guests told us that he no longer bathes, so that his body odors follow him down the street and into taverns where he abuses the serving girls and throws things at the cook if the food doesn't please him."

"And he is a drunkard," concluded Johann. "So you shall not go to that concert, when for only a few florins, we can attend the Bergtheater, where something edifying is being performed—Haydn's Creation."

She took Maximilliane to her crib and turned down the light. When the men left, she took her daughter in her arms and wept tears of despair.

On the journey back to Frankfurt, she became ill. The coach had to make many stops beside the road so that she could relieve herself. Franz became angry and embarrassed. He had to tip the coachman generously because of the extra stops, and apologize to other passengers for the delays. "You do not take care of yourself," he said to her when they stopped at an inn. "You do not eat what is served to you; you do not sleep—no wonder you get sick."

In Frankfurt she saw the doctor who confirmed what she had feared. Her flow of blood had ceased; she was pregnant. Any thought of Vienna in 1805 was hopeless.

Chapter Thirteen

"No Man Knows Who Begat Him."

Louis had taken a vintner's cottage in Oberdobling for the summer. From a window he could look at the Danube Canal and, beyond it, past a gorge, another village—Heiligenstadt, where he summered the year before and meditated about his death. At the piano he brooded over the new symphony, his third; it was causing no end of trouble: an opening allegro followed by the tramping of heavy feet. It was the *marche funebre*—a mystery still.

Best he take to the fields: answers came to him from the meadows, the streams, the rains that fell from cloudbursts in the sky above. With a few books in hand he set his face in the direction of the canal. A large rock jutted out a few feet into the water; he sat on it, cooling his feet in the flowing water as he ran his fingers through his loose hair, over his blunt nose, and onto his square jaw. What a fine death-mask could be made from such a head. He knew a man in Vienna who made such things.

Before long, workers from nearby fields came by to take their lunch and relieve themselves of the noonday heat. They gathered under the trees and spread their belongings: bread, cheese, tomatoes and wine. One of them had a flute and began to play, as the young ones sang and danced. When the heat was too much for them, they stripped and plunged into the water, where they bathed and splashed over each other. One girl caught Louis' eye: Her hair, golden and glistening wet in the sun, fell about her shoulders to her waist; her eyes glinted steel blue like the sky above; and her breasts hung like peaches ready to be plucked. She beckoned to him to come join them.

He dared not. The young men with her, handsome and muscular, sporting in the water or standing tall as oaks on the grass, would see his inadequacy and laugh at him. As still as a statue he sat on the rock, his face set in stone. When the girl came up from her bathing, she looked for her skirt and blouse on the grass and bent over, her back to Louis. Her ass was shaped like a heart; a fissure ran the length of it top to bottom, where it met a small crop of hair almost hidden between her legs.

They picked up their belongings, and when their footfalls and their singing and their shouting had disappeared into the fields, Louis took his notebook and sketched the perfect ass alongside scribbled notes for his grand new symphony.

He lolled on his back near the rock and read a passage from Homer's Odyssey that he had marked.

My mother says that he is my father;
for myself I know it not,
for no man knows who begat him.

These were the words of Telemachus to Athene; he began to tremble at the thought: Yes, who can say what happened when he was yet unborn? A man knows his mother, for he came from her womb and sucked at her breast. But his father could be anyone who stole into the mother's bed.

How often Maria cringed to hear Johann's name. How seldom she used his name. She did not love him. Someone else must be his father, therefore, and that is why Johann hated him and beat him. Someone made his way into the marriage bed. Someone made love to Maria while Johann made love to the whore.

This someone had to be Cressener. How else explain the relation between the two men: one an aristocrat, the other a good-for-nothing drunk? Yes, Cressener saw Maria at the court chapel and decided he wanted her; he paid Johann for privileges in his bed. Johann needed the money, he would do anything. And Cressener paid the whore to come satisfy Johann. Of course—Johann had no money for a whore.

At dusk he made his way back through the grassy fields to the house, where he failed to notice a two-horse carriage standing near the gate. As he entered, Christiana sprang to her feet. "Louis," she said, "we came to surprise you. Here…" She handed him a book.

He looked at the title: "Alfred the Great." With a snort he threw the book against a wall, breaking its spine and littering the floor with yet more paper. "An English King? Why should I read about an English King?"

"Because," said the Prince, "the English may be our saviors. If they go to war against Napoleon…"

Louis exploded. "The English have no hero like Napoleon. Here, I will show you his portrait in music." He thrust at him the first sheet of the manuscript: *Sinfonia grande, intitolata Boneparte.* "There, my third symphony, the grandest of all, honors the liberator from France."

"O dear," Christiana sighed. "Let us not talk politics, my dear Louis."

The Prince picked up the tattered pages of the book. "Louis," he said, "my intention was to give you the plot for an opera. Yes, Louis, you are ready to write for the stage. It will establish your fame in Vienna and silence your critics."

Their voices came to him as if from the bottom of a deep well. He moved closer and cupped one ear with the palm of his hand, pretending to scratch the back of his head. They said he should write an opera?

They knew he was hard of hearing. The Prince took paper and wrote: "The new director of the Theater-an-der-Wein will offer you a position in the theater. You will take charge of the orchestra and you may live in the theater's upper wing and retain your lodgings at the Pasqualati house, if you will compose something for the stage. We thought Alfred a good text because so many Austrians fear Napoleon and favor the English. But consider other books if you wish."

"I must finish the Third." He pounded his fists on the keyboard: two immense chords split the air.

The Prince took another paper: "Of course. But think of this: Schikaneder, our new man at the Wein, and Braun at the Court Theater, will stumble over one another to produce a Beethoven opera. They have titles to suggest."

Louis read the paper. He raised his arms to summon two more chords, but Christiane had slipped behind him; she wrapped her arms around his neck and kissed the top of his head.

"Command over the repertory?" he asked.

"Yes," responded the Prince. "You can schedule your own works."

Louis felt Christiana's solid bosom between his shoulders, and her warm breath on the back of his neck. "What titles?" he asked.

When they left, his thoughts turned to Napoleon Bonaparte, a powerful leader who claimed to free the world from slavery, lies and corruption. If "Boney" took Vienna and the nobility fled the city, including Prince Karl and Christiana, who would support him? So he would seek the graces of this great savior. The new symphony would be of heroic proportions and he would dedicate it to the new ruler of the world. The Eroica Symphony, he would call it.

But his raptus-angel gave him a better reason. It was the angel who marked for him the passage in the Odyssey that he studied over and over. And the angel told him of another passage:

Few sons are like
their fathers; most are worse, a very few
excel their fathers.

He should have known! Johann was a second-rate court musician and a drunk. How then could his son be a genius? Johann could not be his father. Someone else must have fathered him. Again, Cressener. Yes—he had seen the Englishman at the house talking to Johann. What else did they have in common but the big bedroom?

Another strange thing: he always believed that Johann lied about his age, claiming that his son was one or two years younger than he really was, so that he could parade him as a child wonder like Mozart. Johann's lies required that he be born in 1771 or 1772. But once he peeped at the register and saw the date of his birth: it was December 16, 1770. Johann's lies were thus confirmed...or were they? Somebody was born in December of 1770; someone named Ludwig van Beethoven, but what if that were the stillborn Ludwig, the firstborn, whose death broke Maria's heart? If so, where was his name in the register? It was missing. Either it never existed, or it was removed.

Who could tamper with a court register? Only a man of authority. Belderbusch or Cressener. Or someone greater than either.

He began to believe in his illegitimacy, that he was the love-child of some great and noble person. It was right and just, therefore, that he call himself von Beethoven, and that he dedicate his new symphony to a great man. Napoleon's name would be a symbol of greatness, of heroism. Thus he would honor his unknown father in this powerful new music.

Of course, Napoleon was his hero, a savior of mankind; not his real father, to be sure; Cressener was his father...or was he? If a greater than Cressener warmed his mother's bed on those nights when Johann was out a-whoring, or even when Johann was in the bed too, it could have been any of the great men who come to the Bonn court; and among the most noble of them was Friedrich Wilhelm 11 of Prussia, and his uncle, Frederick the Great. Any of these men could have been his father. Who could deny it? He himself could not, because no man knows who begat him.

At the piano again, the piano that earlier in the day failed him, he contemplated a finish to the new Symphony. A third movement and a finale were needed. But what music could follow on the heels of a funeral march that would consume twenty minutes of playing time and leave an audience fatigued? Opening his notebook, he gaped at the crude drawing he had made of the girl by the canal. Her ass was a marvel of symmetry and enticement and promise: in his head he heard the stamping of peasant feet and voices raised in song as these folk celebrated the simple joys of life. Their lives were *allegro vivace*. What better way to celebrate the death of Johann than for him to set peasant feet in motion as if they were his own?—yes, music that was an erotic dance around the grave, the grave into which he had lowered Johann. No more thoughts about his own death; the grave was not his. His fingers flew over the keyboard.

Helene must be told of his despair and his new resolve: he wrote

Dearest mother, I have not written for the longest time, for I wanted to keep from you that which would have given you cause to grieve. The ringing and buzzing in my ears, and the lapses into deep silence, get worse. I can hear some days better than others, but when I am at the piano or before an orchestra I make mistakes. This summer past I near despaired of my life and thought to throw myself in a canal. I wrote my Testament, but so far I have given it to no one; it stands here on my desk, undelivered. What saved me? My raptus-angel during a stormy night sent me a vision of a starry heaven. I thought of Schiller's poem, Ode to Joy, how a loving father dwells beyond heaven's vault. Even so I could not believe, for what loving father would lay upon me a command to make music, then smite me in my most sensitive faculty? What loving father would plant lust in my loins, but shame me so that I cannot make love to a woman? I will believe in such a father only if I can prove him in tones.

I am writing a new Symphony, unlike all others composed by me or anyone. If only you and the boys—Christoph and Stephan— could come to Vienna to hear it performed—in a princely palace at that! It is a march to the grave, but full of life before and after. I do not know who lies in the grave, but I know that life overreaches the grave and triumphs over it. Thus it is that I live and will go on living. The new symphony saved me, but the music proves only my fortitude. It fails to prove Schiller's loving father beyond the starry vault.

Hardly had he settled into his suite at the Theater-an-der-Wein, when he summoned Schikaneder and ordered an all-Beethoven Concert: the First and Second symphonies.

"Ach," the director replied. "So soon?"

"I shall rehearse the orchestra myself," Louis said, unmindful of the director's raised brow and pursed lips.

Schikaneder knew it was useless to argue. "Very well. Now I have some titles for the opera. I shall leave these texts with you…" He placed a stack of books on the table by the piano.

"No. It shall be *Leonore*."

The director tilted his head and squinted. "*Leonore?*" He had heard of it, a second rate text by a Frenchman named Bouilly. Not stageworthy. "Why *Leonore?*"

Louis heard not a word. But he understood what the director was getting at. He rose and brushed the pile of texts from the table onto the floor. "When you hear the music, you will understand." In his mind, the matter was settled.

Schikaneder knew he had a struggle on his hands against the monumentally stubborn composer. Even Mozart would have refused a plot like *Leonore,* so wooden, so slow paced. Beethoven had no experience with stage matters or plot movement. And there was another problem; many musicians in Vienna refused to play in an orchestra that Beethoven conducted, or even in a concert of the man's music, so bitter were they over his treatment of them and their fellows at the premier of his Piano Concerto. The man was not entirely an asset. But he would speak to the Prince and Princess about it; they had a way with this difficult man.

Louis wasted no time. The first concert was set for early spring, and his two symphonies would be brought before the public for the first time. He worked feverishly to produce an oratorio on a biblical theme—to excel Cardellieri's piece by far—and a new concerto for piano. Prince Karl, upon hearing of the plans, fretted over past incidents involving rehearsals and temper flare-ups by Louis; he offered the musicians tips to play for Louis. Even so, the rehearsal could not begin until the very day of the concert. Karl arranged for the hall to be opened at eight o'clock, in the unheated hall during a cold snap. The men were moody and cranky. Karl showed up with bread, butter, cold meat, and drink, to improve their moods. Then he took Louis aside and gave him a stern lecture.

The C Major began with a shudder that shook the audience; but the music's high spirits overcame all. Louis's sharp eye took in many slips and poor ensemble at times, but he said nothing. By the end the audience seemed pleased. Then the D Major. He wondered if the audience would appreciate the novelties in it: the Introduction, a lengthy piece by itself, served to set up the themes, not of the first movement, but of the second, the true heart of the work; this required the audience, when they heard the second movement, to recall the motifs that began the work. And there was a subtle kinship among the themes of the four movements, along with brilliant bridge passages, that held it all together. The audience applauded, but it seemed more out of courtesy. Following an intermission the forces gathered again on stage for the Oratorio. Things did not go so well: the singers and instrumentalists missed cues and made false entries. He sensed failure and he laid the blame at his own feet; it was not his best work; he had composed in great haste, but he had to compete with the Italian—and with Haydn, too, whose Creation was being performed that very evening at the Burgtheater—a spiteful move, he thought. Finally, near the end of the long evening, he sat himself at the piano for the new concerto.

The Concerto in C Minor was no piece of fluff. Louis considered that its imperious stride and noble bearing resembled but transcended Mozart's last concertos, and at its core he composed an incantation that should elevate spirits and make woeful hearts to sing. But he and the orchestra were at odds: he could not play and conduct at the same time; he often made a down beat for an accent in the wrong place, and sometimes he would rise from his bench as from a stage trap to wave his arms and leap about to rouse the full strength of the band, then he had not time to scramble back to the piano in time for his entrances. Yet, mindful of the Prince's admonitions, he made jokes: "Oh, I have unhorsed the most excellent riders," and finally, "Never mind, it will go better next time," he said at moments of crisis.

The following week a review of the concert appeared in the *Zeitung fur die Elegante Welt*. The author liked the First Symphony; it had an "unforced lightness" about it. The Second, however, was too heavy; it aimed for the "new and astonishing" and was of less worth. Another critic said of the Second Symphony that it put him in mind of a mortally wounded dragon that resisted death to the final rattle in its throat. As for the Concerto, "Herr v. Beethoven did not perform to the satisfaction of the public."

"I have decided upon a new path," he declared to the Prince, who had dropped in on him at the theater the week following the reviews. "I will write for the stage—you were right, it will help me win over the public. But as for my new symphony, it will disturb even more than the second, but hang the critics, I write for ages to come."

The Prince shook his head: "It will disturb if you dedicate it to Napoleon. His armies get closer every day; we will have to run for our lives."

When the Prince had left, he sat at the piano and meditated upon his new creation. A vibrant allegro full of conflict and strife, followed by the *marche funebre*; then the rustling and stomping of peasant feet in joyful and erotic arousal. For the Finale, a simple tune, elemental, from the earth, like the stamping feet, but rising from the earth like a tower set in marble—the hero has achieved his life's call.

Yet he wondered: if it was father Johann who died, he had marched him to his grave. He was his father's murderer.

Chapter Fourteen

"For All the World to Know."

A young fiddler sat amidst the string section of the orchestra as the men struggled with the new Beethoven concerto. Things were not going well. There had been little time for rehearsal; it helped that Prince Lichnowsky gave out food and drink earlier in the day, but the musicians were cold and uninspired. Anton Schindler, however, was inspired: not by the music alone, but by the composer himself, the composer who stood before them, eyes on fire, his body making ecstatic leaps into the air, his face aglow with passion. Yet the great man made errors: he often missed the beat. Why? And he would knock things about, like the music desk; and drop things, even when merely approaching the orchestra. Why? He had to know.

He was trained for the law, and he would pursue a career as law clerk; but he had other interests, particularly persons of stature: aristocrats, nobility, great artists, musicians and poets—they were like gods to him. As a small boy, he felt inferior to persons of elevated station in life and even to those among his peers who were more talented than he. He studied people of this sort, wondered about them, admired them from a distance.

When the concert was over he inquired about the receipts. The great composer, he was told, had inflated the price of a ticket. Twelve ducats for a loge—up from four! That was more than a simple law clerk made in a year. A notion began to stir in the back of his head: the Master could afford a personal secretary. And if the Master was hard of hearing—as he suspected; how else account for all the missed beats?—he would need help.

The following day he stood pounding at the door of the Master's flat. He had been at it for half an hour. The Master was at home, surely, for he heard the piano: something royal and commanding was issuing from the Master's brain. But the Master, hard of hearing in any case, could not be expected to hear his puny fist over the powerful tones of the fortepiano. Suddenly the music stopped. He raised his fist to pound on the door again, but checked his blow: he heard the soft voice of a woman. Then the piano began again, something delicate and sweet, played with no expertise. Ah, the Master is giving lessons to a lady, he whispered to himself. And who might she be? he wondered. He pounded again.

The music ceased and the door flew open. A bright-eyed young woman—hardly half the Master's age—passed him with lowered eyes. Inside, the Master resumed his magisterial music-making. Hat in hand, he waited at the open door until the music subsided. He had a note to place in the Master's hands, a note he had labored over; he wanted the note to speak well on his behalf when he introduced himself and pressed his cause. But the Master suddenly reached for his coat and rushed out the door. Their eyes met.

"Who are you?" demanded Louis.

Schindler thrust the note at him but Louis had slammed the door and was on the stairs. "I am not a collector of bills," Schindler called after him, forgetting that the Master was hard of hearing. The note in hand, he followed the Master down the street and into the City of Trieste Tavern, sat down next to him, and put the note on the table beside his glass of ale.

Louis read the note: "Herr von Beethoven, I will be your correspondent and secretary for a few hours each week, to assist you with your affairs, so that you will have more time to compose your glorious music. I will be most reasonable in my need to be remunerated; my chief reward will be the honor of doing a service for you and the music lovers of the city."

"Correction," Louis exclaimed, "... for the music lovers of the world."

The Master seemed interested. Schindler brightened: "Ah, of course. For the world!"

"But I have no need for help," Louis said, as he ordered his ale from a comely serving girl. With a wave of his arm, he dismissed the man as he would rid himself of a fly that landed on his sleeve.

Schindler left the tavern and contemplated the scene he had witnessed in the flat. The young lady...who was she? He would remember the face if he saw her again. In the meantime he would nose about. And he pondered the clutter and litter that made the flat unlivable by all civilized standards; the stench from the kitchen—it was not to be endured: no wonder the Master ate in taverns. And he had caught the crimson that rose to the Master's face as he caught the eye of the young thing who served his table. It seemed that the Master knew to go directly to that table where the girl would come to him. Did they know each other?

The following day Schindler waited at the City of Trieste Tavern and ordered an ale at the same table. Soon the Master entered in the company of a man whom Schindler recognized as Nikolaus Zmeskall, the secretary at the Hungarian Chancellery. This was not an opportune moment; he had hoped to speak to the Master alone.

"You see, Schindler, I have Zmeskall here to tend to my needs."

The man beamed with pleasure.

"And," added Louis, "we have just come from a chamber concert in this man's house. Could you do all that for me, Schindler, and do chores and run errands as well?"

Schindler knew when he was the butt of a joke. Surely Zmeskall—a man of property and endowment—did not do chores and run errands.

As if to disabuse Schindler of the doubt that must have shown behind his metal spectacles, Zmeskall said, "Oh, it is true. I sharpen Herr Beethoven's goose quills so that he can write."

It was believable. The Master had a reputation for being clumsy with practical matters, knocking over music stands in his publisher's rooms, dropping pens and papers, losing his spectacles, inept at striking a match to light a lamp. What could he, Schindler, do that Zmeskall could not?

The serving girl, the same as before, passed close by the table. "Here," said Schindler, snatching her by the sleeve, "a round of ale for my two friends—and serve the great Master immediately; he must not be put off." He gestured with a grand motion so that the deaf Master would understand that he, Schindler, could admire him as much as Zmeskall. The girl made swift steps to fetch the ale. Zmeskall smiled.

"Herr Schindler," he said, "The gentlemen who approach our table at this moment are friends of the Master also. Does your generous offer extend to them as well?"

Schindler pushed back his chair and rose to his feet. Lichnowsky he recognized; he had seen the Prince at concerts. Zmeskall rendered the introductions: Prince Ferdinand Kinsky; The Count Rasoumovksy; Stephan von Breuning, Herr Beethoven's life-long friend from Bonn; Herr Ignaz Schuppanzeigh, a close friend; and men named Weiss, Eppinger, Hummel, Mayseder, and Forster. Schuppanzeigh, Schindler imagined, was the leader of the quartet players who gathered often at Zmeskall's or at the Prince's residence, where they played the Master's new works; but he was too stunned to ask, or to make any conversation at all. These were the high nobility; he was but a law clerk, a peasant from the fields who didn't have the money to pay for the ale.

When he whispered his plight to Zmeskall, the matter was settled out of sight: Schindler paid for three, Zmeskall for the others. Schindler returned to the table where he sat for a time, taking no part but listening. A polka band began to play at the platform near their table; soon it was all but impossible for Schindler to hear what was being said. Finally during a pause in the music he seized his moment. From his coat pocket he withdrew a note he had prepared and passed it the length of the table to the Master: "I, Anton Schindler, will be honored to serve our great Master as chronicler of his glorious deeds. I will serve in this capacity with no thought of reward save that of knowing I have done a service to you and to the music lovers of the world."

Zmeskall read it aloud and passed it to Louis, who looked across the table at Schindler as if for the first time. "Why not?" he shrugged.

When Schindler left the table he noticed the serving girl hovering about his Master. As she reached to place another ale before him, her sleeve draped lightly over his arm; then as she turned, her hip made broad contact with his shoulders. Louis appeared to take no notice. A smile crossed Schindler's face as he made his way through the crowded tavern and into the fresh air.

Chapter Fifteen

"Boney at the Gates."

Prince Karl heard through the French Embassy that on May 18th Napoleon Bonaparte declared himself Emperor and in a special ceremony at Notre Dame Cathedral he had himself crowned before the mitered prelates and higher nobility of the land. He was no longer merely the head of the *Grande Armee*; he was head of state. It was an event that Karl had expected, for he believed the man was egotistical and ambitious.

Immediately he was alarmed for Louis, for Louis had sent to Paris, via the Embassy, a fair copy of his new Symphony with Napoleon's name on the title page. Word had gotten around in the city that Louis admired Napoleon: that was bad enough, even though some liberal intellectuals shared his views; but to have dedicated a work of art, whether the public liked Louis' music or not, to a man who was the enemy of Austria and the monarchy and who now proclaimed himself Emperor of France and intended to impose his will upon all Europe—that was folly. He spoke to his friends Ferdinand Reis and Count Moritz Lichnowsky and asked them to meet him at Louis' quarters at the theater so they could break the news. Perhaps they could persuade him to change his mind about the dedication, or to flee before the rowdies and looters took over the city.

Riots began last July, he would remind Louis, even before Napoleon had crossed the Danube, and things were getting worse. People were frightened and hungry because the government had raided the food supply in order to feed the troops fighting on the Italian front. The first outbreak occurred when some young men and boys came upon a group of soldiers helping themselves to bread at a bakery. The men set upon the soldiers with clubs and bedslats, and pelted them with stones and bricks. One of them held up a baker's stick with a linen cloth and waved it like a flag; another beat on an old drum. The soldiers regrouped quickly and fired into the attackers, killing several at the first volley. The flag waver had his head split open by the butt of a rifle, and the drum beater was run through the gut by a bayonet. Over a hundred ran away injured, while others lay bleeding in the street.

They pounded on Louis' door until finally it opened. Knowing what to expect, Karl had his message on a notepaper and handed it to him. Louis took the paper and read: "Your great emancipator, who was supposed to deliver the people from tyrants, is no longer First Consul; he had himself proclaimed Emperor."

Louis tore the note in two and threw it to the floor. With wide sweeps of his arms, he scattered piles of letters and scores on his desk until he found the title page to the new symphony. That too was ripped apart and stomped upon. "So, he is an ordinary man after all, no god. An egotist! A tyrant!" He went on stomping his feet and swearing until his visitors were entirely satisfied that their first problem was gone.

Karl now turned to the other problem: the difficulty of the music itself. On paper, the work seemed lengthy and thick; and that funeral march—the adagio theme was on paper four years ago when he and Christiane first stepped into Louis' apartment, and Louis denied it was a funeral. Well, no more mystery: it was time the music be heard. He planned to assemble a sixty member orchestra at the country estate of a friend, the Count Joseph Franz Lobkowitz and his guest, the Prince Louis Ferdinand of Prussia, for a private performance of the work. They could judge it in its full orchestral dress. If it proved as impossible as it appeared on paper, they could reason with Louis, persuade him to make changes or withdraw it altogether. What he said to Louis, simply, was that he and his friends wanted the honor of hearing the first performance in a private home.

On a Sunday evening, Louis himself led the orchestra at the Lobkowitz estate. It was more rehearsal than performance, as the musicians were seeing their parts for the first time. There were breakdowns: the worst in the first movement where half notes against the beat threw the orchestra into chaos. Karl was puzzled. What kind of music was this? But to be fair, he called the musicians back the following evening to perform it through. He would judge it then.

The musicians came at six and Louis led them again through the maze that had tortured them the previous night. The ensemble was scrappy, and the musicians ran roughshod over some of the most delicate passages; but Louis took long pauses between the movements to explain what he wanted, and the third and fourth movements had to be repeated at a slower tempo. Finally, the long symphony came to an end.

Karl was unable to speak to the musicians to thank them; nor did he speak to his friends, or to Louis. He felt he had been battered by the *Grande Armee*. Without so much as an outer wrap he wandered out in to the evening's cold. The orchestra's din rang in his ears. He walked at a steady pace first in one direction then the other until he had circled the estate several times. Themes and their satellites knocked about in his head. Massive chords and sinuous rhythms stormed and raged. He was stricken by an emotion as old as the death of Adam. Suddenly he was caught up in a barbaric revelry, as if the grave were of no account. Then finer thoughts came to him as he meditated about the nobility of a great mind.

When he returned to the palace, he found Lobkowitz and Prince Ferdinand pouring over the score, pointing to passages, humming them, speaking to Louis at the top of their lungs. Prince Ferdinand wanted another performance the following evening before he returned to Prussia, and he wanted to talk more to Louis. "The likes of this has never been heard," Ferdinand was saying—"you must come and visit me in my country."

Karl fixed his eyes on his friend as if for the first time. Never mind the pock-marked face, the rude manners, the fits of temper, the body odors that wafted through the halls; listen to the products of his mind, for it is great, vast and noble. If this new symphony was about Napoleon, a greater than Napoleon wrote it. Yes, he realized: the real hero of the piece was Louis himself, his rages, his erotic excursions, his visions, his secrets.

Louis turned from the new symphony to the opera, which was consuming him day and night and removing him from the companionship of his friends. The plot, the plot that stirred his blood, was the problem: it got off to a slow start, and he was compelled to write music for low comedy—not his genre. Yet he delighted in it: the curtain would rise upon a domestic scene in which a girl sings of her passion for a man who has come to work for her father, who approves of the possible union between the two. The music for her to sing must be as pure as her panting heart: "O were we two united," she sings, "and I could call you husband! A maiden can confess only half of what she feels. But when I do not need to blush for an ardent loving kiss, when nothing on earth shall come between us,"— she sighs and lays her hand upon her heart—"hope fills my heart with inexpressible delight, how happy shall I then be."

The public premier of the new Symphony at the Theater-an-die-Wein brought him out into the open late in the spring. To the relief of his friends, the name Napoleon was not on the title page; instead, Louis called it "Eroica," the Heroic Symphony. He stood before the orchestra and signaled the two fisted opening that shattered the calm space where the audience— as he knew perfectly well—was gathered for a polite entertainment in the vein of a Cardellieri or Salieri fop.

The orchestra, by now well rehearsed and familiar with the work, dashed through the *Allegro con brio* with no slips. If there was a reaction from the audience, Louis heard not a word. But in the middle of the *marche funebre* a howl from the gallery pierced the heavy silence of the hall: "I'll give another Kreutzer if only they will stop." Karl heard it; so did Reis; so did the entire audience. Louis kept to the beat, his eyes ablaze, his inner ear tuned to the death of a great man.

94

Was it a great man who died? he wondered. If so, it was not Johann. No, rather it was a great man who stood over the grave and contemplated the death of a lesser. Who then was the lesser? Yes, that could be Johann... and Louis the greater. But he could not be sure. Only the raptus-angel knew, the angel who fired his imagination when he penned the music and labored to give it birth.

In the scherzo the feet that at the grave had stumbled and faltered now took flight. The dance was a pianissimo hush for ninety one bars, as if some mighty censor forbad it; then the orchestra unleashed its life forces. In its middle sections, three horns took the dancing feet into the lolling countryside where health returned to the cheeks. They were his feet, his cheeks.

The theme of the Finale was a gift from the raptus-angel, who came upon him when he stared breathless at the face of Babette in the lightened kitchen; and came again as he felt the pulse of the tipsy, swaying merrymakers who came to the side of the waters and beckoned to him. The theme, at first a simple country dance, grew in his mind into a spout of life and spawned the hero theme of the *allegro*, the *marche funebre*, and the patter of feet in the scherzo. The raptus-angel told him that he himself was peasant-stock, and that his life was bound with their life. Peasants have noble thoughts, too; and the symphony delved into a pensive reflection on the subject of all that had gone before.

Then a boisterous outburst, reminding Louis and all the world of the joys of peasantry, ended it. For Louis was a peasant at heart—even if Cressener was his father.

The audience—half of them—rose to their feet and roared enthusiasm. The other half remained mute, while others had already left. Karl said the work needed repeated hearings and all would be well. There was no doubt, however, that Louis was a name on the lips of the people in the salons and in the streets.

In the evening Karl and Christiane held a dinner in his honor. Many of the nobility came, and Zmeskall came—loyal Zmeskall—but not Moscheles nor Drangonetti nor any of the musicians who still smarted from the abuses Louis hurled at them when he premiered the B flat Concerto. During the dinner Louis was congenial, but after a time he lapsed into thought: something about the Eroica remained unsettled.

When he returned to his apartment, his mind returned to his opera. One aria had already been written, the one for the girl Marcellina as she dreams of the man who has come into her life. She believes that he will return her affection; then what bliss there shall be! she sings. Louis too had a dream. His life was full, but his heart was empty. He put pen to paper, as he had done many times, thinking, praying. He wanted a wife for himself. But when? It could not be denied him forever, because it is a man's right and destiny to find a woman; even Popageno, the simpleton in Mozart's opera, found his Popagena.

But Louis, even as he composed Marcellina's music, knew in his heart that the opera told a lie, a lie that he had wanted to believe since the days he had to hide in the attic from Johann's rages and blows. The lie is that all is well in the household where Marcellina sings her blissful love. The truth is that the domestic bliss is sham: the man whom Marcellina loves is no man at all; it is a woman. And the household where they live borders on the courtyard of a prison, where the prisoners and guards whisper about a man in the dungeon below who is fed only bread and water, less and less each day until he dies.

Later that evening he penned a letter to Helene:

My Dearest Mother, November 1, 1805
Prince Karl thinks my new symphony, that I call "Eroica," is about my own heroism as I rise above the loss of my hearing, and that in Heiligenstadt I rehearsed my own death so that I could face it and defeat it. Yes, I live, and I compose; each day is a gift of joy. But if I am a hero, I am a captive hero in some dark place; I cannot hear, which for me is like the loss of sight in others.

I must tell you about my new project—an opera! It is from Bouilly's Leonore, or Conjugal Love. The moment I read the story I knew I must put it on the stage. The emotion I have felt as I composed the arias and choruses has me quite beside myself. My raptus-angel cannot be far.

It begins as a simple love story. A woman falls in love with a man who has come to work for her father. But under the surface things are stewing. The man is no man, he is a woman in disguise; and they all work in a prison, under which a nameless man is chained in a cell near a cistern, close to death.

The man who has come to work in this prison calls himself "Fidelio," but it is really Leonora who searches for her lost husband. She wonders if the man chained below is he.

Ah, yes, my dearest mother, you have guessed it. Leonora's husband, Don Florestan, is indeed the one who is chained in the dark, dank cell. And she will find a way to rescue him from the evil Pizarro, who, out of jealous spite, had him jailed unlawfully and keeps him in the hidden dungeon below the prison's walls. And, dearest mother, you will have guessed this also, that I am Don Florestan, chained in the cell of my infirmities—as you know. But I am a Florestan without a Leonora.

Tomorrow night we will have all the singers assembled on the stage. The most experienced singers have fled the city, but Braun has rounded up a few good voices. Anna Milder will sing Leonora. Braun says she has a voice that is as radiant as her face, and she can be heard over the orchestra. But she is young and will need time to learn her music—which does not rest lightly on the vocal cords, I admit. But we have little time, if Prince Karl is to be believed. He says he hears Napoleon's cannons firing to the west and south of the city, and we see our dead and wounded being carried into the hospital every day. What will become of us? Of my opera? Like Florestan, we must pray for deliverance.

Your loyal son, Louis

Louis, seated at the pianoforte close to the orchestra rail1 looked up at the gas-lit stage where the singers had gathered for rehearsal. Milder was late, but Demmer, who was to sing Florestan, was present, and Sebastian Meyer, the evil Pizarro, was on stage score in hand. Seyfried, a competent musician, was in charge of the orchestra. They began with Pizarro's maddened aria: he has received a secret dispatch warning him that the Minister of Justice will come to the prison to inspect for political prisoners; he sings his determination to murder his prisoner and he bribes his jailer Rocco to dig a grave at once. Meyer sang well, but Louis, unable to hear the orchestra's woodwinds, shouted at him to correct the balances. Matters were thus often brought to a halt as the singers on stage rolled their eyes and shook their heads at the needless interruptions. Finally Karl took Louis by the shoulders and sat him down, handing him notes to the effect that the orchestra was doing its best, and that things would improve by the time of the performance.

When they came to the scene in the dungeon, all were weary. But Milder arrived, and she was in fresh voice. As Leonora, she comes down the stairs at stage rear, holding a lantern. The stage director had placed the gas lights and Leonora's lantern so that her face would shine in the dark; the audience would see her first, then Rocco, while Florestan sleeps in his cell. At his piano, Louis looked up at the face in the lantern's glow; he quivered at the sight. Beside her stands Rocco, bearing picks and shovels. Rocco looks at his assistant and sings "You are trembling, are you afraid?" She sings "No, but it is so cold here." A rock and a mound of earth and stones block the opening to a cistern. Leonora and Rocco sing a duet as they dig through the rubble. Rocco gets his pick under the rock and nods to Leonora, who strains under the weight of it, but at last it rolls away.

The cistern is exposed.

Louis heard little of Milder's pure sweet voice, but his eyes followed her as she put down the lantern and began to dig, then as she took it up again and moved toward the cell.

As they sang, the din of cannon fire was heard in the theaters, the taverns, the beer halls, shops and streets: Napoleon, the nemesis of bedtime stories in nurseries—"Boney," who would come and "get" little boys and girls who didn't obey their parents—was a fiction come to life. Would the Austrian guard hold fast? Or would "Boney" march through their streets in the morning?

Cannon fire was heard into the next day, which stopped when the sun went down; but sixty pound bombs with fiery tails sailed through the night sky and landed on top of houses and in the streets. When a bomb struck, shadowy figures could be seen groping through smoke and dust in the narrow streets and alleys to seek shelter in the cellar of some larger building. From the tower of St. Stephen's church bells rang out at ten o'clock. Louis, in the Walfischgasse, was in the direct line of fire, but he remained at his piano until his new Concerto in E Flat Major was finished, then he ducked through the streets with a pillow over his ears to the cellar of Ignaz Castelli, a friend, in the nearby Ballgasse, where he complained loudly about the danger to his piano. In his hands he held several scores, including the new concerto and some last minute changes to Florestan's aria. In the morning a breeze from the hills to the north lifted the mist and revealed Napoleon's *Grande Armee* camped outside the city gates.

Chapter Sixteen

"Conjugal Love."

Even before the shelling began, people in the street stopped to gape at the sight of travel-carriages dashing from the court, every hour it seemed, to the Danube, where ships waited to take the Empress, others of the royal family, and nobles with their treasures up the river to safety. At the Josephplatz one hundred horses stood ready to be hitched to carriages that would take kegs of gold, the Treasury, the Medallion and Natural History collections, along with fine linens and silver. Pedestrians lined the avenues to snatch objects from passing carriages—shoetrees, pillows, bedwarmers—as if these would save them from the *Grand Armee*. As an act of mercy or prudence, an order issued from the court that citizens who had valuables—gold, silver, jewels—could take them to a ship at the Franzbridge against a receipt; but many thought better of it and chose to hide their belongings in cellars and attics, to store food, and to keep their women and children off the streets: it was rumored that the French chasseurs treated women badly.

On November 9 Boney ascended the ramparts on his horse with 15,000 fighting men behind him and stared down at the city. At five o'clock that evening, Count Rudolph Wreba, one of the few government officials left in the Court, headed a deputation to meet him at the ramparts and negotiate for the safety of the city. It was agreed that Napoleon would no longer fire upon the city, if the government and citizens opened up to admit the officers and infantry and gave them quarters, food, and supplies to use in their continuing war against the Russians. Prince Murat would preside over the government, giving orders directly to Wreba, and Murat would be quartered in Hutteldorf in the villa of Prince Franz Liechtenstein; Napoleon himself would join him and the Princess that very evening for dinner—porcelain dishes would have to be provided, for that was the way the Emperor and his retinue preferred to dine.

On the 13th the *Grande Armee* marched through the city in triumph. The emblazoned *grenadiers a cheval* in their polished cuirasses, with the proud figure of Prince Murat in their midst, silenced the citizenry that looked down from windows and rooftops. Flags and banners waved from the tips of bayonets; drums and bugles beat time as the victors paraded down the avenues in the order of battle. But the infantry was mudsplattered and unshaven. Many feet were unshod, wrapped in cloth or cheap stained sheets or peasant blouses that may have been looted from a farmer's bedroom. Heads were bandaged, arms were in slings or hung limp from the shoulder. Many men strapped lard or loaves of blackbread inside their shirts; others bore hams or chunks of meat ripped from carcasses. More than one carried a winebottle and lifted it to parched lips; one insolent fellow stopped to light his pipe with Viennese banknotes.

From his steed Murat waved graciously to the onlookers who lined the avenues. His orders were to impress and pacify the citizens, win their good will, and convince them that they should support the French in their battle against the Russian barbarians. To show contempt for the Russians, they ripped the uniform off a Russian officer whom they captured at Ulm and paraded him naked through the streets; when they came to Schoenbrunn, where the crowd was thick, an officer dismounted, took his sword and castrated the prisoner before horrified eyes; then thrust a crutch into his bowels and jabbed and thrust it, forcing him to keep pace with the marchers; blood ran down his legs until his eyes clouded and his head reared back, his agony over at last.

The scruffy appearance of the footsoldiers inspired more fear than pity: men so desperate and deprived—could they be trusted? Word soon got about that one should avoid the streets altogether: the French will strip a horse of its harness, and the horse's owner of anything by way of clothing, jewelry, shoes, money. On the Laimgrube at noon a French soldier who had holes in his shoes grabbed an apprentice and tried to take his boots by force; when the boy resisted, the soldier took his sword and cleaved the boy's mouth. But even staying indoors was not safe: a soldier at The Windmill in Lamm demanded food and drink and lodging; all this was given to him, but when he demanded a girl to satisfy his lust, no such girl could be found; the man grabbed the innkeeper's wife, who resisted, so he shot her with his pistol and she bled to death in her own bed.

Louis returned to his flat in the Pasqualati house and stood at the window looking down; in the distance he could see the Molker Bastei toward Hetzendorf and, below, the Schonbrunn gardens where in the heat of recent summers he had dreamed up his *Leonora*. Now Napoleon's sentries paced the grounds about the palace, for Napoleon himself lodged there and received dispatches and delegations from the Austrian court. It was well he ripped the despot's name from the title page of the Eroica; nothing heroic had emerged from the head of the conquering hordes who had mutilated the body of a Russian officer and terrorized the city. Nor was the despot likely to be edified by the drama of Leonora's noble sacrifice for her unjustly imprisoned husband.

At the theater, Louis, Braun, and Karl argued the fate of *Leonora*. Louis pounded his fist on Braun's desk in rage at the French and frustration with Braun, who was unwilling to risk opening the theater to an empty house. Braun demanded that Louis and Karl guarantee his expenses would be met. The matter was resolved, however, by a bulletin from the Murat-controlled court: theaters, taverns and inns were to remain open for the entertainment of the French officers.

"For the officers and their ladies," said Braun.

Karl required only a moment to grasp his meaning; then he put it in writing for Louis: "The house will be full of whores."

Louis was on his feet: "My Leonora will not be exposed to street trash."

"And how will we keep them out, my dear Louis?" asked Karl.

It was beyond argument: the premier was announced for Friday November 20 at eight p.m.

At eight, the theater was empty. Between eight and nine, French officers, many of them tipsy, but dressed in black and gold with dress epaulets and swords in scabbards, swaggered in, many of them escorting women of the kind Louis had deplored. One of them was loud: he tried to tell the girl something, but she responded only with squeezes and nudges, as the officers laughed and winked knowingly. Louis, from behind the pianoforte, shook his head: how could these men—he didn't care about the women—understand the text of the opera? The theme of it? The beauty of Leonora's sacrifice?

The overture silenced the house for a time, but drew no applause. Louis knew that Austrian music was far from the light, elegant entertainment fancied by the French. He hoped that the comic aspect of the opening scene, a love-tangle with Marcellina's heart panting for a young man new in the house, while her jealous former lover sings his complaints, might gain their interest and stop the wagging tongues. But no—the humor would be lost on the French who knew little German.

In the First Act, Fidelio earns the respect of Marcellina's father, Rocco, who is the prison turnkey. Rocco believes that Fidelio will marry Marcellina and make a fine addition to the family and the working staff. Fidelio plays along with this prospect, for she needs to learn more about the mysterious prisoner and only Rocco goes down to that dreary cell. She must find a way to go with him and see the prisoner with her own eyes.

The audience had thinned out by the Second Act; many officers took their women to more comfortable places, leaving only a scattered dozen or so in the seats. On stage, Pizarro reads a dispatch from a friend in the service of the Minister of Justice, and learns that the Minister, Don Fernando, will come to inspect the prison for unjustly held prisoners. He acts quickly: he calls his guards and gives orders: "Take your posts around the tower. Be strict in your lookout. And you, captain, ascend the tower and keep your eye on the road from Seville; when you see a coach with outriders, blow your trumpet—blow it twice." When the men disperse to their posts he rants: revenge will be his...but how? There is only one way—he must execute the prisoner and bury the body in the cistern. Taking Rocco aside, he slips him a dagger and orders him to do the deed at once. Rocco refuses, but accepts money for the task of digging the grave and keeping his mouth shut. Pizarro himself will plunge the dagger into Florestan's heart.

Louis had trouble hearing the singers; he studied their lips and the motions of the musicians in the pit in order to follow the drama. He turned to see if the officers and their guests were focused on the drama, where Pizarro and Rocco plot the murder. In a dark corner of the stage, and out of sight of the audience, Leonora has been spying on Pizarro; soon, when the two men have gone off, she will burst into the light and sing her brave aria. When he wrote this music, he anticipated a breathless hush would have fallen upon the audience so that every word, every inflexion, of Leonora's aria would sink into open hearts. But he saw that the officers were jabbering away at their women. One of them extended a probing hand into the bosom of a woman whose head tilted toward his shoulder and whose long hair streamed down into his lap. She said something low in his ear and he twisted in his seat to embrace her. In that revealing second Louis stared into the face of his whore.

Anna Milder's face, bathed in light, filled the stage; her voice rang out pure and sweet:

"Ah, break not yet, weary heart! Have you not endured, in these terrible days, new pain and dreadful fear with every single beat? Come, O hope, let not the last star of the weary fade away! Oh you, for whom I have endured everything, if only I could force my way to that place where malevolence keeps you in chains, to bring you sweet solace! I shall follow the dictates of my heart, I shall not falter, I am sustained by the commands of true conjugal love."

After she has sung her heroic aria, Leonora rejoices that Rocco will permit her to assist him to dig the grave. As they sing about their grave-digging task, bloodless skeletons come up from below into the light of the courtyard. Each day these prisoners are permitted a few moments of light and air; they sing "O freedom, O freedom—up here is life, below is the tomb." Louis quivered in ecstasy; he had labored over this chorus with his life's blood; he would lie in his room at night and growl out the words for the whole world to hear. On stage, one of the prisoners whispers, "Speak lightly, eyes and ears are upon us," as the shadow of a guard patrolling the rampart falls over them.

The light and air are cut short: Marcellina dashes into the courtyard to warn Rocco that Pizarro is coming and he is in a rage. Rocco slams the door on the prisoners who have filed back into their cells and turns to face his master. "Are you still here?" Pizarro demands. "You have a job to do—go to it at once!"

At that the curtain was lowered on the Second Act, and ushers lit the gas lights that lined the hall. Louis peered over the top of the pianoforte. The French officer rose from his seat, tall and handsome in his uniform; he put on his bearskin headdress with the wool tuft and red plume that was worn by the *Guarde Imperiale*—a high ranking officer, he was, Louis noted—and with dignity the officer proffered his hand to the whore and helped her to her feet. Yes it was she—he was sure of it: the toss of her head, her sure-footed jaunt. He studied them as they moved to the exit. The officer had turned his back to Leonora. Leonora! And the whore—her very presence profaned this chamber of conjugal fidelity. Never would he go back to her. He would be faithful to his Leonora.

Backstage, Deemer was complaining to Karl that he would have to sing to an empty house. He wanted to call it off and go home. Louis came upon the clamor and when he understood the issue, filled the room with chilling scorn. "You are Florestan," he said, "You are chained in your cell, you cannot leave until your Angel sets you free." Karl and Deemer were taken aback: Louis spoke as if Florestan were a living person present with them, as if the stage sets were a real dungeon.

Seyfried lifted his arms before the orchestra to signal the prelude to Act Three, and Deemer scrambled to his place in Florestan's cell just as the stagehand pulled the cord to lift the drape. Louis took his seat near the pit, a solitary figure whom the singers and musicians must pacify. The prelude begins. It knows no tonality; uncertain of its harmonic world, it gropes in the dark; like the dungeon itself, it admits no light or logic. Soft drumeats like stealthy footfalls warn that gravediggers will come, then the murderer himself. The strings tremble and wail; the horns shriek in horror.

Florestan rises from his stone and sings: "God, how dark in here! How terrible this silence!"

Louis heard not a word, but he followed Deemer's lips: "How terrible this silence!" He had conceived the music for Florestan's aria in the silence of his mind, a dark cell untouched by the summer sun in Hetzendorf, untouched by the brilliant sky over the canal where he dipped his feet in cool, flowing water. In his music he gave to Florestan the gift of hope; but the gods had denied the same to him.

Florestan sings: "In the springtime of my life I was cut down. I dared to speak the truth, and these chains are my reward." He takes a locket from his bosom; he cannot see it, but his fingers caress the portrait it holds. "Ah," he sings, "those were lovely days when my gaze hung on yours, when, with my heart beating joyfully, I held you in my arms." He sinks down upon his stone; his hands cover his face.

Louis' hands flew to his face; if the gods will it, a Leonora will come for him.

Leonora and Rocco come down the dark stairs at the back of the stage: she carries a lantern and a jug; Rocco a shovel and pick. "How cold it is in here," she sings. Leonora's face glows in the faint light.

Terrible things happen in the dark, Louis knew. This is why his raptus-angel came to him in the dark of night. When he ran through the streets of Bonn to escape the face of Johann's whore, his mother's face interceded in light. She was his raptus-angel. And so was Babette of Bonn, her face aglow in the kitchen while he stood in the cold dark. At times the raptus-angel came by day; the sun was in the sky above, but his mind was clouded. On his stage, Florestan, in the ignorance of his night, has no raptus-angel; he sleeps as footfalls from behind approach his cell; soon the cistern will be opened and his prison will be his tomb.

New music poured into his brain. He must write it down; his notebook was somewhere in the dark…but where? No matter; he will embrace the thought in his soul. It will mean another revision and Schickaneder and Braun will object—but he will rage and storm and get his way. An angel must dance on Florestan's tongue. Yes, just as he sings "In the springtime of my life…I held you in tight embrace," a light will pierce his inner dark, bearing the face of his beloved. "My angel Leonora," he will sing; ecstatic and joyful he will open his arms to greet her. But the vision will fade and he will fall back upon his stone.

A boulder blocks the mouth of the cistern. Rocco digs under it with the pick and pries it up while Leonora pushes it from behind; the basses in the pit rumble as the big stone tilts and rolls down an incline. Now they must dig through the rubble. Leonora stands to rest her arms on the shovel. She casts her eyes over her shoulder in the direction of the cell. The figure she searches for cannot be seen. He must be asleep, she thinks…or dead? The orchestra reaches into its lowest registers as she picks up the shovel again and opens wide the opening.

Leonora and Rocco sing their duet. "Yes, it is cold, but we must do our job," sings Rocco. "Hurry, he will be here soon." Leonora, glancing again at the cell, sings, "Whoever you may be, I will save you. I swear before

God, you shall not be killed! Indeed, I will undo your chains, I will set you free, poor man. I will set you free!"

The clink of Rocco's pick against a stone wakens Florestan. He stands inside his dark cell and looks at the face of his turnkey jailer, the only human he has seen in two years. In the deep shadows, another figure leans against a shovel and seems to stare at him.

"Who is that?" he asks.

"God, It is he!" she whispers.

Rocco answers: "He is my assistant."

Leonora puts the lantern on the ground behind the boulder; she does not want her face to be seen by Florestan—not yet. Rocco is about to blow a whistle to summon Pizarro, but Florestan begs for a morsel—a crust of bread will do. Leonora takes bread from her blouse, letting his hand touch hers as he grasps the food and drink. He looks into eyes of kindness: "The boy's deed will be repaid in heaven above." Hope rises in his breast: "Send to Seville," he pleads, "ask for Leonora Florestan. Tell her that her husband perishes here in this terrible place."

"O God," she whispers as she shrinks back into the dark. "He cannot know that she just dug his grave."

Rocco blows the whistle.

What does the whistle mean? Florestan wonders. Rocco looks to the stairs and waits in silence. From the head of the stairs a noise is heard; the heavy door has opened. In a moment Pizarro enters carrying his own lantern; his other hand is inside his vest. Rocco unlocks the cell and retreats to a corner where he crouches until he is needed to do his final task.

Florestan stares into the face of his enemy. He sees Pizzaro's hand slip into his vest and pull out a dagger. Now he understands why he was stolen away from his home, why he perishes in this cell, why he is about to die.

"He who stands before you exacts his revenge," Pizarro exults. "You defied me—now you shall die!"

"A murderer, a murderer, stands before me!"

The orchestra churns and slashes in protest. Leaning against the rail, Louis felt the vibrations through his limbs; when he composed this music he was Florestan himself, trapped inside the cell, his arms crossed over his breast to take the death strike.

Leonora has been hiding behind the boulder. She inches forward to the cell door that was left open and sees Pizarro polish his dagger with a cloth. When he throws the cloth to the ground she knows he is ready to strike. She slips between him and her husband and raises one arm to deflect the blow. Her other arm curves around his neck as she presses her bosom against him. "First stab this heart of mine," she cries.

Florestan shudders: what is this apparition that presses a woman's bosom against his body and dares the monster to strike at its heart before his?

Pizarro hurls her aside. "Are you mad? You shall be punished for this."

In a moment she is on her feet and before him again. "First kill his wife."

Pizarro backs away for an instant, then raises his dagger. "His wife? Then you both shall die!" The dagger is ready to plunge into her bosom, but she holds his eye: "Yes, I am his wife. I swore to save him and ruin you."

"Ha, I am afraid of a woman?"

She pulls a pistol from her doublet and points it between his eyes. "One word and you are dead."

On the tower high above the prison walls the captain aims his spyglass down the road that leads from Seville. A four-horse carriage speeds toward the prison gate bearing outriders who wear helmets and carry arms. Other carriages trail behind. The captain lifts the trumpet to his lips.

Leonora, shielding Florestan, tightens her grip on the pistol. From a distance, the trumpet is heard. She sings to her husband, "Ah, love will set you free."

At the second blast of the trumpet, Pizarro rushes up the stairs. Leonora falls to the rubble in a faint. Rocco, stunned but loyal to his employer, grabs the pistol and follows Pizarro to the courtyard. The dungeon is dark except for the light of one lantern. Florestan, still bound in his chains, calls to his wife who lays before him: "My Leonora, what have you endured for me?"

They hear a great commotion above. Fearful that Pizzaro will return with the pistol and kill them, they embrace: "We shall die happy in each other's arms," they sing.

In the courtyard, prisoners stream from their cells, casting off shackles from ankles and wrists, for Rocco has gone down corridor after corridor, opening cell after cell, releasing prisoner after prisoner. Those whom the prisoners have longed for—their lovers, their friends, their children—have come in other carriages; for the Minister of Justice, Don Fernando, heard that Pizarro had kidnapped those who opposed his evil doings and he declared a festive day, a day of deliverance. He rejoices to watch the men embrace their lovers and sing their thanks to the merciful God who gives them their freedom. Pizarro is led forth, chained to a pole; he weakly pleads his case. The people point at him and shout "Revenge! Revenge!—let the evildoer be punished!" Finally Rocco, having emptied all the cells of the innocent, comes to Fernando: "There is one more," he says, "he and his wife are in the deepest dungeon. They heard the trumpet, but they cannot know what it means."

Leonora, fearful of the crowd that demands revenge, pulls at Florestan's chains but cannot set him free. "Let us meet our death in each others' arms," they sing. The door at the head of the stairs bursts open. A horde of people, men and women, parade into the dungeon led by guards who flood the cell with light from their torches and tapers. Rocco flies down the stairs, half-stumbling, looking over his shoulder, then pointing at Florestan in chains and Leonora in his arms: "Here they are, see!" he exclaims. A tall figure steps into the light. Florestan looks up and recognizes the face of his friend, Don Fernando.

Louis sprang from his seat at the pianoforte. Without a winter wrap, he rushed from the theater and through the dark streets to the gate by the ramparts. The Austrian grenadiers were no longer there; in their place at the guard post stood two French soldiers with bayonets. Two women were there, chatting and flirting. As Louis approached the gate, one of the soldiers blocked his way with the bayonet and pointed at his stomach. "Who are you?" the soldier demanded.

"I am Beethoven."

"What is that to us?"

The women giggled. "Oh, let him pass. What harm? Besides, he has a sweetheart, one of us, and he pays well."

The soldier frowned. "Is his sweetheart outside the gate?"

"Maybe she is. Let's look and see."

The soldier was unmoved. "We cannot permit this man to pass. And I cannot leave my post."

The women winked at each other. One of them grabbed the soldier by the belt and led him through the gate and into the bushes where she began to loosen his trousers. The other led her catch into the privacy of the guardhouse. Louis understood. In a minute he was on the moonlit path that led through the forest toward the canal.

The moon hid behind passing clouds; he had no light to guide his feet which became tangled and trapped in the brush and roots; he fell often but he rose up quickly and sped on mindless. At last he came to the rock that jutted out into the water. He began to strip, but no—the night was cold as Florestan's cell. He lay upon the rock, his face to the few stars that peered through the dense clouds. How easy to slip away into the water. Not far, he knew, was Heiligenstadt, where he had thought to do away with himself. The Eroica saved him.

But tonight in the theater, at the very moment when the Minister of Justice stepped into the light, an old fear rose up in him. Fernando was salvation for Florestan. Who was salvation for Louis? No one. The stars above—the few of them—recalled to mind Schiller's poem. Those poets! Always ranting about a loving father who dwells above the starry vault. The only father he knew was Johann.

Florestan was saved, and Pizarro was taken to the dungeon and chained to rot upon the slab of stone. But Louis, lying on the slab by the rushing waters, was still in his prison; his father Johann had been punished and sent to his grave—that was just, but Louis had not been saved. No angel sent by a loving father had come for him.

Justice? Salvation? Fine diversions for the stage, but scarce in a world crushed by Napoleon and littered with mutilated bodies.

He lay upon his rock until dawn, but no raptus-angel came.

Chapter Seventeen

"An Uncertain Trumpet."

A petite young woman in flat shoes with ribbons made her way up the narrow stairs to the second floor of the Pasqualati house and rapped her knuckles on the door. Her hair was unbound and draped over her bare shoulders, and her yellow silk dress flowed to her ankles but did not cover them. It was her nature to be bold, not only in her dress but in her brash acts—and this was one: unannounced she had come to see for herself what the great but eccentric composer was like. Was he indeed an unbridled womanizer?— such was the reputation thrust upon him by all the wagging tongues of Vienna.

She rapped again and again, then paused. How silly, she thought: the man is deaf. She thought for a moment: sometimes, people said, he would bolt himself inside his flat and answer for no one, not even nobility. But did he not have a man-servant who might open the door for visitors? They said he did. Again she rapped, louder. No answer. Disappointed, she turned to leave. On the first landing she heard the door open behind her; a bulky figure emerged and hurried down the stairs. If it was the great man, she thought, he had not opened to her rapping; he was intent on an errand, oblivious to her presence. She turned and blocked the narrow stairs.

The landing was dusky, but she recognized the dark brow, the imperious gaze of his black eyes, the tangled mane. He was shorter than she remembered from the concert at the Theater-an-die-Wein a few days ago when he led the orchestra in his new C minor Symphony. Before the orchestra he was an immense presence whose slashing arms and barked commands dominated the musicians, the singers, the world—and her.

She thrust a card at him on which her name was engraved.

"I am Beethoven," he thundered. "You must come to my room." He turned and led her back up the stairs and into the flat.

She was unprepared for the sight. Sacks of straw—his bed?—were spread out in one corner. Stumps of pianos and dirty clothing littered the room. An unemptied chamberpot stank from under the one piano that had four legs. Her eyes discerned a fine nutwood desk; it was the only decent piece in the room, but it was cluttered with scraps of paper, tattered pages of books, and an ear-trumpet. A clanging noise issued from another room, which appeared to serve as a kitchen: on the wall was suspended a painted clock with iron weights; only a deaf person could endure that noise. He threw his filthy coat into a heap on the floor along with other articles and stained undergarments. Light from a large window exposed pock-marks and red blemishes on his face; no wonder they called him the Black Spaniard from Bonn. And his belly was swollen: too much beer and grouse at the taverns? Yes, he was ugly, as they said. How then did he make his way into the bowers of so many women? Or was that all lies? Well, she had entered his bower; she would see for herself.

Without a word he sat at the piano and began to play. Soon he was singing a song. His voice was loud and gritty and grated on her ears, but the melody was soulful. When he finished, he turned his deep eyes to her: "It is yours, I composed it for you." His charade was transparent to her: he played from a score that had been written before she entered the room. So, she concluded, this is how the great man captures the souls of his women.

With a roar of laughter he exclaimed: "As you suspect, I wrote it yesterday. It is called *Do You Know the Land*? Poem by Goethe." Quill in hand, he added, "But today I dedicate it to you because you danced into my room with fairy feet." He wrote a dedication over the score and gave it to her: *For Bettina Brentano.* "Now then," he said, "I fear I cannot entertain you here in the way you must be accustomed. My servant is out and he failed to leave me a clean house. Some other time?"

So, she thought, he will attempt no seduction here in the flat. Perhaps he prefers to enter the homes of those whom he beds; that would be a necessity, for what woman would join him in that sack of straw? The gossips linked him to some countess or other from Prince Lichnowsky's circle. Those nobility were immoral; but no more so than she. But other tongues linked him to the most vulgar type of woman; only a strumpet from the street would lay down with him in the straw that lay in the corner, that he called a bed. She pursed her lips; she could set tongues a-wagging, too. Yes, his eye darted toward her bosom. Yes, she could capture him; her bosom was the equal of any. "Well, then," she said, "you shall come with me. I am told there are fine coffee houses along the Prater. We shall talk on the way and become fast friends."

"Ach, regrettably, I must go to the Count Moritz von Fries, where I have urgent business."

Puzzled by the man's playful indifference, she helped him back into his filthy coat and led him by the hand down the stairs and into the street, where a more conservatively dressed woman was waiting for them. The woman's full length dress fell to the tops of her high heeled shores. Her golden hair, tightly bundled behind her head, was partly covered by a bonnet, and her bosom was modestly concealed by a parasol.

"Herr von Beethoven," Bettina said, "I wish to present Madame Brentano of Frankfurt."

Antonie gave him the courtesy of a chilled smile. Bettina handed him a card with her name engraved on it and an invitation in her hand: "Herr von Beethoven," it read, "My sister has just returned home to Vienna for a time. This evening we will offer musical entertainment to some guests. We shall have a pianist and some string musicians. May we have the pleasure of your company? *98 Erdbeergasse, Landstrasse.*"

"Ach, a pity. This evening I must see the good Count von Fries. I will be giving a concert soon and the Count will sponsor me. You see," he added with a grunt, "this is how it is for a musician in Vienna—one must have sponsors."

He raised a hand of each to kiss it in the most formal manner and took his leave of them. The two women stared blankly at his backside as he sauntered across the street where a carriage picked him up and he was gone. "You did well to stay here on the street," said Bettina. "His place stank like certain streets in Frankfurt."

Before he went to the Count von Fries, he intended to go to his publisher. Although Breitkopf was usually reliable, he had become slow lately in making payments. In the Neuer Market he came upon the family of a shopkeeper at a table selling off their belongings to raise money to feed their children, who stood by with hollow faces. He bought six cravats. At Breitkopf's he stormed at the manager, who could do no more than shrug and write his answer on the back of a music sheet: "With the French running rampant and forcing up prices, who can afford to buy music?" But Louis was adamant: "If one pays 30 gulden for a pair of boots, why should he not pay that much for my sonatas?"

"My dear Beethoven, the French occupation has made life harsh for us all. Precisely because the boots cost that much, people are unable to buy your sonatas."

"But I am famous—the Eroica, the Fifth. All Vienna sings my praises."

The manager knew it was pointless to go on. He shrugged again and went back to his desk, his ears ringing with Louis' last words: "Liar! Cheat!"

At von Fries the Archduke Rudolph was present, one of the few nobles who had remained in the city. Louis went on about his money troubles and reported his conversation at Breitkopf. The Count agreed. "Yes, Louis," he said, "you are famous now. I heard that a French poet who heard your

Fifth Symphony was so swept away that when he went to put on his hat he couldn't find his head. Unfortunately, your fame comes at a time when Vienna cannot afford you." The Count proposed that Louis give him music lessons as a source of income. Putting aside his dread of set duties, Louis accepted the offer.

Louis brought with him a gift for his new friend: a trio for piano, violin and cello, dedicated to the Archduke, who was immediately delighted; he took the score to the piano and played the piano part at sight and went into raptures: "It is lordly music," he said. "I must have a copy of every piece you write hereafter. I will amass a library of your productions."

The praise was gratifying, but the income was token. The remark at Breitkopf's still stung. And the publisher was making errors—errors that he himself, the composer, had to correct, with the ensuing headaches and eyestrains. Another visit to Dr. Malfatti was in order. These visits, more and more frequent, concerned not only the eye-strain, but as well a matter of the heart. The doctor had two beautiful nieces, one of whom, Theresa, Louis met when he attended an affair at the home of a mutual friend, Gleichenstein. Theresa's sister, Nanette, was there, who was fascinated by Gleichenstein, a tall well-groomed aristocrat. Theresa, although much younger—only fifteen—had come along with her sister with an eye to discover who might adore her, too. Louis was instantly smitten: her locks of black hair, her slender figure, her charming way with men—pure untutored nature in the young girl. But that Theresa was a novice flirt whose smiles cut a wide swath across the room meant nothing to Louis, who believed that a single glance in his direction was a pledge of eternal love.

How to approach her? Her family summered outside the city—where was she? A consultation with Malfatti was in order. The doctor was tight-lipped: "She is away from the city," was all he said, as he peered into the ailing composer's eyes and ears.

The following morning he took his first bath in a month, scrubbing and scraping with a stiff bush. Schindler winced as he saw the darkened effluvia run down the master's body onto the floor and through cracks into the flat below. Lacking a towel, he required Schindler to fan him with an umbrella. He looked at himself in the mirror he borrowed from his friend Zmeskall and hurled it against the wall; he had forgotten the scars and pock marks, the scarred member and wrinkled bag under the large belly. But today he would see Lind the Taylor who would cover the belly with a handsome new suit, and Gleichenstein had sent him some handsome Bengal cotton shirts. One of the new cravats would match the shirts well, just as he thought.

He had another task for Schindler, to be done immediately. He carefully penned a letter to the registry at the Bonn Court requesting proof of his date of birth, and he was not to be confused with the older Ludwig who died. When Schindler was out the door on his way to post the letter, he picked up his quill again and set his mind to another letter, this one more pleasing:

My dear and charming Theresa, I have asked your uncle to send this letter to you, for I do not know your summer plans and your whereabouts. I hope this finds you in good health and spirits. I lead a quiet and lonely life. From time to time, however, things awaken me and my natural longings. Thoughts of marriage are not far...

He put down the quill. A question nagged at him. Would Malfatti break the seal and read the letter? If so, would he send it to her? Malfatti! The doctor had kept the girl's whereabouts a secret from him—he must have a reason. What? His age? No, only peasants worried about age difference; that was no concern to the upper classes. No, something else...

Malfatti had become his physician when Schmidt died, and he did a physical examination last year. He frowned at the scarred penis and shrunken testicle and put his question in writing: "Have you consorted with women of the street?"

"I have no dealings with women of the street." He shook his head vehemently.

Malfatti stared at him: "How long have you had the scar?"

"From childhood. My mother said I had the red-spot disease." Louis bellowed his protest: "I cannot have syphilis. Only the lowest type man..."

"I suppose that is possible," the doctor said, "but that disease usually affects only the face. The penis?" He frowned again: "A terrible stroke of fate, if true. Are you sure...?"

Each word was seared into his memory. The pen fell from his hand, his head slumped to his desk. His case for Theresa was hopeless.

There was one to whom he could write and she would understand:

Dear Mother,
You know my sorrows more than any other. I have needs like all men, yet I am denied. I must learn to be resigned: "Accept and

Submit," is the wisdom of the eastern wise men. But neither my body nor my spirit will be resigned. Your Louis will search the world for a lover, a faithful one who will be his spouse. Even Popageno found his Popagena, as you recall from that opera.

My physician gave me grief. He saw that part of me that you have seen, and he refuses to believe it is a childhood affliction. He suspects I got it from a whore. You know the truth, and you alone. Yet I feel the shame of my whoring—never will I go to her again—my solemn oath.

Your Louis

In late summer his spirits rose when Karl and Christiane returned to the city, and Braun at the theater suggested a revival of *Leonore*. Braun had terms: would Louis consider a few changes?—just a few notes here and there—and he added that the Prince supported the new production and had invited Louis and the artists to his palace for an evening to make plans. The prospect lifted Louis from his doldrums, and the promise of Karl's support for the project decided it; he could tolerate a few changes if it meant getting the work back on stage.

Braun fired his first volley by telling Louis that the libretto was slow paced and dull in spots—nothing wrong with the music, of course. Cuts could be made—just a few—and these would require that Louis drop or rewrite only those few passages.

Karl's mother, the Princess, though ill, came down from her bed to play at the pianoforte. In fact, she came down because Karl told her they would need her calm presence because Louis, when he understood the extent of the cuts, would bellow and bang his fists in defense of every bar. A great lady of winning amiability and gentleness, but pale and wan in the wake of great suffering—both breasts had been removed—she took her place at the pianoforte and looked for Louis to place the score before her. Louis sat reclining in an armchair, the fat score of his opera spread out on his knees. Court Secretary Heinrich von Collin was chatting with the men and women singers who had come to sing their parts. Anna Milder was Leonora, as before; Mlle. Muller was Marcellina; Weinmuller, Rocco; and Steinkopf the Minister of Justice. Deemer, the Florestan, had lost his voice—to the strain of being Florestan, Braun hinted—and was replaced by a young singer from Salzberg, August Rockel, who was inexperienced but eager for a chance to please the famed composer. His voice was thin, but Braun knew that all voices were thin. All awaited Louis to place the score on the stand before the Prince Mother. But Louis' hands were upon the score before him, his eyes closed as if in prayer.

Finally Karl took the score from Louis and placed it on the music desk. Braun clapped his hands: "We are ready to begin," he announced. All eyes were on the clock, because it was already late, and they had yet to begin. The diplomatic Prince Karl made a gentle beginning: he wrote, "When Pizarro determines to murder Florestan, the atmosphere of the opera becomes tense. We must not let the audience forget that a murder is in the works."

"Yes," added Braun. "And we must bring the audience quickly to realize that murder is our theme. That pretty little aria from the first scene must go."

"Exactly," Karl agreed. "Things must move quickly. That is why the three acts must be fused into two."

Louis was on his feet. "Never." He seized the score and pushed Karl and Christiane aside as he made for the door. Christiane grabbed him by the coat sleeve and held him back. "Louis," she said, "be patient with us. We want to save your work, make it immortal." He heard little, but read her eyes. Resigned, he returned to his seat and let Karl take the score to his mother.

"We shorten the First Act," Braun continued, "and we shorten the chorus of prisoners so when Pizarro orders them back to their cells that brings us close to the end of the Act." The Princess Mother played the piano score for the first two acts, as the artists sang and agreed where the cuts could be made.

Christiane carried written reports to Louis as the discussion progressed. "Only suggestions, dear Louis," she said. Louis fumed and raged, but a look from the Princess Mother kept him in his seat.

"In the last act," Braun said, "the trumpet fanfare is unclear to Florestan and Leonore; they waste time meditating about their fate. We can make the scene more alive by having a voice from above announce that the Minister of Justice has arrived, and the lovers can rush immediately into each other's arms."

Karl added: "Yes, and we can emphasize the lover's salvation by having the last scene taken out of the dungeon and played out in the courtyard above."

When these ideas were put to Louis he spoke at last: "You have murdered my masterwork." His eyes, fixed on Braun, whom he believed to be the chief conspirator, spoke more than his words.

"If the opera is shorted," said Rockel, "the audience will be swept up in a great emotion. And, unlike Deemer, I will not have to sing to an empty house."

Christiane thought to pass over the tenor's words; but Louis had seen his lips move, and demanded to know what his Florestan had said. She put the words on paper and held it up to his face.

On his feet again, Louis charged the music stand to grab the score. But the Princess Mother dropped to her knees before him. "Beethoven," she said, looking up at his face, tears streaming from her eyes. "No. Your greatest work must not suffer. God, who has planted tones of purest beauty in your soul, forbids it. Maria Magdalena's spirit joins with mine to beg you, to warn you. Make the cuts."

Stunned, Louis turned to Rockel. "Sing it again," he demanded. The weary tenor picked up his music again and the Princess Mother returned to her piano. "How dark in here..." the tenor sang; "In the springtime of my life I was cut down..."

For the first time, Louis reached for his ear-trumpet. Christiane and Karl knew what this meant: the aria was life itself to Louis, for he too was cut down in the springtime of his life by a malady in conspicuous evidence as he put the trumpet to his ear. When Rockel finished the demanding aria, Louis called out: "Again, sing it again." The tenor looked to Karl, then the Princess Mother. They nodded.

As the tenor sang, the ale coursed through Louis' blood and gave rise to a new thought: Leonora, not Rocco, should have brought the jug of wine down to the dungeon, for an angel should bring food and drink. The gods drink in heaven, do they not?—the god Bacchus, not the god of the priests. That priest in Modling—fool that he was—despised the young men and women who drank and danced and sang their lusty songs and rushed into the bushes to play. The poets knew better: Schiller would have faulted Leonora that she brought no wine; but the same Schiller would have seen that the wine passed through her hands to warm her husband's cold breast.

Yes, the poets! If Schiller were here he would approve the changes: Florestan must greet his angel in a raptus-vision before he slumps to the ground; Leonora must put down her shovel and hold a gun to Pizarro's head as Florestan looks into the face of his angel; the trumpet will sound and Pizarro's defeat will be known not to him alone but to all. In the last scene the Minister of Justice will call them before him to the courtyard above, for he is the loving father who dwells beyond the starry vault.

The night wore on; limbs stiffened and voices cracked. It was well past midnight when they completed the entire opera, with several repetitions of the aria from the dark cell.

Louis trembled with something hidden in the dark cell of his mind. Braun and Karl knew better than to speak; they left that task to the great lady who sat at the pianoforte. The Princess Mother finally turned to Louis with pleading eyes: "And the cuts?" she asked.

"Do not insist on them."

As the great woman who had invoked the spirit of his mother looked upon him he felt an enchanted presence in the room. His mother's face passed before him radiant in white, like the saints of the Bible—pure and unsullied in their robes of glistening white. Angel wings stirred. Yes, Florestan, before he falls to the ground, must see an angel and he will sing "My angel, Leonora," in the sudden radiance of F Major. Yes, the opera must move swiftly toward that moment; and when the trumpet is heard from the tower, those below must know at once that Florestan's angel has saved him. Leonora will rush into her husband's arms: "O Nameless Joy," they will sing. Louis looked at the face that beamed compassion for him. "Yes," he said, "you are right."

Karl clapped his hands. Servants flung open the folding doors to the dining room where a bounteous repast awaited them.

Louis sat at the table opposite Rockel, saying and eating little, while the tenor devoured his meal with hasty hands. "Ah," said Louis, "when you sang so beautifully, you were starved, just like Florestan. You may have only a scrap of bread before each performance."

His joke aside, he said little during the meal. His eyes clouded over with dark thoughts: his angel Leonora pretended to Marcellina that she was a man and that she returned her affections. She lied! And not only did she deceive the girl, she also—by the same act—betrayed her husband. The most faithful of women? Then she took a shovel to dig a pit in which to bury him. An angel of rescue?

He noted that Christiane, seated next to Rockel, took great interest in the tenor: her eyes aflutter and her wrist bent, she tapped him on the shoulder and pulled his head toward her mouth to receive her whisperings. The stage Florestan would be tonight's victim. Karl seemed not to notice.

Florestan as victim! Pizarro turned his springtime into a winter's death. Then his beloved angel came to his cell with shovel and pick to bury him.

At the far end of the table Karl and von Fries were talking politics—Christiane's excuse for joining Rockel. Karl was saying that the French were distracted by the English and had begun pulling out of Austria.

Perhaps the city would rest quietly under a new peace. If so, the time was right to put a new *Leonore* before the public. The men glanced constantly at Louis: something was going on with him—they knew him well.

Louis shook his head to rid him of his thoughts. Christiane looked his way, then fetched him another ale. A touch of compassion. But she turned back to Rockel. Women are fickle, as the cynics knew well: first this way, then that way. His own mother, Maria Magdalena, was two-sided. Married to Johann, she nevertheless submitted to Cressener and spoiled the marriage bed. Her very name...he remembered the whore's voice: "But isn't she named for a whore after all?" A priest at the court chapel answered his question—with raised eyebrow and quizzical eye—about the biblical woman: "She was a sinful woman," he said, "until she met Christ. On the first Easter she came to his tomb where he was buried, and Christ greeted her with news that he lived beyond the grave."

Christiane was named after the Christ; yet here she was across from him at the table seducing Rockel; and the tenor would be humiliated like all the others. He stood and marched to the serving table for another ale; he would not accept anything again from the woman's tainted hands. The room was very like the world: overcrowded with lust and betrayal and unhappy love.

She suddenly giggled and brushed silent lips against Rockel's coat shoulder and cheeks. With effort and breathing hard, the tenor stood and extended his hand to her; soon the two were turning to leave. Louis gazed hollow-eyed at the couple as they made their way on unsteady feet to the door. In sullen fury he hurled his goblet over their heads, splattering them with ale: "Bitch. Cheat," he roared. Karl came to his side: "Let them go," he said. "What they do is no harm to me or to you."

In bed that evening, his head spinning from draughts of ale, he held in his hand the score of Florestan's aria, wrinkled and scented and bespotted with ale. He meditated upon the aria, but no angel came. Instead he heard faint taps of a drum: four notes and a fifth as a violin soared high above. Never before had he attempted to compete with Herr Mozart's violin concertos; but this theme, pure and noble upon its pedestal, captured the innocence of Schiller's world; it knew no stir of frailty or deceit. The common and sturdy on-the-beat taps would support the theme throughout the course of a long, lyrical movement.

The pages of Florestan's aria, without the angel, fell from his hand onto the floor.

Chapter Eighteen

"A Heart-Shaped Image."

Schindler threw open the door and burst into the flat, ignoring his Master's wish for a hard rap or two. There was a time he did knock but the Master, being deaf as a stone, never answered. Why should he pound his fists until they bled? He begged for a key, and finally got it. Yet, the Master always seemed startled and annoyed when he opened the door. He was here at the usual time, was he not? The Master could be difficult.

Schindler thrust a note at his Master. Louis stared at it. It was soiled— it had served as a napkin at some tavern, he guessed. He could hardly read what his secretary wrote, the note shook so in the man's hand. Something was on the fool's mind, some nonsense as usual. "Hold still, you fool," he bellowed.

Louis seized the note and held it to the light. A few bars of music—the opening of his Fifth Symphony—and the words, "A yellowhammer on wood, is it not?"

A knowing smile curled on Louis' face. Usually at this kind of stupidity he would call his man-servant an idiot, a dolt, and return to his work. Not this time.

"Yes, yes, you are right. A yellowhammer, to be sure. A yellowhammer at the fence post—that post outside there, see? Keep watching, the bird may return."

Schindler beamed with self-satisfaction. He took off his snow-speckled outercoat, draped it over a wooden bench atop his Master's hats, lit his pipe, and positioned himself in a chair near the Master's desk. An object had caught his eye the other day when the Master had a conversation book open and was scribbling in it—a drawing…where was it now? Could the Master have hidden it? He would have been wise to, if it was what he thought it was. But something was under a brass paperweight—yes, it was a book, among a clutter of unpaid bills, eyeglasses, and an ear trumpet… could that be it? When the Master began work again at the piano, he would thumb through it quickly. He would easily recognize the drawing.

Louis interrupted his thoughts by banging out the four note motif that his factotum had mistaken for a bird-call. "You have told the world, I suppose?"

"About the yellowhammer? No, Master. I would not presume—not without your permission."

In fact, Schindler had just come from a tavern where he had announced to his friends that he knew the inner workings of the Master's mind, the secret meanings of his music. The notion that the opening of the Fifth was a bird call came from his hearing the F Major Symphony, where the idler by the brook hears trilling flutes, oboes, and clarinets that speak to him as a nightingale, quail, and cuckoo. The Master had been quick to denounce that opinion: "Not birds themselves, but a dream about the birds, —you dolt." But the four note motif was surely inspired by a bird, he thought. He made his point by banging his tankard against the tabletop: knock, knock, knock, KNOCK; knock, knock, knock, KNOCK. His friends agreed with him.

Louis returned to his music-making. A catchy new tune came spinning out of his piano; it caught Schindler's ear and he listened with mounting interest—although his eye never roamed far from the desktop and the brass weight that rested atop the book. When the Master became deeply absorbed in his composing, that would be the time for him to sweep his hand across the desk and uncover the object of his obsession.

"You like this tune?" Louis shouted.

"Yes, yes. It is magnificent. For a new symphony?"

Louis turned and faced him. "The greatest ever. You must tell the world."

Schindler raised his brow and took note. It seemed to him the tune was from the taverns or beer halls or the trenches, even from the French anthem that Napoleon's foot soldiers sang as they marched through the streets. But he knew his Master was capable of taking some folk tune or military air and making something of it, as he did in the *Eroica*.

When his Master turned back to his music, he adjusted his monocle and slipped his chair closer to the desk. One quick move and he would see it. If the Master happened to turn and catch him, he would explain that he had merely reached for a quill so as to write down the Master's immortal words. When the Master began what sounded like a lengthy fugal passage, his hand flew to the desk and lifted the weight; he fastened his eyes on the image that haunted him and fired his imagination.

Louis stopped suddenly and handed him two pages of sheet music: "Here, take this. Show it to your friends at the taverns. These are themes for my greatest symphony."

Schindler took the pages and grabbed his coat. He had seen the image; someday he would tear the page from the book and take it, when he had a chance. For now, he knew what to do.

When the man was gone, Louis roared his pleasure. He had given the fool a few bars of the new music, a pot-boiler of French and Russian military tunes that he might someday be able to sell and reap a great profit, if only the Russians defeat the French. It was wretched music, written for the gallery, but Schindler would not know that—he was gallery. If the fool thought the *Fifth Symphony* was inspired by a bird's beak, he would believe anything. Let him peddle his nonsense at the taverns and let all the world know that he was a fool.

The theme of the *Fifth* sounded again in his head. The premier had been a disappointment: he could see that the musicians were not in ensemble. The better musicians scorned him, and would not play for him. His music was abused by the second-raters. But there must be some who felt the music as he himself did. The summons of fate! —stand fast, do not give in! It was created for those whose ears discern essences: for them, this music will banish their terrors and give them a new world in which to dwell. Hoffman the poet was one such: he said that when he went to put on his hat, he couldn't find his head. Yes, let the Schindlers of the world peddle their nonsense in the beer halls, so long as others drink of his new wine.

Schindler pushed open the swinging doors of The Red Hedgehog and found a seat near his friends. Soon he was lifting his beer and singing bawdy songs along side the rustics and soldiers who gathered there to gamble, drink, sware, and lift skirts. He himself had no way with women; for that reason he led a solitary life. He enjoyed watching others—like these Austrian and Bavarian soldiers as they quaffed their beer, put down their muskets, bounced serving girls on their knees, and made off to an upper room with their conquests.

He took a blank server's bill and sketched from memory the image he had seen on the Master's desk and words that were written beside it. A man next to him took an interest in his drawing. Schindler held it up to him. "What do you think this is?" he asked his friend. The man stared at the heart-shaped image that was split by a crease down its center. "It is a woman's ass. A beauty. Whose is it?"

"This broad-assed bitch is Herr von Beethoven's taste in women," he said. "He likes to throw them down on his sack of straw and take them that way."

Chapter Nineteen

"An Immodest Stare."

A wedding cortege pulled up before St. Stephen's church heralded by bells and cannonade. Inside the church, sacristans had prepared the altar; and when the groom, a military man with sword in scabbard, marched into the sanctuary, an acolyte snapped his fingers and priests began their entry. A red – cassocked acolyte swinging a thurible sent clouds of incense into the air, as he led three priests robed in gold-lined white albs and chasubles, who on their way down the center aisle blessed the assemblage with holy water while an overhead choir sang the introit of the Nuptial Mass. Louis sat near the back of the church under the choir loft; but it was not the music that had brought him to the church; rather, he needed to please the groom's father, who was one of his patrons. As for the music, he knew from experience that they were singing an old chant of staid beauty; but he could best it with something more dramatic. He had already composed a Mass in C that was scorned by the church; but he could do better, one that would be outlawed by the church—but appreciated by lovers of the art.

His eye roamed about the church, taking in the altar trappings, the icons, the stained glass: much like the court chapel in Bonn, but more ornate. In Bonn, he had bent the knee and groveled along with the congregants, to satisfy Neffe and hold on to his position. But no longer would he honor a deity that had denied him the sound of his own music, denied him a manly organ like unto those that hung from the tall men who stripped on the beach, denied him the love of a pure woman.

The wandering eye caught and held a fierce stare from a young woman ahead of him and across the aisle whose eyes refused to drop in proper modesty. Her head was uncovered and like Louis she stood when the others dropped their knees to the marble floor, and sat when the others stood. This woman was not of the priestly tribe, he noted, for her devotion was directed not to the altar but to him. The fire in her eye, so familiar even without the yellow frock and the bare shoulders and the ribbons on her shoes, spoke to him of their first meeting, fleeting as it was.

The priest droned on about a seal, a mantle, and a crown. The seal, he said, is the sacrament that binds these two and makes of them one. The mantle is a garment of comfort and warmth, for times of joy and times of sorrow; and the crown on their forehead signifies that they enter

God's kingdom as man and wife. Bettina swung her head around again and caught his eye.

From the pulpit the priest, creaky with age and the gout, warned the couple at the altar that they should be chaste save for their nuptial bed; and he warned the unmarried that they must govern the roving eye like a rider governs his horse, and they should resort to prayer at all times. Louis guessed by the priest's dour countenance and the shaking of his head that the congregation was being chastised. Priests! What did they know of passion? Of beauty? That priest in Modling, who scorned the peasant girls who sang and drank and dashed off into the bushes with lusty young men... had he or any of his kind ever seen a breast like a peach or an ass like a heart? No—if one wanted the truth about nature's gods, one should go not to the priests but to the poets.

The couple knelt and received the priest's communion and blessing for the first time as man and wife. The organ sounded from the loft above and priests formed a recessional and filed out of the church. At last the Service was over and done. Louis moved slowly toward the rear of the church, slowly enough so that Bettina would not fail to catch him. "Do you remember me?" she wrote on a pad. "You wrote a song for me last spring."

"Yes, yes...the song I wrote the moment you walked in the door."

Bettina flushed. "Please, while I am separated from the others, let us talk. There's an empty chapel behind the altar. We can be alone."

They were surprised to find Antonie there, alone, kneeling at a prie-dieu by the font. Bettina thought she had left with Franz and his friends, but here she was, her veiled head bent before a hanging crucifix.

She had slipped away from Franz on the pretext of offering a prayer for her father—something even Franz could not deny, not in the presence of his friends. The chapel was dark. It was as she remembered it, but a prie-dieu was set before the font and a crucifix hung from the wall before it. She tried to pray but her thoughts raced: if she had the strength to leave Franz, to whom would she turn? Her father's house was there; she could live in it. But what about money? The children? Her reputation?

It was a jolt when Bettina marched in with the short ugly man in tow. But her manners did not fail: she rose to her feet and extended her hand. "Herr von Beethoven," she said, "I remember how busy you were the day we met. I trust your endeavors were fruitful."

Bettina wrote her sisters words on a pad. "Ah, yes, most fruitful," he answered, as he took the hand and gave it the courtesy of a kiss. As he held her hand, in that moment, he felt a tremor; she was unsteady, he sensed, not because he kissed her hand but because she nurtured some secret, a secret that she shared only with the god that hung on the wall.

With a flashing smile, Bettina moved close to him and took him by the brass buttons of his frock coat, the flaps of which were open wide: "Come, we shall go to a coffee house. You cannot be so busy this time."

The brash move startled Antonie, even though she knew well her sister-in-law's designs upon great men. A reproach on her lips, she tried to catch her eye, but the younger woman had moved swiftly to guide Louis around the altar and into the nave toward the oak paneled doors that led into a vestibule, and they were out of sight. Bettina's breathless passions ought not to be a concern of hers, but the girl was engaged to be married. There was no excuse for attaching herself to this musician, appealing though he may be. She stared at the font for a heavy moment, then dropped to her knees.

In the late afternoon Bettina returned to the Brentano residence on the Landstrasse and met Antonie in the parlor when Johann was not present. "Really, the man is impossible," she said, her hands thrown up in despair. "We talked and talked—with the note pad, you know—then went back to his stinking flat. Not a glance at the sack; he just played the piano." But her face brightened: "Look at this." She held up a page of sheet music. "He romanced me with his music." She waltzed to the piano and sang the song *Do not dry the tears of eternal love*. "Poem by Goethe, music by Beethoven," she exclaimed. "Sung by Bettina." Her face darkened again: "He sang it to me, but I did not hear the panting of his heart."

"Does the man have a heart? From what you have told me…"

Bettina spun around. "Do you know what he told me? Last year he gave a benefit concert for the military. And he says he will do it again for the Hospital for the Poor. There—he is misunderstood by the world."

"All those other rumors…"

"If he throws plates at serving girls, it is because he suffers. We must invite him to our next dinner party."

Antonie's hand went to her lips. "Franz cannot abide the man."

With a wink and a snap of her fingers, Bettina brushed the concern aside: "Leave that to me," she said.

Louis noted the many fine carriages that stood beside the house, which confirmed earlier impressions that the Brentano's were persons of substance and taste. A grand piano was in the salon and in an adjoining parlor, a cello, two violins and a viola—for quartets! The illumination from many candles and oil lamps held promise of a rapt and festal evening of music. Members of the nobility were present; he must impress.

No doubt he would be asked to play. What shall it be? Of course: the *Eroica Variations*—the theme of the hero. What better way could he introduce himself to the Brentano's? But as he was escorted by the household staff into the large salon, he saw the despised Steibelt at the piano—playing he knew not what, but poorly, he adjudged, for he had bested Steibelt in a contest at Fries' home ten years ago. What was he to do: sit politely and pretend to listen? Everyone knew he was deaf.

Bettina greeted him and sat beside him as Steibelt played a Haydn sonata. He chafed at the thought of Steibelt at the piano. He knew how to steal the show from the second-rate pianist. "The Moonlight!" he cried out, "I shall play The Moonlight!" Instantly applause broke out, as the gathered guests recognized the composer of the *Moonlight Sonata* in their midst. It had been, and still was, the rave of the city. Steibelt was urged to abandon his Haydn and take a place in the audience as Louis marched to the piano and raised his arched hands above the keyboard.

He began softly and held a steady adagio pace during the long first movement. As he played, he allowed himself an amused smile: the sobriquet "Moonlight" was not his and it irked him; but whatever fools had associated the sonata with moonlight—as if music could reflect the moon—and applied the sobriquet "Moonlight" to it, had done him a fine service this evening.

The sight of a deaf musician playing the romantic fantasy brought many in the audience to tears. Bettina, comprehending the emotion of the moment, ordered the servants to extinguish the oil lamps. Soon the room was lit by candlelight alone.

Antonie was in the children's room upstairs. With half an ear to the piano below and the Haydn sonata, she had been trying to coax little Phillipe to sleep. When the music stopped and began again, she felt the mysterious motion of a music that bestowed calm. Soon, her little son rested his head on her breast; in a moment she carried him to his bed and tucked him away. Franz was expecting her, so she dressed quickly and went to the stairs. The hallway was dark; why were the lights so dim? Lighting two candles she glided down the stairs and into the candlelit parlor. To her surprise, it was not Steibelt at the piano—it was Beethoven.

At such entertainments the guests were wont, if it pleased them, to turn their backs to the musicians and to carry on with their gossiping and joking and jostling about. But when Louis sat at the keyboard and began his Adagio, they all sought couches or stood rigid, eyes and ears rapt and attentive, afraid to cough or sneeze or clatter a teacup in its saucer. When

Louis lifted his hands and opened his eyes as the last tones melted away, the silence lingered like the charged air after a passing storm.

It was Franz who stood finally and led the applause. Antonie looked on with astonishment: what a change of heart, that he should praise the one he had despised. Now Franz extended his hand to Louis and motioned to others to do the same. A smile of triumph danced on Bettina's face. Antonie marveled: by what magic had she cajoled her brother to become this admirer of the upstart Beethoven? The answer was not far to see: among the nobility present were the composer's friends: the Lichnowskys, the Lobkowitzes, the Archduke Rudolph, who were known to sing Louis' praises the length and breadth of the city.

Hardly could she allow Franz to stand by himself; she saw her duty to him and to her guests; she rose and took her place beside her husband, who was writing in a notepad, nodding and smiling, conversing with the composer. A servant called Franz away for a moment; he handed her the notepad and left her alone with the composer. She must do her duty as hostess.

"People say this beautiful piece was inspired by moonlight."

"No, No—it has nothing to do with the moon."

"Oh, I hear the moon. It is the theme that rises from the earth..."

He shook his head: "No—no moon."

She was trying to make polite conversation but the man, true to his reputation, was being difficult. "I do not mean to offend, Herr Beethoven. I merely want to say that your music soothed me and my small son—he was restless, but just minutes ago he fell asleep to your music."

"Not a lullaby."

"Why, I meant that your music touches the heart."

He looked up from the pad and studied her face. When he first saw her, outside the Pasqualati house, he briefly noted the symmetrical beauty of her facial lines: the high curved forehead balanced by prominent cheekbones, the slender oval jawline and strong chin; and her eyes—large, warm, and luminous under slender arched brows; the small white teeth set in a small full lipped mouth. Now she was transfigured in the light of several candelabra that set her figure in relief before the darkened outer hall from which she had stepped: the natural pallor of her face was accentuated by the black full length dress and black ribbon at the base of her neck that pulled her hair tight behind her—hair that was full and alive with color and light. But when he tried to capture her eyes in his gaze, they darted away.

He could not catch her eye, but he could catch her ear. "The Sonata is not all slumber. It takes a restless turn. Cover your child's ears, and the ears of your guests."

In a moment he was seated again at the piano and the Presto Finale burst from his instrument like a tempest.

Stunned, Antonie fell back upon her heels at the force of it, and retreated to the darkened hall. Some of the women stopped their ears with hands and kerchiefs, while men gasped at the fury that had been unleashed. One woman fled the parlor. If the opening movement was moonlight, this music unloosed the night's secrets and scattered them into the air.

When the guests had departed, Franz came to her importunate, his erection a lump in his trousers, which he stepped out of and tossed aside. She knew the look in his eye; for weeks she had denied him for one reason or another; and he was pent up with rage and frustration; there was no putting him off. He undressed her hastily, pinned her to the bed with his arms, and pressed his urgency upon her. Her eyes closed, she dreamed of better days—her childhood, her long dead mother, Phillipe and the warmth and promise of his kiss. Phillipe! All she had of Phillipe was his name, that her small son now bore. She remembered the heavenly choir at St. Stephen's that chanted of a lovely marriage, a perfect couple joined in conjugal bliss...on what earth and under what sun did man and wife enjoy that? Phillipe and his bride? She flinched at the thought of blessed Phillipe between the legs of a nameless woman. Bettina knew something of bliss, though hers was frowned upon by the priests. But she, Antonie, she knew only the warmth of her own hand.

The next day she awoke to head-splitting pain and ebbing spirits, which so often afflicted her after Franz had his way. Franz patted her head and went to his branch office. She instructed her maids to care for the children and she tried to sleep through most of the morning; but rest did not come to her. A noise—perhaps her maid bringing her tea...no, some voice—she prayed not visitors, not today. Then silence. Whatever it was, let the maid take care of it. In a half sleep, the images of last night drifted through her head: Phillipe, the chapel, the marriage, the choir, and now, the "Moonlight" sonata, its opening Adagio, slow and peaceful, like a giant at rest.

Louis struggled at the piano. Usually in the early morning he found inspiration, or was moved to hike through the woods; but he had not slept well, and the loss of sleep weighed heavily upon him. He looked out the window and saw ominous clouds gathering in the south. A new work eluded him, but he played snatches of the F Major Pastoral Symphony that had

127

so pleased the citizens that they were humming the Shepherd's Thankful Song on street corners, so Schindler said. The Shepherd's Song? —in what world does a shepherd climb his hilltop after a deluge and call to life all the woodland creatures and dispel their terrors? But the Symphony needed a fine ending like that; it could not end with a thunderclap, even though life does often so end. Yes, this is why he composed music, to prove that just endings come from strange and distant beginnings. There!... the third theme in the *Allegro ma non troppo*... it suddenly took on a new guise: in oboes and clarinets it spoke to pain and promised blessed relief. He took up his sketchbook and worked the theme over and over. In mid-morning, exhausted, he fell asleep on his sack of straw. After an hour Schindler woke him with a shaking of the shoulders. Refreshed, he sang to himself as his factotum poured water over his back. Schindler rubbed him with a coarse towel, then cooked him two eggs.

A driving rain kept him indoors, where he brooded again over the revision of *Leonore*, which Braun now called *Fidelio*. The trumpet that sounds from the parapet...it is unclear to the lovers what the trumpet means. They hear angry shouts from the courtyard above. Leonora has lost her gun. They embrace each other, thinking that this moment may be their last. But if a voice from above announces their salvation they will sing in rapture that they are united. What decision will he make? His own life is an uncertain trumpet; he does not know if he will meet his conjugal mate. Theresa is impossible. What woman could bear the sight of him?

He knew that Bettina took an interest in him. She was lively and pretty, with a bulging bosom and a tight ass; but she was a flirt, the type who flutter about from man to man without love for any. If it was ass he wanted, he could get that from the woman at the ramparts. And he had not gone back! Besides, how would Bettina act if she saw his secret infirmity? Yet, he loved the attention from the little flirt. Strange, so little resemblance between Bettina and her sister... or was it sister-in-law? He wasn't sure. The one was busty and forward; the other slender and secretive, veiled.

The day after the evening party he had made an unannounced visit to the Bierkenstock residence hoping to come upon Bettina. Yes, she was a flirt, but her ways flattered him. She was not at home. He was about to leave, but stopped to make a polite inquiry concerning Madame Brentano. The maid Sigrid told him that her mistress was upstairs, ill, and unable to entertain him. Wanting to atone for his course manners, he sat himself at the piano: "Then I shall entertain her," he said. The theme rose from the parlor and filled the mansion: it was the *Adagio sostenuto* from the C Sharp minor Sonata—the one they called the "Moonlight."

By noon he had brooded enough. He needed to tramp the streets, an effort that often brought up answers that were lost in some deep cavern of his mind. Schindler reached for the master's coat and umbrella, but too late: the Master was down the stairs and onto the street, oblivious to the battering of the elements. He imagined himself before the Theater Orchestra; his arms flailed against the drab sky, snatches of uncomposed melodies roared from his lungs and disappeared into the mist. Deep in his mind something about the moon, a starry night, and the words of a poet, clamored to be heard. The woman last night said that the moon rose up from the earth. The earth?—a poet's image. Yes, his mind was an earth from which sprang the themes of his Pastoral Symphony and other miracles: often had he heard the earth's voice in streams, amidst trees swaying in the wind, and in thunderclaps; and felt it under the feet of stomping peasants and in the urges of his own loins.

One cold night long ago he lay under a moon, his arms stretched out toward the dark river. The moon was full, but almost hidden behind banks of passing clouds. Babette, too, was hidden from him; but he could gaze at her through the window and watch as she held a tray high over the heads of rowdy patrons at the Zehrgarten. That night the poet's words came to him about a loving father who dwelt above the starry vault but who, if he existed at all, had hidden his face and left him to the solitary devices of his heart.

The rain lashed at him from all sides and drove him to seek refuge in a tavern—The Black Camel. He stood shivering, shedding water like a spout at the Belvedere. The maitre glared at him, but permitted him to sit at a table and order ale. Serving girls were scurrying about everywhere, but he didn't see the one he splattered with hot stew. And none of the girls resembled Babette of Bonn. When he had finished several steins of ale, he was on the street again, where he hailed a carriage. "90 Erdbeergasse, Landstrasse—at once."

Sigrid brightened to the sight of him. "Is she well today?" he asked.

She shook her head. "No, Sir. She is still resting upstairs. But I believe you know where the piano is." She accompanied him to the parlor and pointed to the instrument. He understood. Again, the grave and mysterious *Adagio sostenuto* filled the parlor and all the chambers and vestibules of the mansion.

The following morning a uniformed delivery man brought him a sealed envelope: "It is from Madame Brentano."

Startled, he brushed aside the eggs and coffee that Schindler had left for him and looked for his spectacles. "My dear Beethoven," the note read, "twice now you have come to my home as I lay upon my sickbed and given me the comfort of your music. If your sonata is not the moon, surely it is the sun, or some heavenly body that rules the night sky."

The idea that escaped him, the idea that drove him from the flat and into the street, into the wind and rain, into the tavern, into his memory…he had it within his grasp: "…some heavenly body that rules the night sky," she said; and she said "the theme rises from the earth." Sky and earth. A new theme, that would rise up from the earth and rule the night sky. It clamored to be. He drummed on the piano and groaned until the sun dropped behind the hills to the west and passersby in the street fled, their hands over their ears.

Chapter Twenty

"Listen for Your Angel."

Often at night citizens were awakened by pounding feet and the clop-clop of horse shoes on granite streets. They understood what these sounds meant: Napoleon's soldiers had burst loose from their barracks and were raiding shops and taverns for boots and beer. Discipline had broken down among the men during Napoleon's return to Paris, and the diplomat Murat, temporarily in charge of the army, had no hold on the men, who heard that soon they would be sent to the cold battlefields of Russia to the north and they were equipping themselves at the expense of merchants, filling their bellies at the expense of inn keepers, and there were desperate liaisons between the soldiers and their new found wenches in the taverns and brothels.

The Viennese heard that Napoleon had demanded that the Emperor Franz release a captured French General, Durosnel; otherwise he would set his drum corps loose upon the women of the city. Durosnel was freed, but the threat gripped the hearts of the populace, who feared for their women. In April, the Austrian Emperor Francis offered his daughter Maria Louisa to Napoleon as a peace offering. Rumor had it that when his bride crossed the border into France to meet him for the first time, he pulled her from the carriage, took her to a nearby wood, stripped, and ravished her within sight of her three hundred attendants. The rumor was unfounded, but believed by the Austrians. Fathers locked their daughters behind double-bolted doors.

Louis heard none of these nocturnal noises but he heard the rumors; and daily he saw Prince Murat, a figure of utmost gravity on his mettled steed, pass under his window on the way to the palaces, and he felt the humiliation and fatigue of the vanquished city. It was not only that his income was devalued—the annuity of 4000 florins was worth only 1000 in common coin—it was also that an armed and suspicious truce weighed heavy upon the spirit. During the assault on the city, he had composed an E Flat Major Piano Concerto, whose proud gait and majestic swelling tones rose above all thought of humiliation. And now he was mounting a stage production, *Egmont*, one of Goethe's inspirations, which spoke of freedom from the rule of tyrants. But work was tedious. The booted tread of French soldiers roaming and looting at will took its toll. Hardly at all did he seek solace at the piano; more and more he brooded over the sorry state of his personal affairs.

It was a bright afternoon in late summer. Napoleon had left Paris and was on his way to attack the Russians at Elba; two of his Viennese regiments were moving out to join him. Louis stood by his window and looked down at the troops bearing their bags and bayonettes. Soon Vienna would rejoice: should he compose a festive symphony for a public occasion? No—Heiligenstadt forced its way back into his thoughts; his heart was a slab of ice. The piano failed him. Yet…if he could run his fingers over the keys again, some new theme—the new theme that had been grieving him for its lack of birth—would bring him back to life. Some passing soldiers caught his eye: a tall officer on his horse took a whip to the back of some laggards. The poor devils; in a few days march they would be meat for jackals. Light from the summer sun struck him full force; his eyes rolled back in their sockets:

She came to his table, a slender golden arm bearing a pewter tray with steins of ale; her green eyes danced and darted about until they rested upon him with a friendly attentive look as if she had been expecting him. Long blond hair streamed from under the bonnet and fell about her shoulders. An animated spirit expressed itself now in a radiant glance, now in a smile that curved her red lips and played over her face. Never had he seen her so close, so warm. Her lips parted and she spoke, but he heard not a word. They were alone in the tavern, the two of them, amidst bottles and kettles—even the widow Koch was nowhere to be seen. As she leaned over his table, small pale breasts rose over the gold-fringed black and white blouse to glow at him and test his eyes; was she thus telling him what her lips could not? He drank the ale she served him, then took her by the hand and led her down the long slope to the bank of the Rhine. There was the tollhouse, the old bridge, the distant purple mountain range. A sudden wind came up from the river; it swept through her hair and stung her eyes. He draped a black cape over her, pulled it close around her neck and shoulders, and drew her close to his warmth. She nestled her breasts inside the shield of his arms, but pulled away quickly; her skirt billowed in the wind as she turned and ran to a tall grenadier with sword and scabbard who wrapped a strong arm around her and took her away into the night.

In the evening he penned a letter to Helene:

Mother Dear, our French masters have begun to move out at last. Maybe the Russians will do to the French what the French have done to us. The city is still under French rule, but my friends have begun to rejoice. They ask me to compose a joyous symphony to celebrate our eventual liberation. But even as others gain hope, my spirits sink. The waters of the canal call to me, and want to swallow me up. Once again I come to you, in my hour of need.

I have remained pure: ever since I saw the despised whore in the theater where my Leonora sang of her devotion, I have sickened at the very thought of her. But my natural desires remain. I thought to propose marriage to a young woman, but I despaired—my doctor believes I am diseased, and he is the girl's uncle!

This afternoon the raptus-angel came to me again: Babette has come to me before, but never so close as this time; she served me ale, and I drank it. Her eyes spoke to me, her lips spoke to me, her bosom spoke to me. But I understood not a word. Then she left me for her grenadier.

Your Loving Louis

He went to his sack of straw. The room was dark, but he did not sleep. Sometimes, when he had visions, he could lie still and the vision, like an icon in the sanctuary of his mind, would come back to shine in his dark. She came, her lips moved. But what did she say? This time she spoke— slowly, so he could read her lips. "*Louis,*" she said, "*let me go. I belong with Hans. Listen for your angel.*"

Bettina lead Wolfgang up the narrow stairs; they paused on the third landing so he could pant and gasp for breath. She expected Louis to be in his flat; she had noted his comings and goings—he should be there now. What a triumph! Two immortals, the poet and the musician, in her embrace. For an hour—for eternity. Wolfgang would be limp from age and exhaustion, she knew, but grateful enough to ogle her bare bosom as she spread her legs for Louis. She cocked her ear for sounds of his piano from the flat above.

Nothing.

"Come, Wolfgang, only two more flights." She prodded him until at last she stood before the door to Louis' flat. The door was unlocked. Inside, the room was thick with trapped humidity and stench from the chamberpot. She hesitated, but with her hand over her nose she ventured in and looked for Louis. Faint slanting light passed through a partly closed drape over the one window and drew her eye to a far corner where, between two stumps of old pianos, was the straw bed she had seen before, and on it was the slumbering genius. Wolfgang, who had remained on the landing, peered into the semi-dark; when he saw Bettina pull her dress over her head, he braved the odors and came up behind her. He reached for her nude body to press her to him, but she had moved toward the bed. The form on the bed was inert, a mound of earth: no breath, no motion. She straddled the body, cradled his head in her hands, and lifted it to her bosom. Her tongue slipped into his mouth, searching for his tongue, but it was curled back into his throat. The sides of his mouth were pulled back, baring gums, teeth and spittle that seeped over his lower lip and ran down his chin. She pulled back and happened to see an empty wine bottle near the piano stump. So—he had been drinking. If she woke him—this much she could do—would his member swell and stiffen? Drunken men, she knew, often failed, and thus disappointed their women.

"He is drunk, leave him be," said Wolfgang, as he came up behind her and cupped her breasts in his hands. She felt warm breath on her neck and trembling knees against the back of her legs. No, first she must waken Louis. How? Water, of course. She shook loose of the poet's hold and dashed into the kitchen. A crockery basin stood on a tabletop; the water was cold, it should rouse him. She grabbed it and, dancing away from grasping arms, poured water over Louis' head; it ran in rivers through his matted hair, washing away strands from his eyes. The eyes were rolled back in their sockets. Never had she seen a man so smitten by his beer.

With deft moves, she tugged at his trousers and brought them down to his knees. Only a flap of cloth stood between her and her object. The poet behind her was not to be denied: he was gasping for air now, his hands at work on his own trousers; and again his hands fondled her bosom as she bent over the bed; never mind, her flesh was ample for the two of them, and that was her intent. But Louis must waken. Kneeling, she pulled aside the flap. There, before her eyes, was the great man's organ. It was small, smaller even than Wolfgang's; her artful tongue, however, would make it grow.

"I beg you, my cherub," said Wolfgang, "embrace me with your lips." Ignoring his plea, she bent closer to Louis' body and took his organ into her mouth. Denied, Wolfgang dropped his hands from her breasts: one hand clasped his organ and pumped it; the other reached between Bettina's buttocks to grope for her inner mystery.

A ridge of scar tissue coiled about the organ from tip to balls. It must be a diseased condition—she had heard about such things that happened to men who consorted with women of the street. Brushing past the bloodless skeleton of Wolfgang, she raced to the kitchen for more water; finding none, she spat and wiped her tongue with a cloth that had been lying on the floor amidst scraps of food and slop.

"My dear, are you ill?" The poet came from behind and gaped at her body, stark and bare in the window's light.

"Not so much as that man on the floor. Cover yourself, Wolfgang—we must be gone." She picked up her garments and dressed outside on the landing.

In the evening, Louis groped among scraps of paper spread out over the floor—not music, but poems: a page torn from Homer, a page from Goethe, a page from Schiller.

With several in hand, he marched past the piano without a glance and sought out a tavern, a quiet one where he could drink his ale undisturbed and read scraps of poems, which he had already marked and underlined in bold lines. Schiller's *Ode to Joy* was a drinking song, earthy and boisterous—"draughts of joy from cups o'erflowing,"—fit for peasant stock. And worms—worms! even—feel life's bliss. Yet heros march among the stars, and angels dwell with God. Earth and sky—in the same poet's breath; and then the poet blows a kiss to all mankind and bids them seek a loving father in the heaven above. Poets!—if only he could prove such bold words in music.

Worms feel life's bliss, but not Louis, even though he is of the earth, like a worm, peasant stock. His pretenses to the contrary—for he falsified his status in the sight of the world—he came from Maria Magdalena, a simple peasant girl, and Johann van Beethoven, drunk whore-monger, who pissed in public gutters and humiliated his wife in the marriage bed. Yet, the poet would have him blow a kiss to a world full of whores and drunkards.

Was there a place where the earth and sky meet? In his music, yes, that was possible. In his Pastoral Symphony he brought God down to earth in the passing wind, the rippling brook, the stomping of peasant feet—but then the thunderclap and all was lost. He needed a god that rose up from the earth, from his own earth, his loins, his breast. He must compose a music that rises from the earth within his peasant breast and takes its place as a mighty globe in the sky above. He hastened back to his flat: he penned a note, then wrestled with the piano until it yielded up the kernel of a new theme.

Sigrid took the message directly from the messenger and brought it upstairs for her mistress. She had been instructed to stay away from the bedroom during these hours, but this was important: it was from Herr Beethoven. She tapped on the door; after a time, her mistress opened the door and took the sealed envelope. Antonie read: "You are right. A heavenly body has risen to rule the night sky."

The coachman, when he picked up the couple leaving St. Stephen's Church at noon, was told to drive up and down the avenues and not to stop for any reason. With a shrug, he set out for the Graben, past the Trattnerhof, the elegant shops, the coffee houses, that lined the avenues. Inside, Antonie pointed to the Pest-Column, built, she told Louis, in 1683 when a plague tore through the population, and the city fathers put up the memorial, thankful for their deliverance. He heard nothing, she knew, but she chatted on, pointing to this fountain or that shop. The coach turned and lumbered down the Herrengasse, where princes and counts built stern edifices of stone; then on to the Prater, and past the Lobkowitz palace with its arched portal. But now the two neither saw nor cared for these sights, nor did they hark to the whip and snap of the coachman above them; Louis had pulled the blinds and the two were silent in the dimness. By mid-afternoon the coachman, tired and thirsty as he passed familiar taverns, despaired that he would be relieved of his chore before nightfall. Finally he stopped so he could relieve his thirst and empty his bladder; but a voice assailed him: "No—go to the Weinerwald at once." At the gates the coachman halted as two guards approached the carriage and demanded to know who was inside. "Do not stop—on to the Weinerwald!" gasped the same voice. Recognizing the voice, the guards waved the coachman through, with a warning to return before the gates closed and he was locked out.

Rattling through the gates, the carriage swept past strollers and cyclists returning from their jaunts into the woods and plunged on toward Heiligenstadt and the Canal. The coachman could not conceive what passion for senseless rocking motion was driving him to lash at his two sweating nags, deny himself relief, and risk spending the night huddled outside the gates.

Finally the man and woman called for a halt; they stepped from the carriage and hastened into the woods. The man eyed them as they removed their shoes and waded across a brook, then he dashed behind a tree and relieved himself. What kind of people are these? he wondered, to be so inconsiderate. When he returned to the carriage, they were out of sight. A few pages of notepaper had dropped from the carriage when they opened the door, he noticed, and the wind was about to carry them away. Curious, he picked them up and pieced them together: bars of music and incoherent scraps of words meant nothing to him—save for the word "moonlight."

They were lovers—that much he had already guessed; their romantic nonsense proved as much.

In the deep grass by the side of the brook Louis rested his head on a knoll by a tree. "Here," he told her, "I heard the gurgling of this brook. Now I hear it here"—he pointed to his forehead. "And I would listen to the songs and sports of peasant troupes who came from the tavern over yonder. I no longer hear their songs, but I remember them. And once while lying here listening to them, I heard a thunderclap. It is the last sound I ever heard. It was the shout of an angry god."

She kissed him softly around his eyes, his cheeks, his lips, and ran her fingers through his shock of hair.

"In the scherzo," he said, "the peasants dance around and around, they get tipsy, they swirl and fall to the ground; the oboist and the bassoonist are tipsy too and they miss their cues. They are innocent and happy. But then the angry god beats his drum. It fells the lesser of them and causes the others to flee."

"There is no angry god here now," she wrote.

He rested his head upon her bosom; she understood and fingered the buttons on her blouse until it parted. His heart beat faster and faster as she blossomed for him like a flower.

"When I put my lips to your bosom I touch your heart and soul."

After a time he sat up and fixed his eyes on her bared breasts as a god might seek his nectar. The shepherd's tune piped in the silence of his mind.

"I must prove my thoughts in music." Waving his arms in grand gestures, he groaned out the roll and clap of thunder. "Those cellos and double-basses, the drums, the trombones, they tell of a stricken world, a deluge—all is lost. But then you hear the yodel of a simple shepherd on a hilltop; his tune says the world is fresh and green. The god has turned his wrath away."

By the side of the road, the coachman lit his pipe and looked up. An evening breeze bent the branches and flowers and clouds raced across the sun's descent in the western sky. It was late. Who would blame him if he returned to the city without his fare? He would call to them from the edge of the wood, a time or two; if they failed to come, it was hardly his fault. At the woods edge he saw them at last, dawdling and cooing—lovers who could not bear to part: she would go home to a difficult or demanding husband and dodge his inquiries; he would go back to—no, who would marry this stump of a man, his face a map of ruddy scars and fissures, unkempt hair, a voice that grated on the ear. Best the woman made amends with her husband before it was too late. He began his weary trot back to the gates.

Later in the summer Antonie took Bettina aside as soon as Franz left the house for his work. "One day," she began, "when I visited here years ago, I needed a lazy day out of the house. I took a carriage ride to the Weinerwald, where I came upon a shaded knoll by the side of a brook. I hadn't known the brook was there, because as a child I was not allowed to pass through the gates. Well, I sat down by myself, and before long I heard songs of peasant boys and girls from beyond a small hill. I wanted so much to go over and join them—I had never done such a thing; but I was afraid. Well…" Her voice trembled in her throat. "…yesterday I went there again—with Louis."

"You went with Louis?" Bettina arched her brow.

"I did. And he guided the carriage to the Weinerwald, and—can you imagine?—we came upon the very same shade tree by the brook where I listened to the songs. I told Louis about that day, and he told me how often he came here himself—to that spot!—and the brook sang its murmuring song, and the peasants shouted and fiddled, and here his Pastoral Symphony was born."

Bettina caught her breath: "Ah, a real brook inspired the music. And he took you there…"

"At that moment, under that tree, I knew we were destined to meet."

In hushed tones, Bettina asked: "Sister dear, did he open your bodice, kiss your breasts?"

Antonie blushed: "I opened my blouse to him and, like your Goethe, tears fell like raindrops and ran in rivers down my bosom."

"That is all? Did you not open the front of his trousers?"

Antonie hand went to her mouth. "Goodness, no."

"A pity," she said, an edge to her voice.

"Whatever do you mean?"

"Nothing."

Antonie gushed on: "He told me that once he was lying in that place listening to his memory of the tipsy peasants and their songs, when suddenly a great thunderclap startled him. He calls it the drum beat of an angry god. It is the last sound he remembers."

She opened the keyboard and played the theme from the *Andante: Scene by the Brook*, which she had purchased in a piano rendition. "The music is peaceful in a way that only a strong man can be at peace," she said. "But he knew no peace when he spoke of some angry god. He blames the god for his deafness. And something else… something that stands between him and the merrymakers."

Bettina noted the crimson that rose to her sister's face when she spoke of Louis. Her sister was in love with an eccentric genius who was warped in body and spirit. Gone was her sickly pallor and heavy heart—true; but she was an innocent child who knew little of the ways of men—least of all, this man. Yet, she had brought his lips to her bosom; she had won him over, whereas she, the buxom temptress, had failed.

Bettina pressed her arms heavily on her sister's shoulders and forced her to stop her playing. "You must listen to me," she said. "When Wolfgang came to me and opened my blouse, he wept tears of joy—I told you—just like your Louis. And he said to me that if he had met me in his youth, he would have been a sturdy lover, not the limp old man who rested his bones between my legs. Now, Louis is no old man, but he says an angry god has wronged him. You cannot know all he meant by that."

"What are you saying?"

"There is something about him. The rumors about whores…and another thing. If you get serious about Louis—and you are already, I see by the flush on your face—let me tell you something else Wolfgang said. He said that it was good he had not known me in his youth, because his spirit would have succumbed to his body's passions, and never would he have conceived a poem. The poet in him would have perished at my breast."

"You mean I would suffocate the musician in him? Why…"

"You would make of him a household pet. No household pet composes great symphonies. Either he will become limp in spirit with you, or he will turn against you and leave you."

"No, No—he is my Louis…"

"Your Louis? Do you think he is yours already? You have not wrapped your thighs around him. And if you do, do you think you can hold him?"

"But we love each other…he says…"

"I have been to his flat. Have you? No. The stink of his chamberpot is still in my nostrils. I have seen the litter, the straw, the decay of yesterday's meal. And in the middle of all stands his piano, the one thing he loves. He belongs to a muse that takes him away from me… from you… from us all!"

Antonie sprang to her feet and pointed a finger at her sister. "You went there to seduce him, that day I waited outside." Their eyes locked. "You want him for yourself. All you talk about is Louis, Louis, Louis… I should tell Achim."

Bettina had never seen her sister flare up. "Better you save your words for Franz, if he finds out." Her words were packed in ice.

"You and your great men—your Goethe, your Beethoven!" As she raged, in her mind's eye she saw Bettina's bosom open to the weeping eyes of the old poet. Did she open her bosom to Louis? How long were they in the flat? Not long, but…"

The next day Antonie eluded Hans and took a coach ride to an artist's studio on the Kohlmarket. Several visits were required, but eventually the artist produced for her a finely styled portrait on ivory. It was daring: the long neckline, the great curl of hair, the hint of bosom. It looked splendid in a locket. Should she sign it? No. Let Louis wonder. She would be the mystery woman in his life. Oh, how silly: he would know for certain. That afternoon she engaged a coachman to deliver it.

Chapter Twenty One

"The God Dreams of a Maiden."

As Louis took his place before the orchestra, he glanced at the audience; Antonie should be seated a few rows back—there!...beside Franz; and there was Bettina with a tall man—von Arnim, he supposed—and an elderly man who must be the famous Wolfgang von Goethe. They would all listen with a critical ear to the Symphony in B flat. The work was not new, but it was first performed at the Lobkowitz palace, where the public—Antonie in particular—could not have heard it; and never here at the Theater-an-die-Wein. It galled him that the musicians would follow the beat set by Umlauf—because they complained that his beat threw them off. But the musicians needed him to give them heart.

In the opening measures of the Symphony his heart beat soft and faint, as if he trespassed in the garden of a sleeping god, a god who dreams of love for an earth maiden. His heart had belonged to Theresa when he composed this music, but now he bequeathed it to the one whose heart beat in time with his own. At the end of the long Introduction he crouched behind his desk, then shot up to his full height waving his arms: the god awakes and bursts from his garden temple with an Allegro for the world—a playful god with a cheery heart. At the Adagio, his eyes shut, in veiled accents he gave homage to this god who sleeps and dreams again; in whose dream he, a divinity, worships a mortal maid.

He was treading on air lest his footfalls wake the dreaming god. His fingers went to his mouth to signal the musicians: Hush... play softly. Six bars of hesitant figuration rose to a chord of the minor ninth in G flat major: the bassoon first, followed by stealthy motions in the basses and a tapping of the kettledrums made an end of time itself.

After an intermission, four singers stepped onto the stage to sing *Mir est so Wunderbar* from Leonore:

"What a wonderful emotion," sings Marcellina. "He loves me, I can feel it..."

But Leonora sings, "What terrible danger besets me...she loves me, I can see it, Oh what unspeakable grief."

Louis studied the mouths of the singers: Milder was a radiant Leonora, her face without guile, her eyes transparent. Good—Leonora must be above all blame. If any doubts her, Rockel, when he sings the rewritten

141

aria, will prove her innocent of deception: "My angel Leonora," he will call her.

Rockel sang with conviction; the audience, hearing the aria freshly written, was moved to applaud on their feet.

At the end, Bettina dashed through the crowd and embraced Louis from behind. Antonie, looking with a sharp eye, saw Louis turn; she studied his face; he was rapt: was it the music—or Bettina? Franz and von Arnim came up and pumped Louis' hand.

Antonie had her notepad ready: "The aria—it is new, is it not?"

"Yes, an angel comes to Florestan to give him comfort."

Bettina grabbed the pad and wrote: "The Symphony—so lyrical, most unlike the Eroica."

Antonie grabbed the pad: she added, "More like the Moonlight Sonata."

Wolfgang interposed: "My splendid fellow—the music was most touching. And I have heard that you play the pianoforte so as to move one to tears. Can you join us this summer in Prague perhaps? Or Teplitz?"

Antonie grabbed the pad again: "Franz and I will pass though Prague on the way to Karlsbad and Franzenbaden."

"Ah, yes," Louis replied. "My physician has advised me to rest my ears in the peace of the mountain spas this summer."

"Good," added Franz. "We shall meet indeed."

On the first of July, Louis' coach took the Prague Bridge across the Vltava river. A stone statue on the Mala Strana side, partly obscured by a tower, appeared to wear a heavy cape—it was probably a cope and mitred bishop or saint, but it put him in mind of the statue of the Commandant in Mozart's opera, the father who was murdered by Don Giovanni, the lecher who had just seduced his daughter. Mozart had great success in Prague, he knew; but his operas were immoral: *Don Giovanni*, with its catalogue of seductions from Spain to Italy; *The Marriage of Figaro*, with its jus primae noctis, deceptions, and adulteries. If Mozart corrupted the morals of the city, however, his Leonora, faithful and true, must have stood as a corrective—and it was well received when performed at the Stadstheater. His mind reverted to his quest: how to meet in private with Antonie. Franz would be a problem, but they would find a way.

In the city, Mozart's music gave him no peace: a harpist on an alehouse bench played *Non piu andrai* and drove him from the place. In the evening, he would be expected to join the Brentanos, for form's sake, at the opera; Mozart's *Cosi fan tutti* would be sung, in which two men pay court to two sisters, then make a wager with some cynic that they can pretend to march off with their regiment to war, require of their lovers a pledge of faithfulness, then return disguised as foreigners and try, but fail, to seduce them. No:—he would ignore the opera, but meet up with their party at supper after the performance. People would forgive him: after all, he was deaf.

He entered the dining room of the Black Horse Inn, where he had planned to meet with the Brentano's. Antonie and Franz were already seated near the end of a long banquet table. She was dressed in a low cut gown of vivid green silk and tissue of gold, with green velvet bodice and a black band restraining her hair. Her eyes were flashing, her cheek was hot as she chatted with their guests at table; she lowered her eyes when she saw him, gave a subtle nod at an empty seat opposite her, then resumed her chatter. He took the seat. After a time she looked up; their eyes met and held.

"Herr Beethoven," a friendly voice called from the far end of the table. The man stood and waved at Louis. It was Verhagen, a writer, and his beautiful fiancé Rahel Levin, whom Louis had met in Vienna. It was well, Louis thought, to have them as a diversion, lest Franz consider him inordinately occupied by his wife.

Verhagen wrote in the notepad: "Your Violin Concerto," he said, "I heard Clement play it at the premier. He played at sight, they say. Is that true?"

"Yes, and he may well have ruined it, for all I know." Louis flushed at the memory of the event, which had drawn the ire of some critics.

"Oh," said Rahel, "he played it beautifully. And those four taps on the drum—how clever to get attention like that."

Louis winced. The beginning of the concerto came to him when his brain was drenched with ale and the gods had denied him the peace of his bed. But now the theme seemed to him a dream of peace soaring over drum taps that sent soldiers marching to some unseen war.

"More than a trick to get attention," Antonie intervened, dropping her interest in her conversational partner and taking up the notepad; "The beat of the drums hints of a new theme's arrival, and its rhythm is everywhere in that long movement, is it not, Herr Beethoven?"

He read her words and admired her hand: so elegant, each letter perfectly formed. She took the pad again and wrote, "And what could have been harsh—the beat of a drum—is soft and lovely. Is it not, Louis?"

Her words searched deeply into his soul: she was right; a mighty storm had been stilled when the inspiration came to him; no war at all, not even distant. The raptus-angel spoke after all. "You are right," he said. "Soft and lovely."

143

A sommelier came to pour wine. She took her glass and returned her attention to the table gossip on either side of her, not forgetting to say, "Franz, what do you think of this?" and "Franz, what do you think of that?" from time to time; but she peered over the rim of her wine glass with each sip and her eyes searched for his as she turned her head from side to side.

Across from her, Louis drank his ale and with rare patience entertained a bevy of admirers who were told that the famous composer from Vienna was in their midst. Some students tried to entice him into a political discussion: they had heard his new overture to Egmont, and asked if more numbers for the drama were to come from his pen, and what were his thoughts about political freedom. Louis ignored their questions: he had indeed written more numbers for Goethe's drama about the 16th century hero, Egmont, who stood up against the Spanish Inquisition. But politics was not on his mind.

The ale rushed to his head. His eyes fastened on her, followed her lips—what was she saying?...words wasted on others…her thoughts, her lips, belonged to him…he alone could immortalize the treasures of her heart. No!—No! Fool! She belonged to another—to Franz. There…there was Franz, by her side: his lips, thick as a purse, as a sow's ear, must have sucked at her holy breasts. He stared at her with glazed, hopeless eyes: she could never be his—she belonged to Franz. But he could make love to her in a way that Franz could not: in music—only in music—he could make love to her.

Some one began to play a piano at the far end of the dining hall: not a Mozart aria, thank god—but something earthy; he recognized it—a Bohemian song about drinking and skirt-lifting, unfit for Antonie's ears. Several of the guests began to sing along, swaying with the beat, hoisting their steins in salute to the pianist. Louis struggled to his feet and lunged toward the pianist—a burgher whose fingers moved over the keys with boorish haste. "Stop that vulgar tune!" He pounded his fists on the keyboard. The fat man, stunned for a moment, rose and thrust his jaw at the intruder: "Who do you think you are?"

"I am Beethoven."

"Ja, and I am the Emperor Franz." The man made to pick up the piano stool and throw it at Louis.

Varnhagen stepped in between the two men. "My dear fellow," he said to the pianist, "be so kind—" he tipped him a thaler—"let my friend here play a few tunes while you have yourself another ale or two." The man grasped the offering and retreated.

Louis sat and lifted his hands over the keyboard. The dining room was stilled, the guests unsure what might issue from this brusque newcomer who had interrupted their pastimes. Was it Beethoven?

The Moonlight—of course, that is what he would play. How regrettable, he thought, that he had dedicated it to Giulietta Guicciardi, that fleeting fancy of years ago. Antonie—she was the true proprietress of this music. In time, he would dedicate to her a great masterpiece—greater even than the Moonlight. After the Adagio, a song he had composed for her in Vienna, would do: "To the Beloved." The text was written by a poet named Stoll, who could never know how his words had affected him. Now it was time to present it to her. He improvised on the melody, then settled into the verse: he began to sing:

The tears of your silent eyes,
With their love-filled splendor,
Oh, that I might gather them from your cheek
Before the earth drinks them in.

One of the guests began to stomp his feet and call for the fat piano player. Louis, unaware that some in the room found him tiresome, was prepared to improvise at length; but he glanced up at Antonie, who nodded toward his empty seat. Her silent eyes spoke to him! She wanted him near her again! In a moment he was with her; he had with him a page of the fat man's music scores, on the back of which he wrote out the music and text for the song "To the Beloved," and presented it to her. Many at the table, sensing a romance, applauded. Antonie took the sheet from Louis and aimed a sweet smile at Franz: "Look, dear—Herr Beethoven has honored us with a gift of his music, a setting of Stoll's poem—you do know the poem, don't you, Franz?"

Franz knew nothing of poetry. He shook his head, and went back to his drinking. Not often did he drink like this; but it was the beginning of their vacation. It meant he would fall asleep and leave her in peace. It meant also that she could speak to Louis—if he too was not too far gone into his cups.

There was much she wanted to say to him. She had prayed, much as the sisters in the convent had taught her, but with more fervor—and her prayers at last were answered. Louis was her Phillipe. She would entrust her all to him, body and soul. It mattered not that the world would condemn her, or that the priests would condemn her. Even if people should say that the new growth in her womb was not the seed of Franz, but the seed of Louis—she would defy the whole world, priests and all. She took a pencil from a serving person and wrote in his notebook: "Dearest Louis, do not let the earth drink in my tears. Take me from Franz. I am yours."

PART THREE

BOHEMIA

(1812)

Chapter Twenty Two

"Not Wholly Yours"

The postcoach driver studied the gathering clouds and shook his head. "If it rains again today," he said to his anxious passenger, "we will have the devil's own time getting through the high pass of the Mittelgebirge range. We have only four horses, you see, unlike that Esterhazy fellow there, whose coach has eight—they can make the climb." He nodded in the direction of an elegant private coach that had just pulled away from the curb. Louis restrained an impulse to yell at the Prince's coach—but there would have been no room for one more, even if the Prince had wished to oblige.

"We will go an easier way." The man pointed to a sketchy map. Instead of Schlan, Budin, and Lobositz, we will take Schan, Laun, and Bilin, then to Teplitz. It will be dark when we get there, but we will get there—unless we get stuck in mud." He shrugged and motioned to his assistant to help Louis lift his bags and strap them to the back of the coach.

The road from Prague turned away from the Moldau and began to wind west toward Schlan. Louis settled in and reached for his sketchbook. A new life, a new theme. But the new theme was not right—not yet. He hummed and groaned and chanted—still, it was not right. Antonie, however…she was right. His eyes fell shut: her face beamed at him: her face—oh, the face! It was flawless; her mouth a gentle curve, her eyes moist tender soft light. So much like Babette!—in her tavern girl's outfit, she perched on the piano seat, her wheaten hair falling down over her shoulders, a tiny mole on her left hand, two more on her collarbone, over her breasts. So fetching! And a larger mole on her forehead. And she played music—his music, the Moonlight.

She was perfect; he was not. The sketchbook slipped from his hands. He feared the night in which lovers mate; but even more he feared the harsh light of day, when her eyes would behold the spectacle of his deformity.

Somewhere a long way off a roll of thunder sounded: the men in the driver's bench heard it, but Louis meditated on his personal fears. If only the theme would come, she would love him for the perfect creations of his mind—his body would not matter to her. The coach came out onto a wide plateau covered with short grass: an odd grove of crosses stood out blackly against the sky, leaning at different angels—some twenty or more feet, he judged—like trees that had been left to seed. Crosses over the heads of the dead, crosses fixed to the backs of the living, he thought. At Laun they stopped at a guard post to register their passage through the Imperial Dominions: "Best not go through the forest at night if it rains," called a voice from the guard house: "We won't be able to help you." The driver stared at the sky: it was dusk, hard to see the clouds that were forming above their heads. He looked to his passenger for a sign. "Let us get on with it," Louis bellowed. The man shrugged: "Very well, the sooner I start, the sooner I finish this day's work."

The night grew cold. He pulled his knees to his chest, hunched back against his seat, and threw a blanket over his shoulders. How long before Teplitz?—he did not know. A terrible thirst rose in his throat; he began to sweat and shiver. He pressed his hands against his head: an ache as wide as the earth, something—almost anything, the noise of the wheel against stone, the call of a night bird; or in his head, a memory, a smell, a clap of thunder…jumbled his senses. The coach ran into a rut and swerved off the road, the door flew open. He lurched out into the sudden rain and retched. The driver overhead cursed God, mud, and His Imperial Majesty's mail service.

At four in the morning the coach arrived in Teplitz. It was small comfort to learn that the Esterhazy coach had been trapped in the high pass and would have to be pulled out by a rescue team.

He took to his lodging at the Oak No. 62, where he slept fitfully until dawn. When he could confine himself to the bed no longer, he picked up the pencil that Antonie had left with him and began to write: if he hurried he could get the letter off in the daily post—it would reach her in Karlsbad in a day or two—and have done with the wretched affair:

On the 6th of July, in the morning.

My angel, my all, my very self,

Only a few words today, and those in pencil (with yours)—till tomorrow I cannot have my room—what a waste of time for such a matter—why this sorrow when necessity speaks—How can our love continue except through you change it that you are not wholly mine, I, not wholly yours? Oh! Gaze upon nature in its beauty and solace your heart with a sense of the inevitable—love demands everything, and rightly so, thus it is for me with you, for you with

149

me, only you are so apt to forget that I must live for myself and for you as well...

Were his words too harsh? He tried to give her comfort, telling her not to sorrow: he was intent upon his own sorrow. Why has he changed his mind? When they parted in Prague, all was well.

My journey was fearful. I arrived here only yesterday morning at four 'clock, and as they were short of horses, the mail coach selected another route, but what an awful road; at the last stage but one I was warned against traveling by night; They warned me of wooded country, but that only spurred me on—and I was wrong, the coach must needs break down, the road being dreadful, a swamp, a mere country road... yet it gave me some pleasure, as successfully overcoming some difficulty always does.

His mind returned to his first coach ride, as a boy, to Vienna to see Herr Mozart. Then he was just a lad, but he overcame his fear of the journey and the great Mozart. Again a journey: terror overtook him and made him curl his knees as he had when he was a boy. But he no longer had Maria Magdalena to comfort him; her prayers were interred with her bones in some cemetery he dared not visit.

But he had conquered Mozart! And he conquered the wrathful god—if that is what struck the coach on the rutted road. Now he would conquer Antonie. No:—his fear of Antonie. No: his fear of … of what?

Now quickly from outward to inward matters—we shall probably soon see each other. I cannot tell you now all my thoughts during the past few days about my life—if only our hearts were united once and for all I should not have such thoughts. My heart is full of the many things I have to say—ah!—there are moments in which I feel that speech is powerless—have courage—remain my true, my only treasure, my all!! as I am yours. The gods must send the rest, what for us must be and ought to be.

Your faithful, Ludwig

Before he sealed the letter, he held it to the light and read his words: he told her to have courage—but it was he who needed courage. The coach ride was harrowing: he wanted her to understand that he had passed through a gorge, a night's journey—that much courage he had. The journey took him to her. He must post the letter... a few steps, a halt. He turned back. But he started again—this must be done. At the Post Office he read a sign that said letters must be posted by 8 o'clock. Too late. An omen? Relieved, he returned to his room and penned another letter:

You must be suffering, my dearest love. I have just found out that letters must be posted very early—Mondays, Thursdays—the only days when the mail goes from here to K. You are suffering—Ah! Where I am, you are also with me; I will arrange for us both. I will manage so that I can live with you; and what a life!!! But without you!!—persecuted by the kindness of people everywhere, which I little deserve and as little care to deserve.

He donned his shabby green coat, took his ear trumpet and sketchbook, and set out for his walk. His tousled black hair waving in the summer wind, he stalked the wooded promenades and let his thoughts tumble about in his head. When he drew stares from passersby, he returned the stares with a contemptuous glare. Teplitz, a fashionable watering place for notables, bulged with titles: the Emperor Franz and his Empress were there and a well-picked bouquet of hangers-on. And French cannon rumbled through the streets: Napoleon was waging his war against Alexander's Russia. The inhumanity of humanity! Christ, the model of humility, preached against inhumanity—and for his reward they hung him up on a wooden pole where he suffered and died; his only triumph that his cross presides over an army of cracked bones and empty skulls in graveyards. For this he is called the greatest of our race?

At dusk, without a morsel of food, and little interest in it, he returned to his letter.

Humility of one man toward another—it pains me—and when I think of myself in relation to the universe, what am I and what is He who is named the Greatest; and yet this in itself shows the divine in man. I weep when I think that probably you will not get the first news from me until Saturday evening. However much you love me, my love for you is stronger. But never conceal your thoughts from me.

Would she betray him? She said no man had bedded her save her husband; that Franz, the first and only to claim her, planted his seed in

151

virgin soil, save that she had once pined for a young man named Phillipe whom she met only a few times in church, then her father tore her away and gave her to Franz. A virgin soul, she was—and she offered herself to him, Louis, with undying love. No woman had ever so offered such love to him. Was her love for him as strong as his for her?

What would she think when she saw his inadequacy? What thoughts might she have? What was Franz like? Again, the Christ came to mind: those crucifix depictions—did the Roman executioners drape their victims in neat loin cloth? No: they would expose the dying man to ridicule.

Now the night weighed heavily upon his eyes:

Good night. As I am taking the baths, I must go to bed. O god, so near! Is not our love truly a celestial edifice, and firm as heaven's vault?

In the morning his mood had not changed:

Good morning on July 7

Even while in bed, my thoughts go out to you, my immortal beloved, at moments with joy and then again with sorrow, waiting to see whether fate will take pity on us.

Yes, let her believe it is in the hands of fate…

Either I must live wholly with you or not at all. Yes, I have resolved to wander in distant lands, until I can fly to your arms…

Yes, he told her that the Philharmonic Society of London wanted him. England—the fabulous country where Haydn reaped a fortune. Surely she would understand… She would be a millstone…he remembered words in his diary: "In this way everything with A. goes to ruin."

…and feel that with you I have a real home; while you unfold me, I can send my soul into the realm of the spirit. Yes, unfortunately it must be so. Be calm, and all the more since you know my faithfulness toward you, never can another possess my heart, never—never—O God, why must one part from what one loves, and yet my life in Vienna at present is a wretched life. Your love has made me one of the happiest, and at the same time, one of the unhappiest of men—at my age I need a quiet, steady life—is that

possible in our situation? My angel, I have just heard that the post goes every day, and I must therefore stop, so that you may receive the letter without delay. Be calm, only by calm consideration of our existence can we attain our aim to live together—be calm—love me—today—yesterday—how I have longed for you—you—you my life—my all—farewell—Oh, continue to love me—never misjudge the faithful heart

Of your Beloved

L.

ever yours
ever mine
ever for one another

There was need to get the letter to the post, yet he hesitated. Fate? In the *Fifth Symphony* he struggled with fate and he won out. In the realm of music he has conquered fate and rid the world of its terrors. And he had braved the terrors of the night journey through the Mittelgebirge. In truth, however, he was less than a man. Antonie must not know his infirmities, she must not know his terrors, she must not think ill of him. Better she believe that he is a great and noble man who lives for his art and sacrifices for his art, and that she must not be a millstone that drags him to the ground. Yes, she must believe that he is more than competent as a lover, but he must give up this love on the altar of sacrifice.

He put the letter inside the pages of a book he brought with him— Homer's *Odyssey*—and sought out a table in the dining hall where he partook of a solitary supper.

Chapter Twenty Three

"Alone...Alone..."

His financial situation was a subject of concern. In Prague, after the Brentano's left for Karlsbad he had met with Prince Ferdinand Kinsky about the annuity that Kinsky, Archduke Rudolph, and Prince Lobkowitz pledged to him three years ago. He needed the annuity to supplement his income from publishers, even though the Austrian Finanzapatent had eroded its value to less than half. The money had not been forthcoming, but Kinsky gave him a partial payment of sixty ducats and promised he would do all in his power to obtain the balance from the others, even though the fortunes of the other two men were in doubt, Lobkowitz having invested in the vicissitudes of theater. Louis was grateful for the ducats but far from assured that all was well. Meekly, he thought he should have honored the advice of Frau Nanette Streicher, the wife of a piano maker, to put aside money from his earnings.

Then too, he considered if he should have gone to London. In odd contrast to the practical Nanette, there was the eccentric genius he had met in Vienna just before he left for his summer jaunt. A "scientist" named Johann Nepomuk Malzel had achieved fame when he was Court Mechanician to the Empress at Schonbrunn; he embarrassed Napoleon by defeating the great tactician at chess: inside his "automatic chessplayer" a man was hidden who happened to be a chess master. The man took a great risk at that, Louis remarked at the time; and that drew his interest to the inventor. Malzel went on to invent a machine that measured tempo, a "chronometer," that could beat out measures to precise fractions of a second, and allowed composers to use numeric symbols to indicate their wishes to performers. Malzel had other ideas, too: the "pan harmonicon"— a mechanical brass band contained in a single box. The thing was operated by a bellows, and a revolving brass cylinder with pins set the pitch. He had already sold something like it in Paris and he aspired next to sell the machine in London, and he had asked Louis to join him: the two geniuses would make a fortune, Malzel was convinced. Louis remembered this project: perhaps it was not too late for him to join up with the man.

He sought out a café for his breakfast and sat alone, pondering his status: alone, alone, he sat, amidst couples and groups, young and old—he was aging! at 42!—and he had no one with him…this the steady, quiet life he wanted?

Yes, for his art he needed the steady quiet life. London would serve to remove him from Antonie, and he could explain that in London he could make the money he needed to take care of her: as it was, if she left Franz, he could not take care of her. After all, she was nobility; without money, how could he support a noble woman? He of course was a peasant—he had deceived her. His letters…they too deceived her: asking her to go on loving him, yet insisting on their separation, that he must sacrifice all for his art. The truth was…the truth was that he was alone, alone—like the oboe's lament in the allegretto of his new A Major Symphony, a lonely cry amidst a world of dancing feet and whirling bodies.

With his pencil he tapped the slow pulse of the allegretto on the tabletop: a clarinet began its lamentation with three notes of the descending tonic triad, just as the oboe, in the Eroica's *marche funebre*, began its passage with the ascending tonic triad. It was a musician's allusion; few would hear his pained heart, the heart that he hid from the world's dumb gaze.

The serving girl brought his boiled eggs; instantly he perceived they were underdone, too watery, and the toast not dry, as he had ordered. Her flaxen hair, flowing at length, pierced him with a memory. He pictured her skating on ice, dancing and singing in a tavern, running with her skirts billowing in the wind. She was gone before he could say a word about the eggs.

Suddenly he understood his A Major Symphony. That work was his pagan symphony, a world of carnival and pageantry, where song and dance took place without religion, therefore without guilt; a world where he could imagine himself all sinews and muscles and at one with nature. It was the rhythm of dance: pure, abstract. But it was devoid of people, this world he created; he was alone in it: no merrymakers fleeing from an angry god, no shepherd piping a song of thanksgiving, no panting lover seeking his mate, no hero—not even a dead one being carried to his grave. This world was raw, no emotion, no humanity. Thus the empty sadness of the allegretto. He contemplated aloneness in a world that lacks its soul. One could live in it for a day. No more. He once wrote: "The good, the beautiful, needs no people. Without any help from others, there it stands." How wrong. Better the world in which he now lived, with its imperfections, its population—and Antonie, the soul of his world. If the gods give him a new theme, he will create a paradise that is populated, that has a human heart.

Should he meet Antonie in Karlsbad? His letter might lead her to expect him—"We shall probably soon see each other," he wrote. Should he post it?

Done with his eggs, he ordered more coffee. As the pretty young server poured for him, her sleeve brushed against his neck, and he felt her warm breath. Was that innocent...or was she a flirt? Either way, the girl had confirmed his new judgment: the good, the beautiful, needs loveable beings whom he can embrace, if only in his mind.

The following day he was taking a brisk walk through a country lane. Suddenly two warm arms embraced him from behind. Bettina! She slipped him a note: "Guess who just arrived at the inn and wants to meet you!" He knew—Wolfgang von Goethe. "He is having breakfast with his wife and invites you to join us. Come!"

On the way she explained: "His wife's name is Christiana. She is unpleasant, but do put up with her. Wolfgang will insist she go on ahead to Karlsbad for the bath cure; she has gout or something. Soon we shall be alone, the three of us."

Wolfgang rose when he saw Louis approach his table and—with a knowing glance at Bettina—said, "Well, my dear Beethoven, at last we meet."

Louis took a place at the table and ordered coffee. Bettina, ignoring a fierce stare from Christiana, placed herself between Louis and her husband and wrote the poet's words for Louis to read. "I am honored," she wrote, "that you have set certain of my poems to music: *Mignon*, and especially *Kennst du Das Land.*" She smiled inwardly at the mention of the poem that Louis had playfully dedicated to her. When she had enabled the poet and the composer to converse for some time, she interposed with an inspired thought: "My dear Louis, there is a piano in the dining hall. After dinner, you must play for Wolfgang!" She tweaked his cheek and nudged him under the table.

Louis had long admired the poet from Weimar. What music would be fitting for such an audience? The Eroica Variations, of course: which he had intended to play at the Brentanos, but instead was inspired to play the Moonlight. The variations would be most fitting for two giants such as Goethe and himself.

Shortly after breakfast Wolfgang put Christiana on the morning mail coach to Karlsbad. She wagged her finger at him and warned him to mind his morals, as he all but shoved her into the coach. "You must obey your doctor's advice, my dear, and take the bath cure. You will feel better for it. And you know I must stay here with the Grand Duke. And of course, Herr Beethoven."

Having sent his wife on her way, Wolfgang returned to the inn and listened to Bettina's plan. "Let us take the path to Bilin," she said. "Louis will agree to the walk. And I know some wooded spots off the path where we can't be seen." The poet's face brightened.

Louis was eager for the chance to spend an afternoon on the country lanes with Wolfgang. After a quick lunch at the inn, they set off. With Bettina as note-taker, the two men conversed about Napoleon's move against the Czar Alexander. He himself was here, Wolfgang said, in his capacity as Privy Councilor to the Grand Duke of Weimar; and he confided to Louis why the Emperor Franz was here in Teplitz: he was meeting with military men to revitalize the military and split the enemy's forces in two. And if the English should win out, Napoleon would be doomed.

They had not been on the path long when they saw ahead of them the Empress and her retinue. The path was narrow, surrounded by tall grass damp from an early rain. Louis said, "Let us walk arm in arm. They will have to get out of our way, not we out of theirs." Goethe, hat in hand, stepped onto the grass and made a graceful bow, so that the Empress and her following could pass. Louis, however, his arms crossed over his chest, bullied his way through, leaving the Empress no choice but to moisten her feet in the tall grass. "He thinks he is an Emperor among us," Bettina said to the horrified Wolfgang.

As they moved through clouds of humid air, the walkers perspired and heaved. Louis made demands upon the lagging Goethe: "Schiller says that all men are brothers. Emperor, Pope, peasant, are all as one. Do you agree?"

The poet stopped to gasp for air: "Ah—Schiller. A romantic. Beautiful sentiments, to be sure. But we must have royalty."

"Hush," said Bettina. "Down there, a beautiful vale. Come, we shall be cool in that grove of trees."

"Schiller tells us that there is a loving father above," said Louis. "Do you believe that?"

"My dear Beethoven, you treat my views with inordinate respect. You must speak to the priests about such matters."

"No, No—I speak to you. About Schiller…Schiller! Is there a loving father above?"

Bettina intervened. "Come, Louis, Wolfgang, over here. Let us rest under these trees. We cannot be seen from the path above."

"The poet says that man's love for man is more important…" said Wolfgang.

"And," added Bettina, "a man's love for his woman."

Louis seized the pad from her hand and took in Wolfgang's words and Bettina's codicil. "The poet speaks the truth," he exclaimed. "In his *Ode*, Schiller says, *And a man who has found a loving wife, he above all should raise his voice. If any man can call even one other soul his own, let him join us in our chorus. Else, gnashing his teeth, he weeps bitter tears in darkness, to all the world unknown."*

His two companions were startled by the force of the utterance.

"Ah, my Leonora, my Leonora!" Florestan's theme flooded his brain, and he sang it out. Another theme began to take shape, the one that sought him out day and night, yet fled from his searching spirit.

He took off his outer coat and shirt and dropped to the earth that was mossy and soft beneath him. Above, a chorus of thrushes, finches, wrens, and starlings chirped in the treetops; he could hear their chorus in his soul. If only there were a stream nearby where he could strip and bathe and be close to peasant girls who would join him in the water and splash about and tease him. He would watch them, feel his humanity among them.

"If any man can call even one other soul his own, let him join us in our chorus." The theme drew tears from his eyes. He leapt to his feet and made as if to sweep the clouds from the face of the sun with wild shouts and flailing arms. Before his eyes an orchestra spread out on the stage, seventy or eighty pieces—no less—and behind them, spanning the stage right to left, a chorus and four soloists sang out the theme and dispelled the mists and laid bare the sun burning in the sky.

Schiller! The poet's verses sang of jubilation, a chorus of lovers and heros—men drunken with heaven's fire who come to the goddess on her throne. The fire spread through his body and urged him on like a hero, like an emperor, to his beloved. He would go to Karlsbad.

Behind his back, Bettina stepped out of her petticoat and underthings. She embraced him with her arms and nudged him with her nipples.

Louis stood still as a statue.

Wolfgang knelt behind Bettina; his tears ran down the curve of her back.

She reached around to stroke Louis' crotch.

"Daughter of Elysium," he sang: "not shall I be the one to steal away in tears alone…!" The image of the solitary no longer afflicted him. The god of the poets had come at last.

Bettina knelt and reached around to finger the organ inside its cloth sheath. It remained flaccid. Why doesn't he respond? He cannot be drunk; he has had nothing. If she reached inside…she tried to open his britches… she would not dare touch it, but it must be exposed. Wolfgang's weight was bearing down upon her back and shoulders. Her plan must work; she needed Wolfgang—not as a lover, as a witness… how can Louis go on singing like that?…if she could arouse the composer of the Moonlight Sonata, she would report to Antonie that the man was indeed immoral, and Wolfgang, whose word was like God's, would swear that Louis came lusting after her as she and the poet were making love under the trees, and that only her prayers and threats of Wolfgang persuaded him to desist. And Wolfgang would see the scar—this time in better light. They would prove to her sister that Louis was a whore-monger.

Achim would arrive on the afternoon coach; this was her only opportunity. If she could move around to his front, she could look at his eyes, flick her tongue—but Wolfgang was wrapped around her waist. Finally, she shook him off, leaned forward, and swung around an arm to turn Louis' head toward her. His neck was stiff. She stood and moved around to seduce his eyes. They were rolled up so far she saw only white, red-streaked patches glistening wet. The singing had stopped, but his lips were working as if he was speaking to some invisible presence. Bettina's hand went to her mouth…she knew! Louis had the sickness, that sickness—not only the sickness men got from street whores, but the other sickness, that made someone stop in his tracks and stand still or fall down.

"Come, Wolfgang, look at this!"

The poet took his eyes from Bettina's bushy crotch for a moment. "He has epilepsy! Leave him be."

Bettina's plan had failed; but it mattered not. Wolfgang was witness to something more frightening. She would get a letter off to Antonie at once.

Louis began singing his Schiller again: he sang of heroes who march through the vast abyss of space, and of a loving father who dwells beyond the starry vault of heaven.

Bettina led Wolfgang to a soft spot under the pines and kept her promise.

Chapter Twenty Four

"You must be Careful."

Louis was not fit for any woman in this world, Bettina determined. Only whores would have to do with him, and he must have paid them splendidly at that. What were Louis' plans? Was he going to Karlsbad? She would write at once; her letter must arrive first. It would go out in the next day's post coach.

date July 12, 1812

Toni, dear, I am so sorry we quarreled. Can we make it up to each other? Do not think ill of me, I want only the best for you. I am not sure if Achim and I can join you at Karlsbad, because he has other obligations. But later in the year, when you return, we can meet. For now, this letter must suffice. About Louis, I know you have a tender heart for him. As for me, I am happy with Achim. I have no designs upon Louis. I admit I found him compelling, and, yes, I wanted to test my powers of seduction that first day I went to his flat and you waited patiently outside. But he did not respond to me. This speaks in his favor, you see. But, my dear, I must pass on to you what I fear because I know you are innocent of the world and its ills. I give you the same advice I would give any woman.

I warn you, if you decide to become intimate with Louis, you must be careful, as you would with any man. Certain diseases affect men: they may take the mercury cure, or arsenic, but it rarely helps. No man will tell you the truth; you must be alert and look for yourself. I mean, look at his male member in the light, before you take it into your hand or into your personal place—I have not seen Louis in that way, this is simply a precaution I would issue to you, because I care for you.

And you must pay attention to some of his habits: you say that sometimes he stands still like a statue of a god and listens to heavenly voices like angels that sing to him and inspire his music. My dear, have you ever seen this happen? I have not, but others have—do not ask who—and they say it is a disease. Please understand and forgive me if I am wrong; I have only your interest at heart. I will never speak to Franz about you—I swear it!

Your sister, Bettina

She posted it. There, she had done her honest duty. Now she owed her sister nothing.

Chapter Twenty Five

"The Letter."

At mid-afternoon dinner Antonie ordered brook trout, which she could eat quickly and so excuse herself from the table without drawing undue attention from Franz. He ate as he always did: slowly, methodically. First he would cut the meat so that each piece was the same size, like the butcher at a shop in Frankfurt, who was exact with his meat cleaver; he would chew each piece an equal number of times; then wash down each piece with two swallows of ale. When he was done he would finish his ale, rinse his fingers in the lavabo, fold the napkin neatly and place it to the left of the plate. He was precise about everything.

"You must excuse us, Franz. Maxie has a problem. I will take her and tend to her."

Franz, still engaged in chewing, scowled at his daughter. When he had taken his two swallows, he said, "Yes, she soiled the tablecloth with soup spills. Three times. That reflects badly upon me."

"I mean she has another problem. Come, Maxie."

Maxie had no problem other than need to relieve herself in the toilet.

Each day, except for weekends, the mail coach arrived in mid-afternoon and an errand boy from the inn took a guest list with him to the post, gathered up all mail and brought the items to the innkeeper's office, where they were sorted, bundled if need be, and placed in slots that bore the names of each guest. In the two weeks they had been in Karlsbad, Franz always went to the office after dinner to collect his mail. He would take it to his suite, place it on his desk, open the first piece, read it, and move on to the next—just as he consumed his beef. It might be the next day before Antonie got anything that was hers. And she had been waiting for a word from Louis.

She had to hurry. With Maxie in tow, she swept into the office and looked for their mail. She found it, but it was a thick stack, bundled and tied—a lot of work from the Frankfurt office, she imagined. If she had time to open it, would she have time to tie it up again? Would the innkeeper think it odd? Flustered, she said, "I will just take the bundle to my husband and spare him the walk in this chilling drizzle." The moment she spoke she felt foolish: a brisk wind had blown the clouds away and the sun was

162

crowned atop the mountain range. The man stared at her. She grabbed the bundle and dashed out the door.

"Are you expecting a letter, Momma?" asked Maxie.

"Why...I don't know, dear. Most of this is for your father. If a letter is for me, he will give it to me later. Hurry now, we must get to our rooms."

"Well," said Maxie, "if you get a letter, I hope it isn't from Herr Beethoven."

Her heart contracted. "Why, Maxie. How can you say such a thing?"

"He talks so loud, and waves his arms—like a crazy man. And at table he spills things."

Antonie put her finger to her lips: "Hush dear. Never talk like that. He isn't crazy, just deaf. Deaf people can't hear how loud they are."

"Well, if he can't hear, why do I have to hush?"

Antonie smiled: her daughter was not the obsequious infant she had been for years. "He is a good man, Maxie. I will ask him to compose some music for you—especially for you."

Maxie made a wry face and curled her lip. "Would I have to play it? That would mean practicing, wouldn't it?"

"I will speak to him—it will be playable."

Inside the suite at last, she placed the bundle on the desk and studied it. The cord around the bundle was tightly knotted; it would take time... how much time did she have? Franz would be along in a minute—if he found she was poking through his mail...all mail was his, he thought. No, she dare not risk it; she would have to wait. Another errand was on her mind; she placed Maxie in the keeping of an inn attendant who managed children's entertainments, and rushed into the center of town.

When Franz finished his ale and returned to the suite, Antonie was nowhere to be found. She must have taken Maxie out for a walk. There was the mail on his desk. Lighting a cigar first, he cut the cord and took up the first piece: it was from a business associate in Frankfurt who was managing affairs during his absence. He opened it and studied a detailed financial report. By dusk he had got near to the bottom of the stack. One letter he noted briefly and put it aside: it was for Antonie; the name von Arnim was on the envelope. What did this mean? Was von Arnim coming to Karlsbad to join them? He detested the man. *von* Arnim, was he? Nobility. And a poet—and devilishly handsome at that. It seemed that when they were together—in the church, was it?—the poet took a long look at Antonie. What about her? She had been strange of late. Could it be...? He studied the letter in his hand. How could he open it without her knowing?

Antonie was pregnant, he remembered: suddenly it struck him odd that she who put him off so often, pleading this excuse, that excuse, now is bearing a child. He had bedded her in the early spring. Was von Arnim in Vienna then? Bettina was…yes, the poet had come often. He resolved to go to her immediately with the letter, and demand she open it in his presence. If von Arnim was amorous, he would teach her an instant lesson: she belonged to him: he would throw her onto the bed, spread her legs, and prove his point.

Maxie came rushing into the room. "Papa, I must find Mamma!"

The child was no end of distraction. Where was Antonie? "Very well, we shall go look for her. Let us try the promenade."

The small Catholic Chapel near the Coach Station posted hours when the priest was available for confessions and spiritual counsel. A bell was suspended from a rope near the red painted front door of the old stone building. Antonie pulled on it, once, twice, and finally a young bespectacled priest in a black cassock appeared. She hoped he would not be harsh on her. She remembered the kind priest who spoke to her at St. Stephen's that terrible day.

"Father, I do not wish to make confession. I have come to ask your counsel in a spiritual matter."

The priest invited her to a small study near the back of the church.

"Father, I have heard that for our sins God does not punish us in this life. Is that true?"

The priest crossed his legs under his cassock and clasped his hands over one knee. "Why do you ask such a question?" he asked.

Taken aback by his directness, she stammered, "Why, no reason at all…"

"Come now, there must be a reason." His eyes narrowed suspiciously. "Are you in trouble?" He stared at her belly. "Are you married?"

"Oh, no, father—it is nothing like that…" But it was something like that. She had begun a conversation with a priest, and didn't know how to go on or get out gracefully. It was like she stood before Father Wolf at the altar at St. Stephen's and felt the need to oblige her father, Franz, the church, the whole world. At that memory, she bristled. "Father, I came here for answers. Will you please answer my question? Is a person punished in this life or the next?"

"That is a difficult question. God punishes us directly in the next. But in this life there can be natural consequences of our sins. For example"— he removed his glasses to polish them with the sleeve of his cassock—"if you offend someone, he may seek vengeance against you, and you would suffer. That is nature's way. But it is not God's direct act. That comes in the afterlife."

"Nature's way? Or the way of vengeful men?"

"Well, vengeance is wrong of course; the Bible says '*Vengeance is mine, I will repay, says the Lord.*' We must not do what God proposes for Himself."

"So God is vengeful?"

The priest removed his glasses and squinted at her. "No. God punishes out of his sense of justice."

"What would be the difference?"

He scowled at this impertinent woman: she was old enough to know not to joust with God about weighty matters, and young enough that she must be in some womanly kind of trouble. Did she wear a wedding ring? His eyesight was poor.

With his glasses wiped clean he was able to see her better; he stared and spoke. "You must tell me. Are you bearing a child?"

"Father, that is impertinent."

"Has someone done you wrong?"

She stood and glared at him. "Yes, Father. My husband…my father… and a priest."

When she returned to the suite, Franz and Maxie were not there. She pressed her hand to her meager bosom. If Louis came and they wanted to make love, would she be good enough for him? What is it that pleases men? Franz never said; he just plunged into her, wiped himself like he dipped into the lavabo after his dinner, and went back to his desk. Do men estimate the size of a woman's breasts? Men ogled Bettina, she knew. And what about her thighs? She was slender, not fleshy. Franz often said she should gain weight.

Well, if Louis has not written to her, she will write to him. She must. She will declare herself in writing; he must respond. She must know.

My Dearest Beloved,

Everyday I long for you, and look for the mail, hoping, praying to hear from you. I even pry into the mail wrapped up on Franz's desk—he is so slow to pass my letters on to me. Today is Friday; no more delivery until Monday, so I must suffer until hope rises in me come Monday. Only a word, a word only, from you, would lift my spirits to the heavens. If only I knew why you are now distant when you were so close and made promises that I cling to in hope.

165

*You touch my heart, you tell me I am your angel. But your angel
Leonora languishes in prison waiting for her Florestan. Louis, is
there someone else who makes you happy? I could accept it if you
were happy, and suffering no longer. Yes...No! I am not so strong.
Oh be gentle with my heart.*

Toni

Dare she post it? She read her own words: she had not used the word
love. That beautiful word passed her lips rarely: only in her mind did she
dare speak it, when two blessed men passed through her thoughts: first,
Phillipe—she never did tell him she loved him—and now Louis. She was
afraid...afraid. "I care for you so much," she had cried, in the carriage,
with her arms around him. Perhaps he needed to hear the word. Again she
picked up her letter. Where could she add the word love? Ah, before her
name—

Love, Toni

No, that would not do. She needed to say "I love you" in the body of
the letter—those precious words. She had not said them; neither had he.
Where...?

She heard a pounding at the door. Franz! Quickly she slipped the letter
between the covers of a book—no, it was a book he had been reading, he
would find it. She looked about: under the pillow. "In a moment, Franz."
She undid the latch.

Franz entered the room and sat on a chair by the bed. "Maxim is
outside playing. We can be alone now. You have something from the von
Arnims," he said. "Here."

She took it, puzzled; Franz usually did not show interest in her mail.
"I will open it later," she said.

"Why not open it now? I'd be interested if they plan to join us—either
here or in Franzenbaden."

Maxie was heard entering the suite. Having tired quickly of the
supervised games and stories, she returned to the suite to require
attention.

After a moment of thought, Antonie responded: "I will tell you soon
enough if they plan to join us."

"You are being curt with me."

"Not at all. I simply prefer to read my mail as you do, after I have done with other things. Now Maxie needs something to do. I will take her to a piano recital."

Franz ordered Maxie to go: "It is only across the court. I will watch you from the window. Maxie, you are ten years old—go by yourself."

Maxie stared at him, defiant. "I don't want to listen to piano playing—every day I have to take lessons…"

"I wish to speak privately to your mother. You must do as I say."

Antonie said, "I will take her, Franz…" But she hesitated—what if he finds the letter under the pillow? She had best stay here.

He pounded his fist on a tabletop: "Do as I say."

It sounded like he was yelling at both her and Maxie. "Franz, give me a moment or two alone with Maxie, here in the bedroom. I will arrange things. Come here, Maxie." Her thought was she would take the letter from under the pillow and take it somewhere…she didn't know where, but outside.

Franz clapped his hands at Maxie like a commandant on the field of battle: "Do as I say!" Maxie shrieked and ran to the recital.

With a swift move he locked the door behind the fleeing child. Facing Antonie, he drew the letter from his coat pocket and held it up before her. "If you do not wish to read it, I shall open it and read it to you. Which do you prefer?"

"I will read it."

"Very good. I shall sit here and await the news."

She opened the envelope carefully. One page. Her eye ran down the cursive and took in Louis' name. "Oh," she said, "Bettina simply chats about the concerts that she and Achim have attended, and they ask about us and the baths."

"That is all?—you hardly glanced at the letter."

"I told you…that is all."

"You deceive me!" He made as if to strike her, but held his arm above her head. He expected her to cower and shrivel. Then he would demand to see the letter.

Her eyes defied him. "You do not dare strike me."

Only once before had he seen her like this—that was when she was shaming herself with her fingers. The sight of it burned in his memory. He took her by the shoulders and shook her; then he reached inside her blouse and snaked his hand around a breast and clasped it, pressing his hardening member against her stomach.

Was God's justice upon her already? She went to scratch his eyes, but the letter…it fluttered to the floor. If she bent to reach for it, he would be the more infuriated—or all the more aroused. His hardened member had taught her many a lesson. "No, Franz—I am pregnant, remember that!"

Her words went unheeded. In a moment he had her on the bed, her dress over her waist. Powerful arms pinned her down. But her underclothing was intact; he could not enter without removing his arms for a few moments. When he did, she would reach for the letter…and what?

The ale had affected him; all subtlety, all sense, was gone. Urgency had set it. He fumbled with his britches front. "Whose baby is in your belly?" he demanded.

Stunned, she said nothing. Could he suspect? But she and Lewis had done nothing…nothing—if only they had, if only the child that grew in her womb was his.

"von Arnim…it is his…is it not!" he gasped; then he was unable to speak, so desperate was he to enter her.

von Arnim? What has von Arnim to do with this thing he was doing? She answered not a word; he would have heard nothing, so intent was he to do his deed; and she dared not resist—he would bear down and hurt her all the more. God!—she mustn't let him disturb the pillow; her letter to Louis was inches below her head.

So he thought the letter was a love letter from von Arnim! Good— let him suspect von Arnim, not Louis. Franz would never confront von Arnim—he was intimidated by nobility.

Franz began his breathless siege against her dignity. His member thrust and bored between her legs, his belly smacked against her stomach, his weight crushed the breath from her lungs, his teeth bit into the soft tissue of her mouth and lips. With her right hand free, she reached to the floor and brought up Bettina's letter: impossible to read it, but she cared little for her sister's words. She got the other hand free behind Franz's heaving back; she tore the letter into shreds; she turned her head sharply from his assault and she swallowed the letter as if it were a piece of pastry left over from the evening's meal.

Chapter Twenty Six

"The Hidden Drawer."

With the Master's spare key Schindler let himself into the flat. The Master had required some duties of him during his vacation in the Bohemian mountains, such as arranging for a cleaning woman to come and clean the flat. But for Schindler it was also an opportunity to accomplish something else, something that had eluded him for some time. He rummaged through the drawers of the fine nutwood desk. Not sure what he was looking for, he took everything out and scrutinized each object, each scrap of paper, in hope of finding evidence. In one drawer, a book was jammed against the back partition: Fergar's Small Poetic Hand Apparatus. It was dirty, well-used. One page near the back was covered with scribbling. His Master's hand was always difficult; he took the book to the window, wiped his spectacles, and made out some of the words: *"Give Amalie a fiery kiss for me when no one is overlooking us."* And along side of it, on the next page, he read a crude poem in the same sprawling hand: *Ludwig von Beethoven, whom, even if you sought to forget, you never ought to.* Then, *These words written in A's album, June 1811.*

The words—*Give Amalie a right fiery kiss when no one oversees us*—puzzled him. *Us?* The words made no sense unless the Master intended to say...*when no one oversees you.* Perhaps when the Master wrote the words in her album, with some third person in mind, he got it right. In any case, it sounded like his Master had sent Amalie a reminder through some friend that a heated kiss had once joined their lips and tongues when no one was looking.

He pulled a chair close to the window and in the afternoon light he poured over the many notebooks that he found on the desktop or under the desk or near the piano. Where was the perfect heart-shaped ass...and whose was it? Then he came upon mysterious words: *"That way, with A., everything goes to ruin."* Now he knew something: his Master had a lover and her name began with the letter "A." Ah, this would suggest Amalie Sebald.

It was a commonplace among musicians, tavern-keepers, and coachmen, that the Master often went at night to the ramparts where he visited one of those women who loitered about the guard posts. These were the worst kind of whores—filthy, disease-bearing creatures of the streets; he had seen them himself at times when his coach happened to pass by. Of course, there were higher type whores who would come to a man's own rooms; yet his keen eye had never discerned that such a woman had been present in the Master's flat. Then too there were rumors that women of high rank had offered themselves to him, but he had scorned them. Mysterious indeed, was the Master's way with women. But, as he had long suspected, there was someone special. Her name began with "A." Amalie?

But perhaps not. The dates of the two notebooks told of years separating them. The first was old, stained; but the words about going to ruin were recent, in a book the Master had used just before he left for the mountains. And something else: in the newer book he sometimes could make out something about a woman whose name began sometimes with "A." and sometimes with "T." Or were these two different women? At once he thought of the Countess Anna Marie Erdoty. She and the Master were on friendly terms. For a time the Master had even taken living quarters in her apartment building in the Krugerstrasse. And, yes, the Master had charmed the Countess with his two trios for pianoforte, violin and cello. But the Countess was married and often bed-ridden; and she dragged about on swollen feet day and night to meet the demands of her three cantankerous children. Would the Master fall in love with such a one? He stroked his chin. Perhaps...perhaps not. Then there was Antonie Adamberger the actress. Yes! He had seen her at the theater. She was exciting, fetching, alluring.

What sense then, should he make of a small package that had just been brought to the flat by a uniformed coachman? It was from the Countess Gallenberg, the man had said. He knew who she was—she was Giulietta Guicciardi, the little scamp who ran past him at the door that first day, her hair a whirlwind of dark curls, who lowered her eyes and turned her face from him. He had long suspected a romance between this girl and his Master. Yet, her name did not begin with the letter "A" or "T." He held the package in his hand. Should he open it? Yes, it was a necessary service for him to manage his Master's affairs in his absence—the Master has used just those words. He opened it. A portrait in ivory, the Countess herself—the wild curls of hair over her head. And she a married woman! She was bold...he gave her credit for that! And young: she was only nineteen when she married Count Gallenburg...perhaps only eighteen or even seventeen when she began her music lessons in the flat. Or on the bed of straw, no doubt. There was another who was young...who was that? Yes, Theresa Malfatti, the famous doctor's niece. She had the honor of receiving the dedication of one of the Master's sonatas. The Master took great interest in the young ones, did he not? And Theresa…a "T." Theresa had not married; she was called one of the most beautiful girls in Vienna. She should not be ruled out.

There was another "A," he remembered: Antonie Brentano. Impossible: the woman was married to a strict no-nonsense husband, a merchant from Frankfurt; she was pale of face, cheerless, and hindered in her movements by children, the oldest of which clung to her like a burr. Besides, she was a devout Catholic: every day, people said, she attended Mass at St. Stephen's.

What was he to do with Giulietta's portrait? Simply, he would write to the Master and tell him of its arrival, and say nothing more.

He returned to his probe of the desk drawer. In the back corner, his hand came upon a thin metallic object. It proved to be a bent nail that blocked his way to something that lay behind the drawer's back panel. With a quick jab, he pulled the nail out and reached into the small space; something hard and round…he pulled it out and stared at a medallion portrait of an attractive woman with a half-smile on her face, a mass of hair curled atop her head, and an open neck that was quite daring in a portrait. Amalie? Another portrait of Giulietta? He took both to the light of the kitchen window, wiped his spectacles, and studied the two images. Yes, both could be Giulietta, but he couldn't be sure.

In the same drawer, more conversation books and fragments of letters and notes were wedged against the backing. He tore into these with hasty hands. In one, he was elated to find the drawing of a woman's ass—heart-shaped, a prize specimen—just as he remembered it. He tore off the page, replaced the book and the other items inside the compartment, secured it with the nail, and turned to leave. His friends at The Red Hedgehog would be impressed when he showed them the ass and a page of the Master's own writing to prove it was indeed the Master's own sketch. Yes, nothing fascinates the minds of small men more than the sex lives of great men, he thought, and this authentic revelation would make him, Anton Schindler, a great entertainer at the taverns as he challenged them to guess whose ass it was that had so smitten the Master. They would assume he knew the answer, of course; but he would tell them that in loyalty to his Master and in consideration of the lady's dignity, he must not let on.

He reached for his key, but a knock on the door stopped him. Not the Master!... he froze with the key in his hand, afraid to take a breath. No, impossible. The Master was far away in the mountains, he remembered— it must be the new scrub woman he hired to come and clean the filthy flat, the first one who agreed to come since the last one quit in an indignant fury. It was not easy to find someone to come to this infested hole and empty chamberpots and shake out a flea-besieged mattress of straw. What was the new one's name? Yes, Freida. He opened the door.

There she stood, a speck of a woman, of poor countenance, old before her time. With her was a younger woman—a girl, really. Her daughter?

"Come in at once the two of you. You have found the right place."

He would linger in the flat a while to make sure the work was done to his satisfaction. And he must be sure they took nothing that did not belong to them. He would watch them with the eye of an eagle. As for his friends in the tavern, there would be time enough later for him to show them the woman's ass. His eyes took in the young one's trim figure. She could be no more than fifteen, a ripe fifteen. Perched at his Master's desk, he assumed the posture of one who was busy and important. From the corner of his eye, he watched the two go about their work.

"Well, who is the pretty one?" he asked.

The woman arched her brow and stared knowingly at him. "Yes, my daughter is very pretty, as you see. And young." After a thoughtful pause, she added, "A scrub-woman's life is very hard and the pay is poor."

He emptied his pocket and thrust thalers into her hand.

The woman squinted. "Oh, this hardly comes close to her worth— look! Maria, take off your blouse for the gentleman to see."

The girl shook herself out of her blouse and tossed it on the bed of straw.

"And she is a virgin," the woman added.

He quivered at the sight of the girl's two beauties. His hand trembled in his pocket, as he managed to produce five more thalers. "There! Now have the goodness to leave us for a time."

"Ach, I am busy as you can see. I must finish quickly and then go elsewhere. A gentleman is expecting us." She intoned "gentleman" as if to convey her disdain of Schindler, whom she regarded as no gentleman.

He took the precious morsel by the arm and led her to a corner where the Master's bed of straw was the only refuge. She slipped off her shoes and unwrapped her skirt, let it drop, and stepped out of it. In a moment she was naked on the straw with her thighs spread wide apart.

"Well then, what are you waiting for?" she said.

The damned old woman was peering out of the corner of her eye. A low type, she would no doubt enjoy the bedding of her daughter. Well, he would give her something to talk about. Holding his urgency in check, he struggled out of his britches and moved toward the girl. Suddenly he was too late. Like a schoolboy he ejaculated before he could get on his knees. The fluid ran down his bare legs onto the floor. The girl smirked, grabbed her clothing, and was out the door.

At the Zum Rosenstock he joined his friends and ordered his ale. After he downed two or three drinks, his humiliation dimmed and took on a new shape. He passed around the image of the pretty ass and boasted of his conquest.

Chapter Twenty Seven

"Accept and Submit."

Louis began his morning walk in the Castle Park and happened upon Rahel and Verhagen, who also enjoyed brisk walks early before the mid-day heat. The morning air was balmy; a light wind came down from the mountains and stirred in the treetops. Rahel had a notepad with her, anticipating they might meet up with Louis. They stopped often as she penned her questions and comments. As they came to a turn in the path, two young peasant girls in bright dresses and hair braided with willow straw approached them with basketfuls of cherries for sale. Louis reached into his pocket to pay for three baskets, but Rahel clasped his arm in hers: "Please, Louis, let me." Louis shook his arm loose: "No," he insisted. "Beethoven will pay for the cherries."

"Oh," said one of the girls, "You are Beethoven? We heard your country dances played by our village band. We danced and danced…"

"And you composed the Moonlight Sonata!" said the other. "How beautiful. All the world knows your music, you are famous." She handed three baskets to him and held up her hand to refuse payment. As the girls went on their way, one of them glanced at him over her shoulder and blew him a kiss.

As the day's warmth settled in, the three rested under a tree and began to eat the cherries. The meeting with the peasant girls stirred Louis' memory of Schiller's words:

O you multitudes, here's a loving kiss for all the world. Surely you know that beyond the starry sphere there lives a father who loves us all. Yes, but who gives a kiss to Louis? And he remembered the words: *If any man calls even one other soul his own, let him join us in our chorus. Else gnashing his teeth, he weeps bitter tears in darkness, to all the world unknown.* Unknown?…No, he was famous, the girls said so. They danced to his music, they said; and the music moved them to make love to their men, he saw it in their eyes. He moved them to love! He sprang to his feet, scattering cherries over the trimmed lawn. "The new theme must rise up from the earth and be pure and holy," he shouted. "Not holy as in church—not a hymn, but holy in a natural sense…that hoary-headed priest in Modling, he despised the girls who served him coffee—he who makes his living baptizing babies born of lusty affairs that he condemns with the voice of Jehovah out of a cloud." Passersby stopped to gape at the spectacle of the small man with the thunderous voice who disrupted the peace of their pastoral stroll.

Rahel and Verhagen looked at each other. Was this one of his spells? Bettina had warned them; they thought she embellished things, but this was frightening. Now he was ranting, "I am the one who steals away weeping…" His hands trembled; he reached for his trousers front and opened the flap. Horrified, Verhagen seized his arms from behind and forced him against the tree, his back to the gathered strollers. Then, with Rahel's help, he pulled him down to the grass and they pinned him down with their weight.

While Verhagen fastened the front of his trousers, Rahel pressed her cheek against his: "Louis, what can I do to help? Tell me…"

He senses a shift in the wind. It is gusty. Overhead high branches sway and limbs snap. At his feet small animals dart about in fear of swooping hawks; but the birds themselves flee from the coming storm. The sun is blackened as winds sweep clouds in the vale. A sudden flash of light then a thunderclap assaults his ears: his hands rush to his head, but the crash of it shakes him to his boots. From afar, but coming closer, peasant dancers stomp their feet: they throw down their fiddles and pipes and run for shelter—but there is no place to hide and they are swept away by the deluge. Their footfalls, their terror, come to life in tones: dissonant shrieks pierce his ears, drums roll, trumpets flare like shafts of light that split the sky. It is the Pastoral Symphony, but with a new and frightening dissonance. Suddenly from the deep basses comes an almost human cry; the instruments surge and press forward in restless motion; they search for a thought, a voice.

Rahel's hands flew to her face and covered her eyes for a moment: then she caught Verhagen's eye as if to say "This certainly is one of his spells. Bettina was right." They stared in horror: his frame was rigid, his eyes like hollow globes, his hands clasped to his ears in an awkward and senseless posture. They held him under the shade tree until the sun had made its way far above the mountain peaks and cast its warmth directly upon the earth. Finally Louis shuddered and opened his eyes: "I must go to the post office, I expect mail." They took him by the arms and lifted him to unsteady feet.

On the path he began to sing, *Hail to joy, immortal beauty from Elysium.* He stopped often to make entries in his notebook; then he would begin again with quickened pace. Rahel felt she was attending the birth of a new symphony.

At the post, a packet of three pieces awaited him, sent on by Schindler. One was from Schindler himself; Louis put it aside. The first he opened was from the Art Society of Graz; he knew what that was; he put it aside. The second was from Streicher; he would deal with it later. Nothing from Antonie.

Thankful for the presence of his two friends, he invited them to his room. "Look," he said, "this man Streicher…his letter is about a graphite bust he had made of me for his piano showroom. It sits atop one of the grand new pianos. I am famous, you see." He gave them the letter to read. "But," he said, "am I loved?"

Rahel wrapped her arms around him again and kissed him on his hot forehead. "Before long the whole world will love you, Louis."

The second letter was a note of gratitude from the Art Society for his gift of two violin sonatas for their charitable concert. Then he opened Schindler's letter. He read it and passed it to Rahel: "You see, someone does love me, but I cannot say who."

Master, all is well here. The woman has come to clean out the flat and did a fine job. Of course I paid her well and tipped her on top of that, so that she will want to return and she was most agreeable to that. So this matter is settled, let us hope, once and for all. I am enclosing a package with a few items of mail. The usual bills I have dealt with, although funds are running short—if so no mind, I will replenish the account and make good until you return and reimburse me. Now an item of interest. A delivery man came yesterday with a gift for you from the Countess Gallenburg. I did my duty and opened it, as you indicated I might do, so that I may evaluate matters and send you reports concerning developments. The gift is a miniature portrait on ivory of the lady herself. A sealed note accompanied the portrait; I dared not open that, of course. I have put it aside for you. You may count on me as always. Your trusted servant,

Anton Schindler

Oh, one small matter: the cleaning woman, the new one, after I had stepped out to pay your bills, decided to dust inside the drawers of your desk. When I returned I caught her staring at a portrait inside a locket, that must have fallen from some compartment deep inside the desk. I reprimanded the woman instantly and would have dismissed her on the spot, had it not been for the considerations I have indicated above. The locket was not damaged as far as I can see. Now, you know what gossips these scrub women can be—it might be wise, lest any reputation be compromised, if I were to return the locket to the person whose portrait it is—for safekeeping until you return, so that nothing can be used against her or you. You need only tell me who she is and I will do so with utmost discretion. Consider me your loyal servant as always. A.S.

Louis read the letter: "You are right," he said, "someone does love me." He passed the letter to Rahel.

Her hand went to her mouth. "But Louis, she is married—to Count Gallenburg."

"It matters little. I do not return her affections."

"Then you must discourage her interest. Require that Schindler return the gift at once. You must consider reputations—and the reputation of the other woman also."

"Ach, that countess—she sends me this message now that I am famous. Well, I shall require Schindler to return the gift at once—you shall see. Here, I shall relieve your fears…"

He went immediately to the tabletop that served as desk and penned a letter to Schindler. "There!" he exclaimed. "You see. I have no need of this woman's attentions."

Schindler, what is this about an ivory portrait from Guicciardi? The woman is married to Count Gallenburg. I gave her music lessons for a time when she was very young. Not much talent for music, but a great talent for romantic fables. Yes, she is quite foolish!—a married woman, yet she sends me a portrait of herself as if I were her lover! I have become famous—that is what inspired her to this foolishness. But we must not offend the poor soul, so do not return it. Place it in that drawer—it is concealed behind a bent nail. You should find it. When I return I will decide what to do with it. Beethoven

Rahel read the note. "Yes, Louis, you must discourage this young woman's flirtations. Now tell me, Louis, is there none other…?"

He looked up at her with fevered eyes: "I can no longer abide the solitary life," he said. "Here, read this poem; it is by Schiller." In the notebook, he penned the entire poem.

When she read the words, *"If any man calls even one other soul his own, let him join our chorus. Else, gnashing his teeth, he weeps bitter tears in darkness, to all the world unknown.."* she knew she had found this man's soul. "Louis," she said, "I—we—shall pray for you…each and every day."

"I have always been the one who crept away alone. Yes, it is I who am banished from the feast."

"Louis, what are you saying?" Tears burned in her eyes.

"The one who deserves to be banished is my father Johann—not me. Yet it is I who am alone."

Verhagen stared helplessly at Rahel and quizzed her with his eyes, as if to say, "Did you see how those two peasant girls looked at him? They would have given away more than cherries. Why then is he alone, if women throw themselves at him?" Rahel seemed not to heed the questions; she ministered tenderly to Louis, wiping his fevered brow with water from the pitcher. Suddenly she knew…

"Louis," she wrote, "you suffer an unrequited love. You love someone and your love is not returned. There is room in your heart for none other."

He lifted his eyes to her, then hid his dazed and contorted face against her bosom. Finally he spoke: "Yes, I love someone, the terrible thing is… she loves me, too."

"Ah," said Verhagen. "She is a married woman."

"Marriage! That is an invention of the priests—it keeps people chained to the one bed…" He made a sudden effort to rise from his chair, but stumbled and had to brace himself against Verhagen's shoulder. "Yes, she is married—to a man who treats her with base lust and contempt for her delicate spirit. I had hoped to get a letter from her at the post, but there was nothing, nothing…" With the force of delirium, it came over him that he must save her from Franz, that he must send the letters to her at once. The power was within him to take her small hand and stroke it; to caress her lovely neck and shoulders; to bring his warm lips close—ah, very close— to her ear, her throat, her mouth; to breathe the sweet air of her breath; to whisper his love for her and to declare to her in a soft sincere voice, that she was safe in the embrace of his arms and secure in the knowledge of his undying love…and that she must never speak of his secret shame.

"Louis, we must pray for you…"

"I despise those prayers that priests say in church; and the god they pray to is as deaf as I am."

She wrote a hasty answer: "Read the poem, Louis—the poem you love so much. *Seek Him above, in the starry vault where He dwells among the stars.*"

"Above," the poet claims. "But not here below."

Verhagen interrupted: "Louis, you should remember your Kant; the philosopher says that the power of the starry heavens resides in the human conscience. The divine is in our moral judgments, in our morality. He says a man should always act in such a way that his act should be a law for all men."

"All men? All men? Schiller too spoke of all men: All men are brothers, he says. God has ordained it so, a God whose magic joins us all and brings together even worms and angels to dwell with Him." Louis shook his head. "But these are words, only words. Who can prove them? Kant? No. Only music, my music, can prove the truth of those words—if truth there is."

"Your music, Louis," said Rahel. "If it can be done, only you…"

"You could prove Immanuel Kant's Categorical Imperative?" asked Verhagen.

Louis spat. "Kant, Kant—all I hear is Kant. The priests name their dogs after Kant." For once he agreed with the priests: reason failed to prove things that priests called matters of faith—that there is a God, that He made the world, that He cares for the world He made. Nothing, he believed, could bring God down to earth for all men to see and believe.

Into the night he struggled. The dining hall had emptied out, the last of the patrons having consumed their ale and gone to their beds. The piano was his:

An intimation, a kernel, trembles and aspires to life over quivering strings; it takes shape, bursts from the ground, and assumes immensity— a theme as jagged as strikes of lightening from God's wrath. It strides over the strings that generated it and the strings suffer under its weight; they swirl like dervishes to suck the theme back into the ground where it disappears in a column of smoke. But it rises again. The entire orchestra thrusts it upon the world with unflagging energy; it takes mighty strides over the earth. When it returns at the recapitulation its thunder shatters the world and in the coda it slams its fist upon a few glimmers of hope whispered by soft woodwinds in the far distance.

Exhausted, he fell back into a divan. An unfinished glass of ale on a serving tray caught his eye. When he had finished it, he looked for others and found some. Back to the piano, his intentions more clear, three movements of the new symphony took shape in his mind. After the menace of the first, however, there must be no relief:

A satiric dance begins to...no, demonic forces, like the dervishes that make mischief underground; now they have come to the surface. A kettledrum tuned in octaves accompanies the dumb brute forces that admit of no life, but cast an illusion like a sorcerer's spell. The dervishes retreat as a new dream ushers in a landscape of pastoral simplicity; but they return to insist that theirs is the only truth. All throughout, even in the dream, a sense of striving prevails, a longing, a clamor for a new voice.

Now, he believes, he has found an island of repose:

A static theme rises from the strings in utter contrast to all that has gone on before, followed by a lyrical theme for the second violins. No strife, no clash of mad armies, no lusting after whores, no memories of Johann: perhaps a dream of Antonie in his arms but this too is illusion. A fanfare interrupts the peace, and forte strings cry out in protest. These strings are a weak voice over against the full orchestra that calls him from his peaceful dream and would impose its doom upon the world and upon him, Louis, for his death is immanent. A second time the fanfare calls him to pass death's portal; his soul slips away. Suddenly another fanfare is heard: it is dissonant, urgent; it is the sound of fleeing feet; peasants drop their fiddles in the face of the storm that sounds in the heavens. Again, a protest: this time from basses that sound from deep within the earth.

He rose from the piano and shielded his ears with his arms. Who sends this deluge? It is the thunderous voice of a god whose wrath comes upon him because he composed a pagan symphony in which a dancing, feasting, fornicating world forgot its religion; because he consorted with the woman by the ramparts; because he failed to honor his father and save his mother; because he lusts after a beautiful and noble woman.

In the C Minor Symphony he struggled to save the world from a base, senseless assault; by dint of his courage he won out, he saved himself and the world. In the Pastoral Symphony the god's wrath sent catastrophe; but he survived and gave the world a shepherd's song of glad and grateful feelings. But the assault will come again.

He recalled that in Bonn, the university students who gathered at Helene's introduced him to Schiller and his poem *An die Freude*. So long ago…the thought of Helene brought back the land of childhood and Babette Koch. How old was he when he saw her through the window? Fifteen? Sixteen? Even then, he had honored the poem: he had taken a snatch of it and set it to music in a cantata; and somewhere in a sketchbook he had begun to set to music the words: "There surely dwells a dear father…" He had set the entire poem to music! Where was it? Not in the desk drawer, he was sure. Now he remembered—he crumpled it, took a match to it, and burned it along with some other poems the censors had banned. No—he was not afraid of the censors, not even then. He burned it for a reason more mysterious.

Babette! At night so many times she came to him, her long golden hair about her shoulders, sometimes seated at a piano, the score of the Moonlight by her side, next to a long red candle. When next she comes in a dream, he will take away the score of the Moonlight and he will put Schiller's words beside her, set them to music, and give her an immortal name—Babette!

A loving father above would have endowed him with a healthy organ so that he could hope for the consolations of conjugal love. Even if he were whole, Antonie belonged to another. What then was the voice of the raptus-angel, who spoke through Babette's sweet voice, and told him to look for another? Why should he look for a pure virginal woman akin to the angel Florestan had seen in his cell below the earth?

More and more the idol of Babette became the living goddess Antonie Brentano. The shy smile, the thin lips, the deep eyes, were Babette's. But Antonie's hair was golden, the color of a field of sun-struck wheat; and the abiding peace in her eyes was hers and hers alone.

In the morning he dressed slowly; thoughts of the preceding day and the night pressed down on him. If Rahel and Verhagen had not gone, he would seek them out for a late breakfast and tell them about the raptus visions that came to him unexpectedly during the day or at night, in the rain, under the trees. He found them taking their breakfast at an outside table, where a light wind skimmed through the pines and Rahel's hair, and a rising sun gilded everything in warm yellow. The aroma of roasted coffee brought him to his wakened senses.

"Sometimes," he told them, "I am walking on the street or in the forest, and an angel spirit takes me away and speaks to me and sings to me. Then she returns me to earth." It was important for them to understand; if they understood, perhaps others might also—like Antonie. "Or at times the raptus strikes me down, and I get up from the street or the forest floor, like a drunk. People mock me and scorn me—I know it as if I heard them with my ears. I want to say to them, cry out to them, 'I am Beethoven. I have heard voices that you do not hear. I hear the thunder of angry gods; or I hear angels who sing sweetly to me.' You must believe me."

A window opened in Verhagen's memory; he glanced at Rahel in a studied silence that she read easily: what angel causes him to reach for the opening of his trousers and expose his member to the world?

"My angel bids me to bind together the world of the gods above and world of men below." Louis went on. "If there is a loving father, only one thing can prove him to the world—that is my music."

His art; his art was his world. Only the whole embrace of mankind could he love; a particular woman, never. Helene would understand:

Dearest Mother,

It has been a while since I wrote you last. I am in Teplitz. The doctors advise the quiet of the countryside as a remedy for my tired ears, and for my digestive complaints as well. But so far nothing helps the ringing in my ears, or brings to life for me the sweet solace of the voices of my fellow men. I may or may not move on from here to Karlsbad, to take the baths—but another motive has come over me, and I do not know which way it leads me. In K. a woman awaits me, who will be my angel. I am drawn, and I am terrified at once. She is married, she is nobility. But something else—you know—my affliction, stands between us. I am afraid she will ridicule me. But she is my only hope, my only prayer. I have written three letters to her but I have not had the courage to post them. I have them in my hand, I read them over and over again—shall I send them or not? I am puzzled by my own letters; I tell her she is my immortal beloved, and then I say to her that we must sacrifice for each other, and then I say that I can never be wholly hers. Oh, I crave her with all my essence, but I cannot promise what I cannot consummate. And my art—what would become of my art if I settled down to domesticity? No— I cannot post these letters. I cannot go on to Karlsbad. I must return at once to Vienna. I must accept what the wrathful god has ordained and submit to his will.

Your devoted Louis

Chapter Twenty Eight

"I am Leaving You."

When Franz got up from her, he set his imperious gaze upon her prone figure, her waxen pallor, her meager bosom flattened by his use of her. Sometimes he wondered why he desired her so, she was so passive, so unappreciative. But she was his, and that was the truth that incited his lust. To prove his position he stood arms akimbo, placed his foot on her belly so that she could not move; she was forced to lie under the arches of his belly and see nothing but the underside of his scrotum and the suspended flaccid member. He would force her to remain upon the bed where he pitched her and laid her, her dress crumpled and gathered above her waist, her lower body exposed, until she had absorbed his lesson.

She considered herself virginal by virtue of rape and pillage: she had surrendered her virtue under the judgment of an over-powering Johann, and Franz had subdued her will; throughout her life she had been witless, preyed upon like an animal hunted for sport—but her spirit remained chaste. She was aware of beaded tears upon her lashes, that her lower lip trembled. Towering over her was a massive barrel chest, hairy belly, with a dangling limp penis, an object that she had abhorred for years. Why was his face still red, his nostrils flared? It was too much to expect that he would be satisfied with his latest pillage; he must have the letter as well.

"Where is the letter?" he asked, his eyes narrowed.

"Which letter?" she responded as best she could, her tongue hindered by the wad of paper. Would he suspect something in her mouth? Then she comprehended her real mistake.

His neck flushed and swelled. "The letter from the von Arnims. What other letter is there?" A fleck of paper on the floor caught his eye. He looked about under the bed, inside drawers—but that made no sense, he had seen it fall to the floor by the side of the bed…she had taken it! When she had her hands free behind his back, she must have…his two hands began to pry at the corners of her mouth.

The wad had gone down, but pieces cleaved to the roof of her mouth. He plunged his fist into her mouth. She clamped her teeth on his hand.

He reared back and struck her full force on the mouth. Blood streamed from the gash, her breath caught in her throat. She knew with the nerves and sinews of her being, that she loathed this tyrant over her spirit. After a few agitated breaths she spat in his face: "I am leaving you."

"You will go nowhere. You are my wife."

"I will go…I will go where I want to go..." She slipped from his grasp and ran to open the door…No, what if Maxie were there to see her father in such a state? She turned to face him, her skirts catching about her legs. He came at her, his chest heaving, fists clenched. She taunted him with his own words: "I am pregnant, remember," she sang out in triumphant song.

"And by whom, exactly, did you achieve such a state?"

"Not by your wretched member!" Let him think what he may. Her words were true: no priest would agree, but she felt that she had conceived like the Virgin Mary, pure, untouched by this man's lust. That was another question she would have taken up with the priest, but the man was an ass.

He had her by the shoulders and shook her: "What did that letter say? I demand to know." She spat onto the floor at his feet. "That letter is between me and the man who wrote it." He crossed her face again with the back of his hand. Blood seeped from her nose and ran down her dress.

"von Arnim is nobility, I am not. That is why you went to him. You have sinned in the sight of God…"

"God? God? What has our marriage to do with God?"

Whatever answer may have come from his lips mattered not: she clawed at his eyes with her nails until his arms went to his head and she was free. But where...? The letter to Louis was still under the pillow…if he saw *that*… "Do not dare let Maxie see you naked with that filthy thing of yours." She threw a bedsheet at him. There was no Maxie but he could not know. Some decency must remain in him. But he had no use for the bedsheet; he groped for the pitcher of water on the bedside table and poured it over his face, all the while cursing and groping for another pitcher. She took the letter from under the pillow, hid it inside her dress front, and was gone. If she hurried, the Post Office would still be open when she got to it. They would give her an envelope.

She dashed across the lawn to the large room where Maxie was being entertained by a governess. With the surprised girl in tow, she cut across the columnaded square, through thickets of bushes and brush, and came out on the lane that took her to the main avenue and toward the Imperial Post, oblivious to the stares of passersby who saw and commented on the blood stains on the front of her dress and the paper she clutched in her hand as if it were an urgent matter for the police.

The imperial doors swung open to her hasty push. The official stared in shock at her appearance, but she cared not at all. She asked him for an envelope and pencil. In moments she had addressed it to Herr Ludwig von Beethoven, at the Golden Lion Inn, Teplitz, Imperial Dominions, and safely handed it to the Imperial Authority. Nothing Franz could do now, within the law, would stop the letter from speeding on its way in the morning.

She prayed Louis would still be in Teplitz to receive it.

Chapter Twenty Nine

"An Angel's Love for the Asking."

The breakfast served at the inn was wasted on Louis: a large broad-faced cut ham, eggs, cresses, beetroot, medlars, and appletart, were spread out on the board; but his appetite, usually robust, had left him. A serving girl poured tea from a proud slender spout, but he demanded coffee, which with black bread served as his first meal of the day. He was unsure if there would be another.

As he took the long walk with slow tread to the Office where he would post the letter to Helene, his life's flow turned heavy and leaden. Yes, he had decided to forgo love for the sake of his art. The curse of father Johann! who dragged him from the warmth of his bed and beat him about the ears until he learned his art. Johann was right—God curse him; it was his fate to be the savior of the world. He stared at the envelope in his hand: the tenderness of her smile, the motherly way she looked upon his infirmity and said "Someday you will find one who will love you and she will not laugh."

He was about to depart for the coach when he saw a sign that advertised a visit to Teplitz that evening by a dance troupe from Munich, to perform Schuhplattein: as the sign said, a Tyrolese dance of clapping hands and music and dancers tossed high in the air. Everyone was invited to attend and join in the dancing. It caught his fancy; he could leave the following day.

A public building near the square had been emptied of its furnishings in preparation for the event, and hanging lamps lined the path to its wide swinging doors. The solid wooden floor resounded to the knocking heels of the men, the trapped hot air enclosed the sounds of clapping hands and music from three zithers on a platform. The clanking of mug-lids, the cry of "Prosit, Prosit," was heard through the evening as ale was served and wines; and a masked entertainer sang bawdy songs and told risqué jokes as he went about like a gnome tapping the women on their shoulder or knees when he came to the point of the joke, which he rendered with an appropriately lewd grin. The men seemed not to mind at all, as long as the ale flowed as free as the laughter.

Louis downed his ale with the best of them and took in the sight of the girls tossed high in the air by their partners. The atmosphere was magical: golden dust shimmered about the lamps which cast eerie light upon the dancers and all the spectators. His attention finally wandered into the pasture of his memories, where boys and girls played and danced and whirled one another about. A tap on his shoulder roused him: a slender, lithe shape glided around from the back to face him with a flashing smile; tiny rosebuds were stitched to her bodice and the hem of her skirt; she entered his nostrils like a field of lilacs. He knew her; she was one of the girls who gave him cherries—she was the one who turned and blew him the kiss. "Herr von Beethoven," she said, "may I buy you the next drink?" At that she perched herself on the bench opposite him and pointed to his glass. "And I will have one, too," she said. He understood.

He passed his notebook to her: she wrote "My name is Elizabeth." The ale came and they studied each other over the table-top as they took their drinks. She was young, not even eighteen, perhaps; but she had a knowing look about her—she was no innocent. What did she want of him...? Her knees touched him under the oaken table. When she finished her drink, she nodded sharply in the direction of the door. She wanted him to leave with her.

Scarcely knowing what he was doing, he let her take him by the hand out the door and into a graveyard where they stumbled among tilted and broken markers, crosses and enshrined saints in carved niches. His spectacles fell off... where were they?... he groped for them, all the while mindful of her urgency. Never mind, he had another pair in his room. He let her pull him to the soft earth behind a giant angel figure whose wings spread out against the moonlit sky. She opened her blouse so that he could admire her fulsome breasts.

The woman gave off an odor of decayed flowers...when she lifted her head she studied him with an intensity that made him tremble. "Whatsa matter kid, you got only one ball?" She looked more closely in the dim light. "My God, whats that rash?" She spit on the floor: "Godallmighty if you made me sick... I shoulda looked first." In the kitchen she retched and cursed. "If you ever do it to a nice girl, do it in the dark, dearie." Suddenly Helene's face emerged from a dark background: "Louis, sometimes when the gods give they take away." She gave him a mother's kiss on his forehead and said, "The right woman will come into your life and when she does you will know. What you have shown me will not matter to her. She will not laugh." At his desk he took her pencil and wrote "My angel, my all, my very self..."

Trembling, he rose and took up his clothes. The girl was gone. His head was light and giddy, his step uncertain; he rambled through hedges and clumps of fir trees whose sharp boughs beat against him and threw little showers of drops and beat his belly with their clusters of sharp needles and thistles that pierced him, and the whip of the hazel became too much for him. He rested against the trunk of a large birch, its ridges and vital knots firm and secure. The hall that had been bright with many lanterns and loud with singing and dancing was dark and empty. He was alone with his thoughts, the tree, and a heap of clothes that was too much trouble to put on. Exhausted and confused, he lay down and passed the night on a bed of hazel under the sheltering tree.

In the morning, he searched for his clothes and stepped into the dew-drenched trousers and shirt. He still had his money; the girl had taken nothing. But what had she done? He made his way back through the graveyard, his mind cast over in dark thoughts. On the door of his room was a note pinned to the door: it was from Rahel: "Louis, I looked for you all night, where were you? Verhagen and I must return on this morning's coach to Vienna. Are you staying or coming with us?"

He took his breakfast at the inn; this time he consumed omelets and toast and coffee. In his room, he took out again the three letters to Antonie: send them or no? He studied them: how intense, yet how reserved. It was Saturday. He could not leave for Vienna until Monday. Nor could he send mail or receive mail until Monday. He wandered about the streets of the village, then out into the fields, where he was happy among the wet hillocks and grassy slopes. This was his world here, among the hyacinths and primroses, where he was confident, supreme—but alone. On his back again, under the noon sun, he meditated about his raptus. The voice of Helene was so clear, so confident; the sound of it filled his being.

Sunday at the piano the new melody still sounded too much like a church hymn, perhaps because it was Sunday, and that would not do. He struggled with the harmony and the tempo. It should not be too fast. One should meditate over it, as he had meditated last night in the graveyard under the angel that spread out its wings to protect him. He played the Adagio up to the point of the violent fanfares and the sudden change of key as if he came over a hill onto a sunlit meadow. What meadow is this? Yes, that is where he died. His soul passed through a portal and came out in a sunlit beyond; he could see it almost, now he could hear it. Voices sing in his ears, all is alive, in motion: stars in their courses, men like heroes marching among the stars and singing, a jubilee of dance and song, peasants and royalty alike, in a chorus of jubilation. No heaven this, no loving father; but the spectacle of men and women with voices raised sounds in his ear. They sing Schiller: they praise a heaven-born goddess whom they call Joy, whose magic brings together all those whom stern custom has set apart, whom the priests and killjoys have set asunder. And he who has won a noble woman let him join our Jubilee. This goddess presides over a festivity in which hearts and hands and voices look to the sky above, where a loving father dwells.

What fools! he thought: the millions celebrate their love and their faith in a loving father—but they are all tipsy.

A Monday morning downpour delayed the departure of his coach to Vienna. Packed up and ready to go, he greeted the postcoach from Karlsbad. There was Antonie's letter:

> *My dearest beloved, everyday I long for you, hoping, praying...*
> *you tell me that I am your angel...Love, Tony*

He pocketed the letter. Where was the coach schedule? She did not say if she and Franz would remain long in Karlsbad or go on to Franzenbaden. Should he go on to Karlsbad at once?—Yes, if she had gone on to Franzenbaden, that was only a short distance beyond. She longed for him, she called to him—she would not laugh at him. Helene's words rang like a prophecy. His letters to her? He would not send them—they were too wavering. He must present himself to his love as a man who knows his mind. Should he destroy them? No—they were precious; he would bundle them and send them back to Vienna. Schindler would put them in the drawer with the miniature from Giulietta.

Chapter Thirty

"A Spotless Bride Awaits."

The swift piping of wind through the trees that lined Franzenbaden's cobbled square on two sides was not lost on Louis as he stepped from the coach. He heard nothing, but he felt the gusty mountain air against his face, and he stared at the clusters of white clouds scurrying across the blue sky. The world that was dumb to his ears, he ravished with eye and scent and an inner knowing; the gods had granted him this in compensation for his loss. He paused in the middle of the avenue where he roared his pleasure and made grand gestures with his arms as if leading the theater orchestra; his world was in rhythmic collusion—the clouds, the sway of trees, the flight of birds overhead. An eight horse postcoach had to rein in to avoid hitting him.

A young boy, anticipating a tip, had picked up his two bags. The boy halted in his tracks and gaped at the sight of the madman in the middle of the street howling and flapping his arms like some wild bird. A quick thinker, he darted ahead to the police station that was across the way, where the official who presided over the arrivals registry would take the matter out of his hands.

"Stop, you thieving magpie!" yelled Louis.

Louis followed the boy into the station and grabbed his two bags. "The boy is a thief, you must have him arrested," he demanded. Out of breath, he sat down heavily on a bench, all the while jabbing a finger in the boy's direction. The boy disappeared quickly, forsaking all hope of a tip.

The official, unbalanced by the vehemence of Louis' demands, managed finally to hand him a quill and point to the registry.

"Do you want to know who I am? Well, I shall tell you. I am Beethoven."

"So you say," responded the man. "Let me confer with my superior about this."

In a moment the Chief of Police came from a backroom and fired questions to the stranger, which received no response other than "I am Beethoven." Finally, the Chief threw up his hands: "Does the great Beethoven wear soiled britches? Does the great Beethoven smell of a distillery? Does the great Beethoven never groom his hair?" He determined that the stranger must be detained lest he offend the gentlefolk who visited

190

the mountain resort and expected him to maintain public decorum. But Louis' smoldering gaze deterred him: "Zwei Goldenen Lowen," he shouted.

Was it possible? The Chief called to another of the young boys who hung about looking for tips, and sent the boy running to the Two Golden Lions Inn to ask if they were expecting Louis von Beethoven on the daily coach from Karlsbad. Louis however could tolerate no waiting; he took up his bags and stormed out onto the avenue, where he was heard demanding "Zwei Goldenen Lowen?" of passersby.

The boy returned in the company of Franz Brentano. Franz found Louis and jotted a few words in a notebook: "We are fortunate to have adjoining suites at the same guesthouse, 311 Aug' Gottes auf der Weise. Antonie and the children are waiting to see you—hurry and resister here, just to please this poor Officer." Louis obliged, and permitted his friend to lead him gently by the arm down the avenue, where he stopped to gaze at passing clouds and thank the heavens that the gods had granted him another day of holy joy.

When he settled into his lodgings, little Maximilliane dashed into his room and threw herself onto his lap. He hummed for her a tune from the easy little Piano Trio that he had written just for her, and she hummed along, not quite in proper key. Then she handed him a sealed envelope, planted a kiss on his brow, and ran out. In the envelope were two notes: one from Franz, to invite him to join them for dinner in the main dining room. The other from Antonie. Clever of her: she must have slipped her note into the envelope after taking Franz's note, and sealed it herself. Her note said, "Tonight I shall come to you, late. A."

At dinner, he ordered a dark beer, Spatenbrau; but the waiter regretted that the house did not carry that beer. When Louis understood, his face turned red. Antonie knew well that a storm was about to burst. Quickly she caught his eye, took her quill, and sped a note to him: "Dear Louis, do try the Moselle with me." Louis perceived immediately the implication of their drinking the same wine; the implication was lost on Franz, who saw only his wife's diplomacy in averting a public embarrassment.

Antonie's diplomacy had already prepared other guests in the dining hall to practice toleration: "The great composer from Vienna, Herr von Beethoven, will join us soon. He is hard of hearing, and he is quite loud. And of delicate sensibilities. You must give consideration... he is great of heart, though he has a temper. The poor man suffers so."

The Leberknodel Suppe went down easily, but Antonie feared the worst when Louis ordered Schweinschnitzel. She knew he was fond of pork and critical of its preparation. "Tender it must be, and moist; yet well cooked, not rare," he advised the waiter. When the pork came, he examined it with a practiced eye, tasted a sample, and cautiously began to eat it. The entire room was immensely relieved. But then he blared: "One cannot be too careful. Herr Mozart ate pork just before he died. He was poisoned—not by Salieri, but by that ass of a butcher, the one who plays the horn. Leutgeb was his name."

Louis ordered Guglhupfen and coffee for dessert. Antonie anticipated no issue with this simple raisin-cake. But as Louis' attention was diverted from his stomach, it moved to her bosom. She understood: he read my note—he dare not speak, he answers me with his eyes. Yes, dear Louis, but we cannot let Franz suspect. Again, his eyes strayed. She could only divert Franz's attention from Louis: "Franz dear, did you enjoy your dinner? Shall we be served coffee in our suite?" But the room was full of Louis' unspoken words.

A thunderstorm broke to the south. Its lightening strikes scoured the peaks of the nearby Mittelgibirge range. Antonie thought: when it rains, he will want to go out in it. He will stand under the torrents and have a raptus. He will forget me, he will forget the world. But the storm will not last the night. The people at the inn said that storms like this come and pass quickly through the valley.

"Let us not curse the rain," said Louis, "if it falls softly." A saying he heard from the wise Neffe came to mind: 'If it must be that rain falls upon a wedding, pray that it be a soft rain, for a soft rain caresses the union.' Neffe had advised students how to compose music for a wedding—soft, so as to caress the union, like the rain if it falls. But Louis saw the flares that shot through the valley air, and feared that no union would be blessed on this night.

Antonie was relieved when Franz announced that after dinner he would join a number of men who were organizing card games and billiards in a parlor. He suggested that Antonie would be pleased to entertain their honored guest; perhaps their honored guest would entertain the other guests by improvising on the fine broadwood piano that was often unveiled after the guests had finished dining.

Louis pounced upon the piano and insisted that Antonie sit near him. "A simple waltz tune," he announced. He played it: a light unassuming piece. "A mere cobbler's patch by Diabelli," he said. "But now you shall hear it again—this time by Beethoven." It sounded like Diabelli for a moment, then it wandered into unsuspected, ethereal regions of tone. Finally he stopped, oblivious to all others, and turned to Antonie: "Ach, it is not ready yet. But someday, dear one, it shall be yours." She understood: on the night of their first love-making, her beloved had promised a dedication to her.

Toward midnight the winds picked up suddenly. The men playing cards and billiards retreated quickly into their quarters as the downpour began in earnest. Franz, having drunk too much wine at the tables and blinded by the lashing rain, stumbled on the path to 311 Aug'Gottes and lost his bearings; when he finally reached his quarters, he collapsed upon the bed and required his dear wife to help him remove his soaked garments. Antonie obliged. In minutes Franz was asleep.

She checked in on Maximilliane. The girl was asleep. Quietly she slipped out onto a canopied veranda that connected several adjoining suites. She found Louis' suite. The door was ajar, the interior illuminated only by an oil lamp that cast a golden glow over the tumbled covers on an old brass bed. No sign of Louis, no note. Of course, as she predicted, he would be outside absorbing the elements. He was a force of nature. And he would be a force in her arms this very night.

She pondered how she wished Louis to find her when he returned. In the semi-dark, her face should glow like an angel's—Louis often said she had the face of an angel. Good! The moment he walks through the door, from the dark into the light, his eyes shall fall upon the face of his angel. She lowered herself onto the divan, the oil lamp just to her side, her face turned toward the open door. No, not right—not yet: Louis' eyes often rested on her bosom. On her feet again, she undressed, letting her chemise fall to the floor about her feet.

Outside, Louis had gone down a slope behind the inn and found himself at the edge of a wood which stretched out to the distant ranges. He lay down on the moss and ferns among the trees and waited for the rain. The wind brushed past him. As a boy, he once visited Rotterdam where sea wind carried the brine and spray into his nostrils and his lungs, and foretold another wind that would sweep over him. Often he had tried to recapture the frenzy of that windswept moment by pouring ewerfuls of water over his head and letting it run down his body. The wind and the water were his raptus, his oracle, voices that called to him and made him want to seize nature by the throat and steal her secrets—secrets that were his by right.

Antonie was his by right. It was timely that the winds were playing about his limbs when he was about to claim his spotless bride, for the voices of nature taught him to love beauty. When he looked at her—any beautiful woman—he could taste God's eternity, he could bathe in the divine comeliness of her hair and bosom. But the voices—sometimes he felt that they owned the very self of him. Helene was surely right, that he had sold himself to them in return for the gift of his genius.

As the winds rushed upon him, he heard again the stomping of peasant feet in tipsy dance steps, and heard again the tympani roll that scattered those dancing feet. It was no ordinary storm he had set to music in the Pastoral Symphony; it was a cataclysm in the heavens. Only he, Beethoven, commanded such mighty, such manly powers over the orchestra, over the hearts of women, over the world. He who composed such music was Lord of the heavens. "I am the god Bacchus," he shouted, "from whose winepress comes the wine that intoxicates the world."

Yes, he commanded the drumroll; but God commanded the thunder; and the thunderous voice of God sent storms that disrupted the peace, scattered the merrymakers, and denied erotic pleasure to certain of his creatures.

The storm vented its anger. He stripped off his vest and shirt and offered his bare chest to the elements. Again he heard voices: their wordless wisdom was in the wind, in his head, in his music. Their wisdom had decided his fate; they denied him the love of a pure woman and afflicted him with lust for low women, women of the street, with whom he could relieve the urges that consumed him day and night, but whom he could never love. He was a Florestan without a Leonora. Until now. Turning his back to the wind, he groped through the thickening rain for the safety and warmth of his lodging.

Chapter Thirty One

"Who is this Angel?"

Schindler, seated at the master's desk, delved through notebooks, torn pages and scraps from inside the drawers and tucked away inside pages of books. Before him was his own notebook; he has been writing his recollections of the Master from the first day of their meeting, when he had to follow him to the tavern and force his attention upon him. All these years he has labored without recompense, often without a word of thanks.

Recompense will be his in time. Someday he will be interviewed for information concerning the Great Man's life. That day may come soon: the Master has been struggling with intestinal disorders, redness and swelling around the eyes, fevers, headaches that would strike him down and send him off to bed, pains in the chest, bouts of nosebleed, overeating, drinking, and moments of paralysis in which he would stand outside in the cold rain as if nothing existed in the world outside his deaf ears. It was rumored that the Master had the unspeakable disease, the one called lues, that men got from bedding street women. Schindler took note of the Master's scribbled words in one of the notebooks that lay open before his scrutinizing eye: *On the Art of Recognizing and Curing All Forms of Venereal Disease* by a doctor L. V. Legumann. When he first saw that almost illegible scribble he had thought nothing of it; then he had wondered if the Master intended it as a lecture and warning to his nephew, Karl, who was a wonton lad and a wastrel, according to remarks the Master had made from time to time. But now he believed that the book was for the Master's own edification.

Something at the door startled him—could it be the scrub woman? No:—she was not expected until later in the afternoon. He will be ready when that happens.

A delivery man handed him a package. He opened it with trembling hands: inside must be a letter; the Master surely will tell him to return the portrait to the lady whose name so far has been unknown to him. Now he will know. Inside, an envelope was sealed; the note was attached to it with a pin.

Schindler, What is this about an ivory portrait from Guicciardi?
The woman is married to Count Gallenburg, I gave her music

195

lessons for a time when she was very young. Not much talent for music, but a great talent for romantic fables. Yes, she is quite foolish!—a married woman, yet she sends me a portrait of herself as if I were her lover! I have become famous—this is what inspired her to this foolishness. But we must not offend the poor soul, so do not return it. Place it in that drawer—it is concealed behind a bent nail. You must have come upon it already—the scrub woman found it for you! When I return I shall compose a polite note and send the portrait back to her in a proper manner. Beethoven

P.S. Fire that impertinent scrub woman at once. And conceal this enclosed packet inside the same drawer behind the bent nail. LvB.

The ingrate—he said no word of appreciation about the tip he gave to the woman, nor did he give thought to the inconvenience of finding a replacement—something near impossible in light of the Master's arrogant treatment of such people, and the palpable filth of the flat. Well, he would have the scrub woman's services for a month at least.

The sealed envelope... he took it in his hand as if to weigh it. Something to hide away beside the portrait? If he broke the seal, he could blame it on the scrub woman, who got to it in revenge for being dismissed. Or it could perhaps be resealed: he knew someone skilled at that. His hands trembled as he opened the first of the letters:

"My Angel, my all, my very self,..."

The angel bore no name, no hint of identity. But he was encouraged: the troubled state of the Master's mind proved that he was in love with this woman. Where was Louis when he posted the letter? Where was the woman? They are planning an assignation, no doubt in the fashionable high hills of Bohemia—this meant the woman might be wealthy, possibly even nobility. He picked up the second letter: ah, something about "K." "Karlsbad?" He had heard of it. His Master will meet the woman in Karlsbad and they will be together. *"I will manage so that I can live with you,"* he writes. Where? Will this woman move into the flat? What will happen to him, will he be deemed useless, in the way, after all these years of faithful service? Or will they live somewhere else? Still, he would be dismissed. Who is this woman? Taking up the third letter, marked July 7, he is relieved: the Master will wander in distant lands—France? England?—before he returns to her. The Master calls her his *immortal beloved*, but he seems to be backing down—he needs a steady, quiet life. Perhaps this is a fanciful notion of the Master, a romance that is tinged with amorous charade. Still, he wondered. But the woman's name was not given. Of course—the letter was written to her; no need to mention her name. She is addressed only as his Angel.

Puzzled, he put the letters back into the packet and turned to another item in the day's mail. Something from Bonn caught his eye: a letter from the court Registrar at the Imperial Court. What could this be? With a knife he slit the envelope and its seal with a clean stroke. The document read:

Herr van Beethoven, As you have requested, I have examined the Court registry. The day of your birth is in fact December 16, 1770. The name of your father is Johann van Beethoven, the name of your mother is Maria Magdalena van Beethoven. I trust this satisfies your inquiry.

What error is this? van Beethoven? The Master was von Beethoven—assured title and claim to nobility. But what if the Court Register was right? The Master's nobility was in question, for van was ambiguous. And why after all would the Master write to the court about the date of his birth? His eyes narrowed. His noble Master a fraud? To impress some noble woman?

His thoughts returned to his list of candidates. Antonie Adamsberger was not of the nobility. Amalie? No. The countess Anna Marie Erdoty? Yes, she was nobility. Her life was peaceful and quiet, except for the children—and her husband! Antonie Brentano? Nobility, yes: but she too was married—and a Catholic. No —it must be someone unknown to him.

He took both portraits to the window, wiped his spectacles, and studied first one then the other. Still puzzled, he shrugged his shoulder; both could be the Countess—or one the countess and the other...?

How could he find out? He could hardly go about peering at the faces of the women on his list. A thought crossed his mind. What about a man? A man, perhaps, who knew the Master well and whom he had offended. There were many such, he knew, but some were nobility—he dared not speak to highborn men. But what about Stephan von Breuning? Now there was a man who knew the Master well; he lived close by and had been to the flat many times. True, he was nobility, but lesser nobility. Most significant: he heard the two had a falling out over a legal matter pertaining to the Master's good-for-nothing nephew, and the two had not been on speaking terms for a time. He wrote a note requesting to speak to him regarding his friend Herr Beethoven—a most delicate matter.

One evening the following week Schindler arrived at the von Breuning place at the *Rothes Haus* and was greeted by Frau von Breuning who called Stephan at once. He was guided to a table near a window that overlooked the lamp-lit city. When Stephan came, Schindler unbuttoned his tight coat and settled into a chair. Clearing his throat gently, he reached into a bag and pulled out the two portraits wrapped in a handkerchief and placed them on the table.

"Herr von Breuning, perhaps you will advise me in a delicate matter, so that I may be of service to my Master, who is presently summering in the mountains. These two portraits were given to my Master by two women—or perhaps by one woman, if the two are of the same person."

Stephan took the two portraits from his guest and studied them. "I suppose they could be of the same woman at different times in her life, or by different artists. Why is this of interest to you?"

"My master has—perhaps unwisely—asked me to keep them in the flat for safekeeping. However, many people come and go, music students, visitors, even the cleaning woman—she is efficient, but gets into things, and I fear she may be a gossip like others of her kind. It occurs to me, if I knew the name of the lady whose portrait it is, I could return them to her at least until the Master returns."

"How safe is the place you have hidden the portraits?"

"It is behind a desk drawer, a compartment secured by a bent nail—that is the Master's hiding place."

"How did you come upon it?"

Schindler froze: the man was interrogating him. "The Master trusts me with such matters."

"That sounds safe enough. How would the cleaning woman find it?"

"She pries into things—and I cannot always be present to supervise her."

Stephan studied the man. The dark eyes heavy with a sense of duty, the cheeks a hollow dark, the bony fingers, suggested scholarly, even ascetic, qualities; yet his eyes darted about and his quick nervous motions suggested some other purpose. He knew little about the factotum, other than Louis seemed to trust him. But this matter didn't smell right.

"What presumption have you made?"

Schindler pulled his clasped hands to his breast.

"Why, I claim that nothing is wrong. I merely wish to protect the Master's reputation, and possibly the honor of some lady who could be an innocent music student who sent the portrait as a gesture of gratitude. But as you know the city is full of gossipers who might wrong both my master and the lady."

"So you want to know who she is? That's what you want, is it?" He caught Schindler's eye and held it.

Something about the man's arched tone, his shrewd eye, made Schindler's face turn dead white.

"Herr von Breuning, I only wish to spare embarrassment to my Master and some innocent woman."

"Your Master does not seem overly concerned."

Things were not falling out the way he intended. He determined not to tell von Breuning that he knew the identity of one woman. He must trick the man to admitting a recognition of the unknown face—the mysterious "A."

"My Master is so busy with his music that he pays little attention to practical matters. That is why he needs me."

Stephan in fact recognized both women: Giulietta Guicciardi, in whom Louis had long since abandoned his interest; and Antonie Brentano. Louis' interest in Antonie was evident to him.

"I am sure that both are the Countess Gallenberg," he said. "Leave the matter in my hands."

Schindler understood that he was dismissed. He rose to leave.

"One more thing," Stephan said.

Schindler felt the sharp edge to the man's voice.

"Yes?"

"I must know the name of this cleaning person you are so worried about."

Schindler did not dare question the man's intent. "Her name is Frieda— I do not know the last name."

Stephan passed him a piece of note paper. "Please indicate here how I may reach her."

What did the man have in mind? Schindler wondered.

As if reading the question on Schindler's face, Stephan said, "Frau von Breuning has need of a cleaning person. You said she is efficient. You have done us a service."

On his way home Schindler's mind turned over the way the matter hand been resolved—if it was resolved. He didn't trust von Breuning; the man was nobility, and his manner bespoke contempt for one like himself, an untitled fiddler. But he had the man's statement that the woman in the two portraits was the same—Giulietta Guicciardi.

Chapter Thirty Two

"O Nameless Joy"

On his way down the sloping path he had passed a large oak, its low hanging branches catching him almost in the eye, and he had tumbled down the slope. Where now was that tree, his only marker to the path above? A sudden flash lit up the whole sky—there stood the tree, like a half-clothed skeleton hidden behind dirty gray veils. He lumbered toward it, falling several times and striking his knee against rocks. Finally he wrapped his arms around its trunk and clung to it as his anchor against the powers that swirled about him. A sudden burst caught his breath and left him gasping. Another flash in the sky opened up the path that led to the house…there! he saw it at last. Gulping for air, he set off limping toward the guesthouse. A soft glow from the oil-lamp guided his feet. The door! It was open…yes, he himself had left it open in his hurry to greet the elements. He shuddered and shook his head as he entered. Water splayed from his long hair and ran from his trousers onto the floor.

In the blue-black of the deepest corner of the suite the glow of the oil lamp rested gently on the fine features of a woman's neck and face. Darkness almost covered the body that reclined on the divan, half turned toward the open door. Her left arm fell limply across her stomach, her hand resting just below her waist. A curve lingered on her lips—a smile, the loveliest of invitations. "Close the door behind you, Louis," she said.

Louis shrank back against the door frame.

"Come to me, Louis."

In the world of his silence, he had learned to read her words as they passed her lips and beckoned to him from her eyes. In this silence he heard her call to him. And her hair—it too called to him: no longer bundled and coiffed, it draped over her bosom and flowed into the semi-dark that both concealed and revealed her figure. It invited him to disrobe, come to her side, touch and possess her.

He stumbled to a chair, sat down, and removed his shoes. Something was wrong: he could not bring himself to remove his trousers. He slumped forward and covered his face with his hands. The door remained open.

In a muffled voice he said, "I must go out."

He could not approach her with content in his bladder. He put on his shoes and tramped though the open door toward the privy. The small house was a brief walk from the inn but in the driving rain the walk was as tortuous as the climb from the forest. Darting shadows rushed past him from the toilets to the main house. Inside the privy chamber he relieved himself and examined his member. It was small and limp. Gone were the big drums of the orchestra and the roll of the tympani. He was alone in the attic, waiting for his mother; he was frightened and had soiled himself.

In the attic—that was where he had to hide from Johann, in the cold, with wet stains in the front of his britches. It seemed that his body ran away from him then, and at other times when he was afraid. When he met the whore in the street, and again when he went to the whore in the upstairs flat, he had left his body for a time and gone elsewhere while time passed. Would he leave his body behind when he tried to enter his beloved?

When he returned, Antonie was seated at the dressing table combing her long hair. She turned to him—again, the parted lips, the moist eyes…

"I must wash," he said.

A sound bulwark, this need to wash. She could not take issue. He rose and hobbled toward the toilet table, his britches around his knees. The washbasin was tipped, having broken loose from one socket.

"Why is it not mended," he raged. He was about to tear it from its stand and hurl it at the window, but he felt her hair soft against his side.

"Louis," she said, "let me pour the water for you."

She had followed him into his refuge. Where confidence had ruled, he now felt a hollowed cavity.

In the soft glow, she caught his eye, then she looked down.

What will she do? he wondered. As if in response, she knelt before him and tugged at his wet britches. He could only obey—he lifted his right leg and she pulled at its cuff and the leg was free. Then he lifted the other, and soon he was without his britches and his undergarment, bare in the blessed dimness. She rose slowly, took the pitcher, and began to pour the water over his hands and arms, letting it run down the front of his chest and belly. With the sponge she scrubbed him, then she took him by the hand.

"Come, Louis," she said; and led him to the bed.

He sat on the edge and did not resist as she reached for his feet and lifted them so that he was prone on the bed. In a moment he saw her figure beside him, then over him as she bestrided him, arms and knees bearing her weight as she bent over him. He felt her hair tease his belly. Her half-open mouth moved over his body until the tongue lighted upon his breast. Her hand, warm and moist, found his member and caressed it. Now she would know his shame, he could hide nothing, the dark availed him not at all.

Yes, she could see his infirmity, but she could not see the shame that burned on his forehead; she could not hear his heart as it panicked and thumped against his ribs as he endured her efforts to arouse him. What must she be thinking? Those lusty nights at the ramparts, with that broad-assed bitch, he was a lion, the way he took her and forced his will upon her.

Antonie sensed the distance between them; it was nothing new. This noble man had always checked his natural impulses toward her because he respected her sacred vows to her husband. But now he has sworn to sacrifice his nobility upon the altar of love; now he has declared himself in his letters and in his art; now he is here, prone under her humble caresses. If his member does not stiffen and rise, it was the last inhibition of his nobility. Soon, her art will make him a man in her arms. She lowered her head, letting her hair tease his thighs, and clasped his member in her mouth.

It was small and soft, unlike Franz. This seemed right to her; for Louis was a smaller man than Franz. But should it not stiffen? She knew that when a man's member changed its shape and became hard, he desired the woman. Louis' member remained inert. Was he not pleased with her?

Her lover was shy, he was slow to rise…those terrible things they said about him and those street trash, they were lies—she always believed in her heart that her Louis was pure; yes, Louis is pure, he is innocent, he is not of the flesh and the lusts of the flesh; he is so pure she must teach him; his soul is not down there—she should have known; she lifted her head from his belly and took his hand to her bosom and pressed her lips upon his; she needed to find his soul…it was in his eyes, his eyes, surely; she searched for his soul in the dark—dear God, if I cannot tell him of my love I must show him my love, my love is in my bosom—she rose and sat on his belly, her legs astride, her bosom and her breathing for his eyes to behold—dear Louis, I am yours, all that I am… my heart, my spirit, my love… open your eyes, lay your eyes upon my bosom, Louis, Louis, look upon me, my love swells in my bosom.

His eyes were shut.

Outside the wind was loud and distant thunder echoed in the valley. She knew that rain and thunder transported him to another world. Often she would join him and a few others as they escaped Vienna's heat and enjoyed Heiligenstadt's wild tangle of trees, shaded bowers, and cool running brooks. Louis would lie down by the running water or he would pause in an open field and let the summer wind pass through his tangle of hair. Once a downpour overtook them; she raced for shelter but he stood still as a statue, his eyes heavy-lidded, his lips moving. Surely he was in the company of angels, and soon thereafter he would show his love by bringing heaven down to earth—a heavenly song, a deathless song, a song of love.

She slipt from his inert frame and knelt beside him: "Louis, you are with the gods. I cannot go where you go. I wait for you here, my dear one, by the side of your bed."

Time paused for him. The wind was now almost spent of its fury. There were occasional cries from night owls, and once or twice the scream of a bird overtaken by some night killer. The wind's wavering voice in the pines, the smells of the night and its seeming stillness, beguiled his inner ear with a strange grace. He heard the rustling energies of the earth recover themselves after the storm, and he felt a presence, a voice that spoke in the dying wind and a face that shone in the pale light of the moon: the voice softened some part of him, something concealed, hard and insoluble, so that it yielded up its secrets to the night.

The gnawings of an unburied memory brought his hands and arms to his eyes: it was unlike other visions and dreams that had disturbed his sleep. In those dreams he had seen Maria Magdalena in the harsh light below throw a gown over her nakedness, turn toward the door that had slammed, cup her hands over her face, and weep bitter tears. And many times in trance-like visions that rose during sleepless nights her warm eyes would beam at him as she reached out to save him from Johann, whose menace was heard like stamping feet behind her. In other dreams he could hear Johann in a rasping voice sing weird ditties full of dirty words. But in this vision he saw her offer no saving arms: her gown lay rumpled at her feet, her face rouged and painted, her breasts blue-veined tumors, her stomach wrapped in stained linens from which red rivulets ran down her thighs; her eyes intent upon him in some other way. He recoiled and shrank into a corner of his mind.

Once he was out late: choir practice at the court had been extended by Neffe, and when it was finally over, as he raced through the night, he passed some building fronts that were of no interest by day; but in the gas-lit glow of one of the shabbier doorways, he saw a man and a woman. They were conversing. He heard the woman's voice: "Twenty gulden and I am yours, dearie," as she urged her hand against the front of his trousers. Her voice—he knew it. Their eyes locked for a fleeting moment.

She was a harlot!—that was the word used by the priest at the court chapel, when he explained the meaning of the icons. A large crucifix was suspended from the rood beam over the high altar, and three women stood at the foot of the cross to gape at the dying Christ as he breathed his last. One was Mary his mother, the priest said, and a second was Mary

Magdalene, who was a harlot until she met the Christ, who redeemed her; she came to honor him with her tears as he died; and she was the first to behold the empty tomb, from which the stone had been rolled away by an angel; and hers the first voice to proclaim the dawn of Easter. The image unsettled him: in the depiction the dying Christ was covered by a cloth about his loins; but even at thirteen he understood that in reality there was no covering at all. The Christ's genitals were on exhibit, exposed to the view of the gaping women, one of whom was his mother and another a whore.

In a vision he saw two women standing at the foot of his bed. One is Maria Magdalena:

Maria pours water over his fevered red-spotted body; her tears fall upon his chest and belly. She consoles him with her caresses. His strength returns; he gets up from the bed and relieves himself at the chamberpot. His little penis grows and he feels like a man.

The other woman is Johann's whore:

She opens her mouth—neither tongue nor teeth are visible; a sickly glow spreads across her face as her eyes swell with fascination at the sight of him, and her lips move as if to say, "Twenty gulden, and I'm yours, dearie." A third woman kneels by his side, her hair draped over his belly.

He is no longer in bed; he is in a fetid cell, chained to the furthest wall. An angel of God clad in light enters the blue-black night of the dungeon. Near the cell is a cistern, its mouth guarded by a large stone. The angle rolls the stone away—has she come to save him or bury him? She approaches his cell—she is dressed as a young boy—and gives him bread to eat and wine to drink. Her sweet voice sings, "You must have courage and faith." A metal door swings open; a man dressed in a black cape enters the cell and threatens him with a knife. The angel Fidelio rushes into the cell and stands between him and the darksome Johann. "First you must kill his wife," she cries. Johann would kill them both, but the angel Fidelio reaches into her trouser front to pull out a pistol which she aims at Johann's head. The orchestra trembles and quakes, but suddenly from a distant rampart sounds a trumpet. The Minister of Justice comes! Strength rises in his breast like a responding chord, as he, Don Florestan, rises to embrace his angel Leonora. O Namenloise Freude! they sing, in ecstatic union.

He dropped his arms and let them fall to the side of the bed. His head lolled side to side; a sudden and visible tremor racked the length of his body. The vision was gone, only the woman who knelt by his bed, whose plaits of hair and sweet breath played upon his belly, was visible. Who was this woman whose sweet tears fell upon his belly? The woman lifted her eyes; the light of the moon rested upon her face. Their eyes met. A slow smile of recognition appeared around his eyes and at the corners of his mouth. Peace descended upon his bed. He had found his Leonora.

*

The two lovers stepped outside to gaze at the high riding moon, whose bright face gave a warm yellow hue to the sloping fields that led to the faraway ranges of timber and rock. Its very silence was golden and gentle and confident, as had been their love-making. A mockingbird broke the silence, singing its song from its perch in a nearby copse. To Antonie, the trilling song came to her from a newly discovered world of grace, a world known to Louis when he composed the Scene by the Brook. Like the brook, the song conferred the unruffled calm of eternity. Louis had always known; now she knew.

His glance rested on her face. The mockingbird's song was in her eyes. The bird's warbling would be like a flute played by the god Pan: surprising, full of unexpected leaps and long, graceful utterances that teetered on the edge of melody, then scampered off to take up new scales. The song, like their love, assured the world of endless tomorrows, and bestowed a blessing upon all yesterdays. They waited until the day broke and the bird's trilling had tapered off into the silence of a lengthy descent. They watched as it soared from the trees and went off sailing and fluttering until it was lost against the lightening colors of the morning sky.

"I must go to Franz," she said, her head resting on his breast.

Her hand slipped from his; he understood.

Chapter Thirty Three

"The Goddess of the Altar."

They met at the canal. He took her arm and led her through the forest to a clearing that was shielded from the summer sun by large oaks. A light breeze passed through her hair; the scent of meadow flowers seemed to come from her breath as their lips touched. Finally she spoke: "Adam may have stood upon this spot when he called his bride to come and lay down with him." She knelt and drew him down to her side. The spring grass was cool and they felt the earth's peace beneath them.

When they rose he pointed to a rock that jutted out into the water. "I sat on that rock one summer day before I met you. Some field workers came to take their lunch. They stripped and bathed and splashed one another in the water. One was a beautiful young girl, who caught my eye; I admired her shapely form, her breasts, her ass. I was invited to strip and jump in with them, but I was afraid."

He took her to the rock and told her about the young men who also bathed in the water, so tall and handsome. "They would have laughed at the sight of me," he said.

"I will not laugh at the sight of you." She slipped from her perch on the rock and swam out. "Come, Louis, we are in God's light."

Her words were distant to his ears, but he read her lips and understood: they were no longer in the half-light of the inn, no longer in the shaded bower under the oaks.

For an hour they splashed each other, dunked their heads under water and bobbed up. She cupped her hands and poured water over him, then rubbed his body with tender hands. His stomach flab, his stumpy frame, his small mangled member, basked in the glow of her love.

On the rock, again, she took his member between her fingers, kissed its head, and looked up into his face. "This is your gift to me, Louis," she said.

He looked puzzled.

She wrote in his notebook: "Your feelings about your body are the most intimate of your feelings. You keep them behind closed lips. But when you show me your body in God's light, you have placed your body and your feelings on an altar."

"And you are the goddess of the altar, who accepts my offering."

They were silent for a time. Finally she lifted up blue, wondering eyes at him, and pointed to the notebook, where she wrote: "I saw the picture of a woman's ass in your sketchbook. Bettina cribbed it from Schindler."

His face reddened, he lowered his eyes.

"Was it the girl you saw that day on the rock?"

"Yes, that is the one."

Her woman's heart told her how to offer him a pure virginity. With a light kiss to his lips, she rolled over on elbows and knees and lifted up her offering. In a moment she felt the sharp pain of his entry, and a fleeting old fear came upon her, then the fear passed as a truth dawned: what she had feared so long was a beauty so fierce and demanding that it defied all reason and containment; it was an ecstasy so bold and consuming that it defied all contempt and inhibition. She knew that Louis felt the ecstasy too; his voice behind her sang the praises of a loving father above as he approached his crisis. She knew that his smallish member had achieved its manhood in the cleft of her buttocks.

Afterward as they lay upon the rock she clung to his breast, murmuring: "My love, my love."

His silence seemed fathomless. She reached for the book and wrote: "What were you singing when you came into me?"

"From Schiller's poem. Your words about the goddess at the altar stirred my memory. Joy is the goddess who brings us to places where stern custom forbids. The words are *Joy, by your magic is united what stern custom parted wide.*"

She perched on her heels and stared at him. "Dear Louis, what we just did was forbidden by morality and religion. Men and woman are not supposed to be joined the way we did. But the joy of you in me set me free from religion."

"From our Johanns, did it free us?"

She pondered his words. "Louis, the way I offered myself to you proves I am free of my father. Are you free from yours?"

He read her words but remained silent.

She picked up the pen again: "Louis, when you came inside me, you sang about a loving father who lives in the heavens."

He sang for her the first song he ever wrote, *An Einen Saugling: You still do not know whose child you are. Nevertheless there is an occult giver who cares for us all, and if I am a believer even he will be revealed.*

Turning toward her, he said, "When I have set the occult giver to music, I will have found my father." Soon the two were humming and singing the words to the simple tune he had composed as a child. Her lips proved to him that she was attuned to him.

"Tell me more about your father, Louis."

"Let us go back to the shade," he said. When they had lain down again, he took her head in her hands and told her how as a boy he had strayed into the big bedroom and saw Johann and Maria and the whore on the bed; how Johann struck him on the ears and sent him sprawling; how he heard a ringing in his ears and could not hear the screams that came from their mouths. "They were waiting for someone else to come into the room," he said, "and that is why they left the door unlocked. I believed that the man who went into that room was Count Belderbusch or George Cressener, the Englishman. One of them paid for the use of my mother; how else could Johann afford his whore?"

He felt the weight of his words at the back of his tongue. "I took pride in that thought," he said, "I even considered my father might be Friedrich Wilhelm of Prussia. That would make me nobility, you see. I didn't want to just a peasant from the lowlands."

She laid tender moist eyes on him. "Louis, you are more than royalty…"

He went on. "A portrait of my grandfather Ludwig hung on the parlor wall in Bonn. Unlike Johann, he had kind eyes. He pointed to a page of music and with those black eyes he seemed to inspire me to study and learn the divine art. I studied to please not Johann, but Ludwig. He was Kappelmeister; people respected him. I must show you the portrait; it hangs now in my flat, behind the piano. I admire the pitch of his head forward, the large forehead, the black eyes and hair…"

"Louis, you have a large forehead and lots of black hair … and those eyes of yours…"

He turned his black eyes upon her. "That is what I must tell you. When I saw the portrait after so many years, it struck me…I am a Beethoven. Not a Cressener, not a scion of Prussia… I am a Beethoven. Ludwig van Beethoven, a peasant."

She ran her fingers through his hair.

When the sun had dropped and lay low in the west, they waited for the moon to rise in the east. They saw it finally, as big as the wheels of a coach and streaked with tints of clouds that moved across its face. The two lovers contemplated the two globes that were separated by the width of the world. "We are lovers," he said, "who were as far apart as this rising moon and that vanished sun. We have overcome the world that stood between us."

She gazed upon his moonlit face. "We have not overcome all the world's inhabitants."

With a slow nod, he acknowledged that she was a married woman.

They rose and began to dress. At last he spoke. "Your words about the goddess at the altar reached me. You are my goddess, but I must find a male god, the one the poets sing about—the father I have never known."

"You will, Louis, you will—and when that day comes I will be with you one last time."

PART FOUR

"ODE TO JOY"

(1825-1827)

Chapter Thirty Four

"The Occult Giver."

Antonie smiled to herself, as the coach pulled out of Frankfurt, and contemplated two ironies. She had no difficulty persuading Franz to let her go. After all, von Arnim was not in Vienna, so Franz had no fear of that; and the tension between husband and wife was such that even Franz felt the need for relief from her vitriolic jibes and withholdings. Nor did she have difficulty taking Maxie with her: father and daughter were on hostile terms. Moreover, Maxie, now twenty one, had a boyfriend, a musician, whom she wished to impress. She had already impressed the young man when she told him that she used to lie on Beethoven's knee when she was ten years old, that he had written a little piano trio for her, and very recently had dedicated a grand piano sonata to her which, she pointed out, was a very difficult and imposing work. Now she could sweep him off his feet by going to Vienna to hear the premier of Beethoven's new Symphony; it was something unusual, people were saying, because it called for choruses and solo voices: he had set to music the words of the immortal Schiller. Antonie's ambition, however, was something she kept to herself; although she told Franz the truth, the truth that she wanted to hear the new Symphony and speak once again to its great composer. That was one irony. But as her coach made its tedious way into Austria, she considered it a poignant irony that art had separated her and Louis when last they spoke; now art would bring them together for this undoubted last time.

Franz understood nothing. Even when the package came in the mail just before she left, she had no trepidation about showing Franz its contents: a score of Louis' latest work for piano, *Variations on a Theme of Diabelli*. The work was full of fantasy, humor, passion, contemplation—traits of Louis himself. And it was dedicated to Frau Antonie Brentano. Again, she smiled. Louis' sacrifice of domestic bliss has yielded another gift to the world.

Her former home was unavailable to her. The Birkenstock mansion on the Landstrasse was emptied of all its belongings: the estate had been auctioned off in 1812, just before she met Louis, and she had left it "an artless tomb," as Clemens Brentano called it. The great collections of paintings, master drawings, and engravings she had taken to Frankfurt for herself, but all else was gone: Johann's library of seven thousand books, maps, manuscripts, and copper engravings—gone, all gone. It would be too painful for her to go near the house. Instead, Clemens, her confidant, had arranged lodgings for her in a villa outside the city, and Clemens would escort her into the city when she wished to attend the concert and meet with the composer. Clemens was entirely discreet; no one was to know of her arrival, especially not Louis—not yet.

It was a warm evening in May, ideal for a concert. When she pulled up in the carriage along with Maxie and Clemens, people were already gathered outside the Karntnerthor Theater, even though the concert would not begin for another hour. Usually on such occasions people did nothing but gossip and show off their finery, and many made a show of being late as they paraded in during the performance. But this gathering was subdued, hushed. They came early for a glimpse of the great composer because they sensed endings: Beethoven was aging, and they knew he was in poor health. She knew more than most of them: Clemens had close friends in Vienna and passed on to her what he learned about Louis' many afflictions. He always had trouble with his bowels—she knew that. From time to time a surgeon named Seibert would puncture him and draw off a quart or two of water, and that would give him temporary relief; but the bowels would become inflamed again all too soon and they would swell at inopportune times. Then there was his eyesight: his eyes were often puffy and red-streaked. More and more, his pains and his bilious disposition forced him into isolation—an isolation already ordained for him by his deafness.

Yet his moods were mercurial: an admirer could risk rebuke by knocking at his door, but be rewarded by a warm eye and grateful greeting. Clemens told her that the esteemed music critic for the *Allgemeine Musikalische Zeitung*, Friedric Rochlitz, visited Louis in his flat recently, fearing that the composer was near death and wishing to pay his respects. Rochlitz, a timid soul, had put off the visit for years, although he was known to follow Louis about on his walks, at a safe distance behind, but finally worked up the courage to go to the flat when he knew Louis was in. Louis was grateful for the visit, to the point of tears. Later, Rochlitz wrote, "The man who solaced the whole world with the voice of his music, heard no other human voice, not even that of one who wished to thank him."

Not all the talk she heard was kind, however; as far away as Frankfurt people said that Louis had reneged shamefully in his dealing with the London Philharmonic Society, which had paid him fifty pounds for the manuscript of the new Symphony, and whose management expected to give the work its world premiere, and for Louis to direct the performance or at least to attend. Louis took the money, but stayed in Vienna. Louis was a cheat, said some. She cringed at the unjust accusation, her Louis was a man of honor; people just didn't understand him, that was all. No doubt the trip would have been a challenge to his failing health; as for the money, he certainly will return it. Louis, she knew, was generous. Clemens had written her that Louis often strayed into The Black Camel Tavern where he would sit still and order nothing, his eyes glazed over as if in deep thought; then he would get up and walk out, saying not a word; but always on the table was a grand tip for the serving girl.

And there was talk that he was mad. When he summered in Wasserhof, a tale was told, he was standing silent as a statue in the middle of a country lane when suddenly, at about the time a pair of oxen driven by a young peasant lad was passing nearby, he burst into gales of laughter and began to sing to the treetops. The oxen bolted, ran into a ditch, and stayed there until Louis had gone. If the tale was true, she reasoned, Louis had seen his raptus angel in the treetops. If people failed to understand the source of Louis' genius, they were no better than the stupid beasts of the field.

Clemens nudged her: "That is Zmeskall being carried in, one of Louis' friends. He has terrible stiffening of the joints." She saw the poor man being born to his seat in a sedan chair. When he was seated, the musicians on stage began to tune their instruments. People were coming in fast; the concert would begin soon. She listened carefully to the musicians as they tuned and practiced; at other concerts she had attended, sometimes one or two of the musicians as they tuned would play a theme or passage from the new music—a portent of the miracle to come. A sudden horn call chilled her and stiffened her back, as if she had been struck. In minutes the seats would be full, and Louis would step out onto the stage and raise his arms before the orchestra.

"How large an orchestra," Clemens remarked. "I count twenty four violins, ten violas, twelve basses and cellos, doubled woodwinds... and look at the size of the drum..."

She noticed one musician mop his brow. "It is too warm on stage?"

"That is Dragonetti," he told her. "I do believe he shed a tear. He was one of Louis' greatest friends until they had a falling out."

"Yet Dragonetti is here."

Clemens smiled. "Yes, and so is Moscheles, another friend he lost. He is here, too. And another—the bassoonist in the corner there, that's Mittag. Many of these men played in the orchestra that premiered the first Piano Concerto, and they swore they would never play for him again or play any of his works, they were so offended by his manners. But they are here gladly. And there!—the Archduke Rudolph and Friedrich Wilhelm."

"Will Schindler be here?" she whispered.

He leaned toward her ear. "Yes, but of course he will not recognize you. And after the concert, he will probably join Louis and the concertmaster and a few others to celebrate the triumph—as most assuredly it will be"

"Are you certain that Schindler won't walk in on me?"

He nodded. "But I shall check with Stephan, when we get there."

She knew exactly where Louis lived. After many changes of lodgings, he had settled in at the Schwarzpanier Haus overlooking the Glacis—the coach had passed by there that day eleven years ago when they took that giddy ride up and down the avenues with the curtains drawn. She learned that he had been all but evicted from a previous lodging when the Landlord wanted him out: the two feuded over smoking flues and storm windows. Louis could be a difficult tenant, she acknowledged—the filth, the banging of the piano at all hours, the procession of visitors wanting in and strangers standing in the street staring at his window for a sight of the madman. She prayed he would be happy in this new place; it was directly across the street from an old friend from the city of his birth, Stephan von Breuning, son of Louis' motherly Helene von Breuning, who lived in the Rothes Haus. She had not yet met Stephan, but she would soon—Stephan, his wife, and his little son Gerhard, whom Louis adored and whom he called "Hosenknopf."

A seventy voice choir spread out on stage behind the orchestra, with four soloists centered in their midst. Clemens whispered: "That one on the left is Henrietta Sontag, the soprano. And Karoline Ungher next to her, the contralto. Their voices will have to carry over the entire orchestra. Seipelt and Anton Heitzinger are bass and tenor—they have strong voices."

In a moment Umlauf and Schuppanzeigh, the music directors who would give signals to the performers, stepped out to take places behind the desk that Louis would occupy. As excitement mounted, the hall grew tense and still. Before the Symphony, Antonie knew, the forces would render three sections of a religious composition that Louis had composed recently for the coronation of Archduke Rudolph, his friend and patron. It was curious, she thought, that Louis would turn to formal religion, having shown mighty scorn for priestcraft in times past. Had he changed? And she had learned that Louis had solicited subscriptions for the manuscript of the *Missa Solemnis,* and of ten subscribers the first to respond was Friedrich Wilhelm, King of Prussia. Another irony. But, thank heaven, Louis had let go of the delusion that any one other than Johann was his father.

Louis came out in a green coat—not black—was this a snub? Or did he not have a black frock coat? Should not have Schindler seen to it...? But he still looked elegant in black silk stockings and buckled shoes. He stepped up to the director's desk as if he owned the world. Yet she could not but notice his grayed hair. He put on his iron-rimmed spectacles; they must have been waiting there for him in the desk. In a moment they would hear parts of the new *Missa Solemnis*. He fumbled for a few moments, turning pages in the score before him. Suddenly his arms split the air:

Kyrie Eleison! Christe Eleison! Those words—*Lord have mercy! Christ have mercy!* Was Louis asking the mercy of forgiveness? For what sin?—his love for her, a married woman? Or the murder of his father? She alone, among all the hundreds in the theater, had such thoughts.

Credo in Unum Deum! Never had she heard these words uttered with such conviction—*I believe in one God!* But Louis had contempt for the god of the church and the priests: he believed in a god of nature who planted lusty urges in the loins of young men that made them swoop up young peasant girls and carry them off to bushes and streams. How then can he glorify the God who forbade him to romp and play in the bushes like other men? The clamor faded into a soft twilight: *Ex Maria virgine... et homo factus est.* In the music Louis contemplated the descent of the Holy Spirit who caressed the womb of the Virgin Mary so that she would conceive and bear a son. Antonie felt the caresses of Louis when she offered him her virginity on the forest altar and by the brook, but the orifice she offered him allowed no seed to enter her womb.

Et Resurrexit! The male voices of the chorus shouted the words at the top of their lungs—Jesus rises from his tomb and begins a new life as his Father's hero son. Louis, when he rose up from her, was a man among men; it was their love-making that gave him the lust to compose this mighty music, music with muscles and brawn and fiber. And their love-making helped him to be his father's hero son. Yes, in this music Louis showed himself a believer—but his belief would never fit inside a priest's confessional.

Agnus dei, qui tollis peccata mundi...Dona nobis pacem. The bass solo sang a dark and heavy laden song of a sinful world that prays God's Lamb will rid the world of its sins and bring peace. Peace? Antonie heard Louis turn his face to God in petition for peace, but distant drums and trumpet signaled the approach of cannon and foot soldiers intent upon war. The chorus took up the chant for Peace with a glorious new melody that brought the music to a close. But the ending seemed to her too soon, too easy.

At intermission she and Clemens took refuge outside the hall. A light rain had begun to fall but they felt hardly a drop. "Louis was strong," he said.

She was silent. Yes, he would crouch then leap up into the air waving his arms at a large crescendo. But when he left the stage he was stooped and haggard.

The orchestra tuned again. This time no chorus was on stage; she knew that the chorus would enter at the fourth movement to sing the *Ode to Joy*. She had read the poem many times over; it was on her lips during her private devotions in church and as she prepared for her evening bed. The audience stirred. Louis took his place still wearing the green coat; he faced the musicians and put his finger to his lips.

Only a murmur at first—a faint tremor in the violins and lower strings, like a candle's flame in a passing wind. The audience strained to hear it; it came from some distant place; yet it was familiar. Antonie was grim and tight-lipped, like the music itself; but she must take heart—Louis was speaking to her in tones. She must endure whatever might come from this mysterious beginning.

The full orchestra thundered a doom-laden theme that it seemed to pull together from notes that flickered in the wind. A sudden downrush of the violins sucked the theme back into a void where it vanished. Could it be that a merciful god decreed the theme too crushing for human souls? But the theme came back and left her gasping for breath: she found no beauty in it, nothing human at all; the god was no merciful god, he was the god of Louis' darkest night. She wanted to reach out and touch him, caress him, open her bosom to him.

She felt the chill of the music, it sank deep into her bones; it was carved from a block of ice. The thing that laid upon his spirit, whatever it was, entered her soul: the thing was rampant, hurling great chords of shock, fright, fear and dread. But she felt also a steely resolve to persist, to hold fast—to live.

The music raged. Thunder and lightening flashes from drums and trumpets and shrill woodwinds split the sky. She pictured Louis standing stark naked in a windswept field as the elements beat down upon him. Did he wish to be washed of his sins? She was sure he felt sin, but is that why he exposed himself to the elements—to be washed clean? No—she believed he took strength from the forces that crashed about his head; he drew nature's powers unto himself. That is why he composed the storm for the Pastoral Symphony, to prove his powers over the god who sent storms into the world. When he let loose his fury, at his friends, his enemies—at serving girls in taverns, even—he was proving that he had those powers within himself.

When the second movement began she heard dancing feet. Not a frolic of peasants as in the Pastoral: these were devils who mocked Louis in his efforts to shake free of the shackles laid upon him by the terrible thing. No light, no rest—only meanace, strife. Suddenly the big drum broke in; its thumping shook her to the core. What manner of beast is this that whirls us away to some place… we know not where? At the center of the movement, however, was a scene of sweet morning air that brought back the memory of times spent by the brook, lolling and grasping one another in the brush, her hair draped over his head as he rested on her opened breast. But that brief respite was brushed away by the return of the big drum and its insistent thumping. The peace could not hold.

The third movement, she knew, would be a peaceful *adagio*. Here was Louis' own heart. No longer did she hear the devils from below or thunderings from the angry deity above; she heard the pulse of a heart that longed for peace. Still holding his hand in memory, she heard her own song too, her prayer of the last eleven years, that she be resigned to the truth, the truth that she would never be wholly his. Yet the music was not cold acceptance: it had a warm heart and a manly pulse. Suddenly her dream was shattered by two raucous fanfares from the orchestra and a change of key that sucked the breath from her lungs. Louis slipped through some portal in the remote sky. He was gone; she was alone.

His death was unthinkable to her. What was life without Louis? A desolation that might beset someone exiled to a strange and baleful land came over her: no warmth, no love, no meaning; no home, no hope, no consolation. Her thoughts were echoed in a dissonant outburst from the full orchestra, a cry of pain, which provoked a cry of protest from the basses and 'cellos. Stand fast! said this new voice from the strings. The orchestra threatened to revert to themes from the first three movements, but the basses, moving in a wistful dream of solemn concords, defied the realism of woodwinds and brass. At length a pair of oboes, timid amidst the confused powers that had been contending, breathed something new. At once the basses caught its spirit and greeted it with the highest powers of their instruments. The new theme was played straight through, then 'cellos and violas chanted it to the harmony of basses and bassoons. Soon the first violins took it up, and then the full orchestra, trumpets blazing, swelled with the pride of it. Once more she heard the beating of his noble heart.

If Louis died in the third movement when the sky opened up and took him, how is he now alive in this noble and joyous new theme? Her question perished the moment it crossed her mind: she knew—he passed from the world not into a grave but into the haloed presence of his raptus angel. She knew at once, she knew, that he would come back to her.

There he was on the podium in front of her, so alive she could almost smell his body's fluids and feel the pumping of his blood as she had in Franzenbaden, where he came to life in her arms; and she could hear his voice barking out the melody, the rhythm of the new theme. He shuddered as if shaking off scales or armor; he was vibrant, alive. Surely he was with his raptus-angel. Yet he did not go rigid and roll his eyes back into their sockets; nor did he go limp and fall to the ground as he sometimes did when he heard those tones and saw his angels. He was awake, alive, and when he came back he would speak to her and all the world with the voices of four soloists and seventy choristers.

The music fell back into uncertainty; the theme lacked the power to go on. A plaintive oboe in a remote key reminded her again of the prophet's doom-saying, and the orchestra, with all the strength it could muster and more violent than ever, sounded the dissonant outburst that began the movement, and the new world that was a-birthing caved in. Then a new voice was heard: not the doom-saying prophet, but a human voice

O friends, no more these sorrowful tones.

It was as if Louis himself spoke to her.

Let us raise a song of sympathy and gladness;
O Joy, let us praise thee.

The pair of oboes piped the tune. Her heart began to dance.

Hail to Joy, immortal beauty from Elysium,
You divinity from heaven's abode,
We come to your presence inspired
To worship at your shrine.

The great theme kept its promise as it embraced Schiller's words; the poet and Louis' music were wedded in perfect union. She and Louis were wedded in perfect union.

The spell of your magic will heal
The wounds of evils past;
All men then shall be as brothers,
As you from the beginning ordained.

By stern custom she was joined to Franz; by magic she has flown to the side of her Beloved. The chorus confirmed her thoughts, sounding from behind the orchestra like all humanity speaking to her and to the world. Yes, come to the shrine where lovers are bound by an immortal spark from heaven.

Joy's great bounty is poured forth
So that friends can be loyal to one another.
And a man who has found a loving wife,
He above all shall raise his voice.

She was Louis' wife, wedded not in a church by a priest but in a forest shrine by their own deed. Louis' voice rang out, soaring above the tumult of the chorus: *And a man who has found a loving wife, he above all shall raise his voice.*

The poet's words clamored to be enlivened by the music's spell:

If any man can call even one other soul
His own, let him join us in our chorus,
Else, gnashing his teeth, he weeps
Bitter tears in darkness,
to all the world unknown.

No longer had Louis cause to steal away weeping; he could call her heart his own. They were welcome at the Feast.

Nature's bosom nurtures with draughts
Of Joy full to the brim, freely given
To the good and the wicked alike.
All living souls are blest by her largess.

Louis had taken her to the brooks and fields, where he drank to the fill from nature's bosom. Nature was his mother. He told her about Maria Magdalena, how she hid him away in the attic, how she tried to save him and his brothers from their father Johann. Maria was his human mother; but in this music Louis proclaimed that Nature herself is his mother and he sucked holy joy from her breasts.

Lowly creatures, even the worm, partake
As do the angels who dwell with God.

By slow and stately steps the chorus rose to God's presence. What the poets knew all along, Louis has set forth in harmonies. His raptus-angel took him there many a time, and now he was calling her to join him on the angel's wings. Never had she heard such power from human voices.

The music hung suspended in air, leaving an abyss:

Joyful as suns that blaze
Across the majesty of heaven,
Brothers, do your duty
Gladly, as heros go to conquest.

A drunken step-march in space: bassoon and big drum led a troupe of heroes who staggered among the stars. The intoxication, she knew, came not from the brewer's art but from the art of the music master, who alone takes men to such giddy heights where the sublime can be expressed only as the grotesque. Her eyes fixed on Louis' immense figure; she marveled as every move of his head or arm brought forth a miracle from the forces he commanded. Louis himself was the hero who led this marching band among the stars. Closer and closer they came. Finally the bass' voice was heard above the din: *"To conquest!"* he shouted. Instantly the orchestra took up the theme of heros marching among sunlit stars and doing battle with unnamed foes.

O you millions, I reach out to you
With a kiss for all the world!

A kiss for all the world! No drunken boast—but magical new wine, to be sure. A noble melody brought the poem to an exalted new realm. Now she understood: when Louis wrote the words, *No longer these tones,* he turned aside from the afflictions of his past—the bitterness of it—because his new Mother embraced him and flooded his soul with new wine. All her children were his brothers and sisters.

Brothers—above in the starry vault
Surely there lives a loving father.

First the mother, then the father. She herself did not bring Louis to the loving father; she had no loving father to share with him; her Johann was like his Johann. As fatherless children they came into each other's arms and together they searched the dark and the light for the father above.

221

Why bow down then, O millions?
Do you feel your creator near, O world?
Seek Him above, in the starry vault
Where He lives among the stars.

Not in church where people kneel before the priest at the altar, but in the fields and meadows where he tramped day and night and amidst peasants with their pipes and fiddles, he heard things that others could neither hear nor see nor name. The god of the starry heaven is in the fields below where young lovers dance and children play—closer than anyone dreamed.

He found the father not only in her arms, she knew; and not in the poet's words alone. In his mind he searched until he found himself bound in a dungeon cell, where he awaited not only his angel Leonora but a righteous Don Fernando, the Minister of Justice, who righted the wrongs committed by his father Johann and brought him to the sunlit surface and set him free.

Certainly, she believed in her heart, he must have come to know that the thundergod who struck him down was no god at all—it was only Johann.

The spell of your magic, the spell of your magic...
...All men, all men, shall be as brothers...

Louis was storming the gates of heaven with an army of children. The text, *The spell of your magic*, set to a childlike strain, was sung by the four solo voices, swinging and swaying in a free round such as children sing; their voices transported her to an enchanted world where children play innocent games and repeat their merry songs. The chorus came dashing in like god-appointed mothers and fathers who rejoice to see their little ones at play. Louis had no childhood, she knew. Her heart swelled with joy to hear the patter of *...the spell of your magic, the spell of your magic... and all men, all men...* The round could have gone on forever and she would not have minded; but the solo voices broke in with a radiant new key: *All men shall be as brothers*, they sang, as their voices rose to ecstatic heights then dissolved into a cloudless sky.

It seemed to her that the voices had gone to heaven far removed from the concerns of men; yet all the while they sang about the joyful life on earth. Louis, in the isolation of his deafness, had found the link between heaven above and earth below.

This mighty Symphony to end in a child's nursery?

No. The pagan throng of dancers from the Seventh Symphony rushed in to join the full orchestra, with cymbals, triangle, piccolo, and big drum—all was frenzy, ecstasy, lusty joy and abandon. The loving father in heaven looked down and smiled.

Antonie was on her feet along with the entire audience; they stood, they roared, they cried, they stamped their feet, they waved handkerchiefs. Louis heard nothing; his eyes were fixed on the score before him. Dear God, thought Antonie, he thinks the music is still being played. Or he is meditating about the music itself. Or he is having a raptus. Karoline Ungher came down and plucked him by the sleeve; gently she turned him around to behold what he could not hear. He looked startled. A gasp went through the audience, as they realized that he heard nothing of his own music, nothing of their love for him.

They were among the first to leave the theater and breathe the moist spring air. The clapping and shouting roared in her ears like breakers against the North Sea coastland.

The driver that Clemens hired saw them at once and pulled along side of the other waiting carriages. With her dress gathered about her ankles, she stepped into the street and accepted Clemens' hand as he drew her into the high carriage; Maxie followed, and Clemens ordered the driver to the Rothes Haus overlooking the Glacis. The three were silent for a time.

It was Clemens who finally spoke. "The outburst that began the last movement put me in mind of the Thunderstorm in the *Pastoral*. Did you feel it thus?"

"Yes," Antonie answered, after a moment's reflection. "No wonder Louis put those big drums in the score. I heard terror and running feet during the whole time, and even at the end when the violins seemed to quiver… I felt it here…" She clasped her hands over her heart.

The carriage came to a stop in front of a large three story red brick building. Antonie saw a child's face in the bay window. "That must be little Hosenknopf," Clemens said. "Louis and he are great friends; the boy goes to visit him every day and brings him cakes and sweets. Louis adores him." They hardly had to knock at the door: Hosenknopf pulled open the heavy door and grinned at them.

The boy's mother was quick to the scene. "Little Gerhard knew you were coming," she explained. "A friend of his Beethoven is a friend of ours, too. He has stayed up late just to meet you." The five year old boy was soon in Antonie's lap, giving and demanding hugs and kisses.

"Is this how he treats Herr Beethoven?" she asked.

"Oh, yes," said Frau von Breuning with a smile. "They sing and dance and play games for hours."

Stephan came down and introduced himself. "Gerhard's eyes grow heavy," he said. "We must take him up to bed, then we shall talk." The boy's head nodded in agreement: soon he was in his mother's arms, his head raised over her shoulder for one more adoring look at the beautiful lady who had come to visit him.

Maxie went up with her to help put Gerhard to bed, leaving Antonie with Stephan and Clemens. "Will Schindler return to the flat?" she asked.

"No," said Stephan, with a shake of his head. "He will be at the dinner party until late, along with the Prince and others. I will be on my way there shortly. You will have the flat to yourself."

"Louis has a portrait of me that I gave him. Schindler must have seen it. Does he know whose it is?"

Stephan broke out in a broad smile. "Louis showed me the locket with your portrait; it touched him to his very soul. Schindler came over here one day, asking questions. He had the locket with him and another; he wanted to know whose portrait it was; he thought the two were of the same woman—Giulietta Guicciardi. I let him go on believing so."

"Still, he must not see me."

He smiled again. "He will not see you. But even if he did, he is such a stubborn man he would not believe the portrait is you. He would go on insisting the two are of Giulietta. He has touted this opinion and bandied it about in the taverns. His reputation rides on it."

She stood and moved to the door: "I will go over now and wait."

Stephan took her across, lit the lamp, and left her alone in the large space. The first object to meet her eye was the large four-square oaken table that Stephan described to her: on it lay writing pads, books, pencils, quills, pipes, a metal handbell, music paper, a chronometer, a metronome, an ear trumpet of yellow metal. A large bookcase leaned against an opposite wall. In a far corner was a sack of straw littered with music scores and manuscripts, pages of books—she heard that Louis slept with his music. The sole ornament in the room was a framed portrait of a man who must be grandfather Ludwig. The resemblance struck her at once: the large head, the black hair and eyes…how could Louis have forgotten it all those years? And the older Ludwig held before him pages of sheet music; his serious but kindly face urged the beholder to study and enjoy the divine art.

In two deep window-niches lined with smooth panels hung two objects: in one niche a violin was suspended from a nail; in the other its bow. Near the windows and on a pedestal, but not so near that it could look out, was his bust, the large bronze head made by Franz Klein—she heard of it from Clemens: it faced away from the windows, as if Louis did not want it to look down upon St. Stephen's church. She sat near the windows for a time and fixed her eyes on the moonlit church and its steeple. Finally she got up and sat at the piano. A music stand was beside it, and a large red candle that tilted. She smiled. Louis must have knocked into it hundreds of times; he was so clumsy. She thought to set it straight—but no, she must not fix things, not tidy up, not domesticate him. That was what he feared most, and that was why they were apart. She did, however, place a bound score of music on the stand. After a moment's thought she moved to the straw bed and dragged it the length of the room next to the piano. Then she turned off the oil lamp and waited.

It was well after midnight when she heard the stamping of feet on the stairs and the turning of a key in the lock. In a moment Louis was inside. He shuffled about—he would be trying to light the oil lamp. Its flame rose, but slowly; it did little more than cast slivers of light about the room. She kept her eye on his dark figure as he sat to take off his shoes then stood to drop his trousers and toss his underthings into a corner. Would he sense the warmth and fragrance of her presence?—Clemens said she smelled like a field of lilacs in the spring. She smiled as he groped about for the straw bed. Not finding it, he turned up the flame. The light must set her face aglow, set before the dark night framed by the window niches. Her fingers moved over the keyboard, but of course he would hear nothing. But the light, the light on her face—it would draw him to her. In a moment he pulled up a chair and touched her lightly on her shoulder. By the motion of her fingers he would know she was playing the *Adagio* from the Moonlight Sonata, and he would see the score on the stand beside her, next to a rose candle, a candle as red as her lips.

EPILOGUE

(March 29, 1827)

"The Thunderclap."

Schindler heard the stomping of booted feet at the bottom of the stairs. Here already? It didn't matter—he had what he needed. As if to reassure himself, he clasped his hand over the coat pocket that contained the letters and the lockets. Yes, the bulge confirmed they were there. Von Breuning was first to meet him. Why did it have to be this man?—he knew about the lockets and the letters too. "How good of you to come—you are here to see to the cleaning? I have already…"

Stephan backed Schindler into the room and closed the door behind him. "This is Count Rasoumovsky, Count Moritz Lichnowsky, Prince Lobkowitz, and His Imperial Highness Archduke Rudolph— and Herr Grillparzer, Louis' very good friends. You must have heard Grillparzer's splendid oration at the church."

"Yes—'a heart expanded to much greatness.' That is true to the Master, to be sure." Schindler looked at the men; he had seen them at various public appearances and admired them for their reputations; never did he dream he would be introduced to such highborn men—and under such tense circumstances. What did they want? He looked toward the door, but the way was blocked.

A band of musicians had come to the house: they stood on the street and played an arrangement of the funeral march from the Sonata Opus 26. The men inside paused for a moment, their heads bowed in reverence.

Stephan broke the silence: "I must thank you, by the way, Schindler. You supplied a reference for our new cleaning woman a few years ago—

Freida; she is still with us. The one with the lovely daughter Maria. Surely you remember. They do good work, my wife says. Of course, the woman is an incorrigible gossip."

Schindler's face went white.

"Now you must do me another favor," he said. "Our dear departed Louis told me that I am to fetch from his desk some letters and two lockets." Stephan's eyes spoke more than his words.

"Why, the Master hid them away...I would not know..."

Stephan flared at him. "You may recall the lockets you showed me a few years ago. You could hardly forget."

Schindler knew he had made a nervous misstep.

Like a hawk swooping down on his prey, Stephan pressed his advantage: "He said something about a compartment hidden behind a drawer, held fast by a bent nail."

"He never mentioned to me..."

"Indeed?" Stephan moved to the desk. In a minute he had pulled out the bent nail and held it up to the light. "I believe we are on to it."

"Ach," said Schindler, "that drawer. I remember now. I cleaned it out this morning and I intended...I was just on my way across the street...to hand you the contents. Here..." He took the items from his coat pocket and handed them to Stephan.

"That will be all, Schindler. You may go to your tavern and join your friends."

In a moment Schindler was out the door and on his way.

Stephan left the others to join his family in the Rothes Haus, leaving the noblemen and some hired helpers to pack Louis' books and other belongings; there were decisions yet to be made—where would the broadwood piano go? Other more intimate possessions?—although Stephan could imagine nothing more intimate than the piano.

Across the street, he found Frau von Breuning serving a light dinner for Antonie and Clemens. Little Hosenknopf was all over Antonie, telling her stories about his great friend Herr Beethoven, how he often heard the pounding of the piano all the way across the street.

Antonie glanced at the boy's mother with an enquiring eye.

"Yes, at all hours of day or night," Constanza said, with a smile. "I only wish Herr Beethoven had composed more lullabies."

Stephan sat down next to Antonie. "Here are the letters and the locket—the one that is yours."

She took the letters with a trembling hand and read them. Finally she spoke. "Yes, these are the letters he wrote to me when I was in

Franzenbaden. When we parted I gave them back to him: I did not want Franz to come upon them—he looks into everything I own."

"Well, dear," said Constanza, "does that matter to you now that Louis is gone?"

The question was daunting.

Hosenknopf begged to hold the locket. "Can I keep the pretty lady's picture?" he asked.

His mother was quick to chastise him. "No, child, the picture is very dear to Frau Brentano."

Antonie looked down at the boy's crestfallen face. "Yes," she said. "It is dear to me. But you were dear to our great friend. Take the locket and keep it safe for me." His mother looked on and nodded her approval. Hosenknopf took it with an eager hand and ran upstairs to hide it away.

She looked up at Stephan with moist eyes. "And the letters too, if you will, please—it is better this way."

When Hosenknopf had been trundled off to bed, Stephan turned to Antonie: "I was sitting here in the parlor," he said, "when this storm first broke. At four in the afternoon a terrific clap of thunder split my ears. I rushed across to the flat. Louis was dead. Two of his friends were with him, so he did not die alone, thank God. I must tell you what they told me."

She nodded: "Yes, I heard the thunder myself, just as my coach passed through the city gates. It made the horses rear up."

Stephan clamped his hand on hers: "They swore that he heard it. He opened his eyes, raised his head, lifted his right hand and clenched it into a fist. Then he fell back dead."

***

Antonie arrived in Frankfurt on a foggy morning in early April, chilled and tired from the lengthy trip from Vienna. She instructed Franz that she had slept poorly during the journey and wished to be alone. He nodded and said nothing. When he had gone off to work, she locked the bedroom door and slept for an hour. It was a restless sleep; something was on her mind.

She rose and went to a closet where she kept hidden some personal items that her husband's eyes were unfit to see. One was a large leather-bound book in which she wrote down thoughts or aphorisms or wise sayings that moved her spirits when she was low: even something from Kant was there, about the sublimity of nature; and Schiller's words about love of humanity. All of it would seem harmless in Franz's eyes, who was wont to finger his way through it at times, she knew—he disturbed little ribbons that she left in certain places. But many of the sayings—most of them—were thoughts she had of Louis, or thoughts he himself held in his mind and shared with her during their times of intimacy.

Had Louis and his God communed in his last living moment? Yes, she was sure of it: but did they make peace, or did the God strike him down? She moved to her piano and played the Joy theme from the Ninth Symphony: children rose up on dancing feet; they sang songs and clapped their hands, innocent in the sight of their loving Father. There she had her answer.

On a fresh page of the book she made a new entry:

"He who truly understands my music will be delivered from all the world's evils and travails."

Louis had said that to Clemens, who passed the words on to her. Under the words she wrote:

Ludwig von Beethoven. Born December 26, 1770. Died March 26, 1827.

GLOSSARY OF TECHNICAL AND FOREIGN TERMS

Abstract or absolute music. Music with no reference to human experience. "Music for its own sake." It is the opposite of "Program music," which imitates, implies, or suggests some aspect of life.

Adagio. Slow tempo.

Allegro. Moderately fast tempo.

Andante. Walking tempo.

Ballet. A ballet is an extended theater-piece for dance. It is similar to opera, but the "text" is danced rather than sung. The composer is challenged to make music serve bodily expression. Beethoven's *Creatures of Prometheus* is his contribution to the world of ballet.

Cantata. A cantata is similar to an oratorio, in that it involves setting a text to music. But cantatas may be based on a secular text, and are usually shorter. It may involve a chorus or soloist only. Beethoven wrote two cantatas: *Cantata on the Accession of Leopold II,* and *Cantata on the Death of Joseph II.*

Concerto. A composition for one or more soloists with orchestra. It is almost always in three movements: fast, slow, fast. Cadenzas, brilliant passages for the soloist alone, are used for effect. Beethoven wrote five concertos for piano and orchestra, one for violin and orchestra; and even one for piano, violin, and cello and orchestra—a daunting work, but not his best. The concerto uses the same formal structures as a symphony: Sonata form, Theme and Variations, etc.

Con espressione. With expression.

Diabelli Variations. Beethoven's Opus 120, written in 1821-22. Beethoven took a tiny, insignificant tune from the composer Anton Diabelli, and built a universe of fantasy and invention from its kernel. He dedicated the work to Antonie Brentano.

Don Giovanni. Opera by Mozart about a dissolute seducer of women (known in lore as "Don Juan"), who murdered the father of one woman he seduced and finally was dragged down to hell by a statue come-to-life of the murdered man ("The Commandant"). Beethoven considered the opera immoral because it openly treated of sexual seductions.

Elysium. From Greek mythology, the abode of deceased heroes. In time, it came to mean paradise or heaven.

Eroica. The title of Beethoven's Third Symphony in E Flat Major, Opus 55. The word means "*Heroic.*" This symphony ushered in a new quality to music with one convulsive wrench. Beethoven began work on the symphony in 1803, intending it as a tribute to Napoleon. When his hero disgraced himself by proclaiming himself Emperor, Beethoven tore the title page to shreds and called the work simply *Eroica Symphony.*

Fugue. A polyphonic procedure in two or more voices in which imitation based upon a special subject or subjects is primary. This definition suggests absolute music, but a fugue can be written for a chorus or have extra-musical associations: Beethoven incorporated fugues into the finale of his Ninth Symphony, one of which is a kind of battle allegory following the text "...as heros on to conquest."

Largo. Slow.

Leonore, or Conjugal Love. Original title of Beethoven's opera. Later it was changed to *Fidelio.* (Note: in the English libretto, the heroine's name is spelled Leonora.)

Marriage of Figaro, The. An opera by Mozart. Figaro is a man-servant in the household of Count Almaviva. His betrothed, Susanna, will be required to spend their wedding night in bed with the Count ("Jus Primae Noctis"). Figaro, however, is clever and highly motivated; he finds ways to outwit the count.

Mass. The chief liturgical service of the Roman Catholic and Anglican Churches, five sections of which are often set to music: (1) *Kyrie Eleison, Christe Eleison* (Lord have mercy, Christ have mercy); (2) *Gloria in Excelsis Deo* (Glory to God in the Highest); (3) *Credo in Unum Deum* (I believe in One God); (4) *Sanctus et Benedictus* (Holy, Holy, Holy..., and Blessed is He who comes in the Name of the Lord); (5) *Agnus Dei ... Dona Nobis Pacem* (O Lamb of God, Grant us Peace). Beethoven wrote two masses, one in C and one in D (*Missa Solemnis*).

"Moonlight Sonata." This sobriquet was applied to Beethoven's Piano Sonata in C sharp minor Opus 27 No. 2, published in 1802. Beethoven's only designation was *quasi una fantasia* ("Like a fantasy").

Ode to Joy. The name of Schiller's poem with its utopian longings: "All men shall be brothers." Beethoven set it to music in his Ninth Symphony.

Opera. A play set to music; the text (libretto) is sung. Beethoven's only opera, *Leonore,* was premiered in 1805.

Opus. "Work." A term that designates a composition in a publisher's catalogue.

Oratorio. A setting of a religious text with a similar structure and forms as in opera. There are no costumes, scenery, or ballet. The soloists are often in fours, SATB. A narrator singing recitatives is a common feature. Beethoven wrote an oratorio, *Christ on the Mount of Olives.*

Overture. In Beethoven's day, a composition for full orchestra that might stand alone, such as his *Coriolanus* overture, or serve as prelude to an opera. It is usually in sonata form.

Program Music. Music that suggests or imitates some aspect of human experience or nature. Beethoven's Symphony #6 in F Major is subtitled *"Pastorale,"* because the symphony invites us to love and enjoy nature as he did. For example, its second movement is designated *Scene by the*

Brook; the third is designated *Merry Gathering of Villagers*; the fourth is designated *Thunderstorm*; and the fifth is *Shepherd's Song: Thanksgiving after the Storm*.

Raptus. A word used by some mystical traditions to signify an ecstatic experience that has transported a person from his ordinary life to a higher awareness or state of being. In the Bible, the Apostle Paul speaks (*2 Corinthians 12:2*) of being "caught up" into the third heaven: he uses the Greek word *harpazmo*, for which the Latin Bible uses the word *raptus*. In *1 Thessalonians 4:17*, Paul says that Christians will be "caught up" to meet Christ in the air. This is called "The Rapture" by some Christian churches.

Scherzo. Literally, "a musical joke." In Beethoven's symphonies it is a fast paced, often humorous or playful piece that replaced the traditional and stately *minueto* movement that composers such as Haydn and Mozart used for contrast in their symphonies. The scherzo gives Beethoven's symphonies greater internal contrast, a buoyant character. The scherzo in the *Eroica Symphony* offers a contrast that wakes up the audience following the twenty minute funeral march.

Sonata. The solo sonata will be written for a single instrument with full range, such as piano or organ; or for instruments such as oboe, violin, or cello, with keyboard accompaniment. These latter should be called duo sonatas. Beethoven wrote thirty two sonatas for solo piano; ten "*duo*" sonatas for violin with piano; five for cello with piano.

Sonata Form. A three part composition in which musical ideas are presented, developed, then repeated. (A.B.A.) The first section is called Exposition: it may contain two or three ideas, called "first subject," and "second subject." The second section is called Development: ideas presented in the Exposition are "worked out" in ways that surprise and delight the listener. In many of Beethoven's sonata form works, the Development explores and reveals inner meanings and essences of the original ideas. The third section is called Recapitulation: the first section is repeated, but with key changes. This form can be relatively simple or elaborate. Key relationships are important. Sonata form challenges the composer to solve certain artistic problems such as "variety within a unified structure," relationships among keys, and development of thematic materials. A Beethoven sonata form work may begin with an Introduction that suggests what is to come in the Exposition, and conclude with a coda—a brilliant finish.

Symphony. This term describes a large scale orchestral composition that is usually divided into sections called "movements," and may combine several forms, such as Sonata Form, Theme and Variations, and fugues. Beethoven's *Fifth Symphony* has four movements: *(1) Sonata form, (2) Theme and Variations, (3) Scherzo, and (4) Sonata form.*

Symphony No. 4 in B flat Major, Op. 60. It bears no title, but the world seems agreed that Beethoven's Fourth Symphony is a species of love music. Its second movement, an Adagio, particularly conveys this impression. The Scherzo is more refined than a typical Beethoven Scherzo, a hint, perhaps, that he wanted not to offend his lady love.

Symphony No. 7 in A Major, Opus 92. Beethoven provided no titles or designations for this music, yet it has an out-of-doors quality, like the *Pastoral*, and resonates with festivity and celebration. Richard Wagner called it the "Apotheosis of the dance." Its second movement happily falls short of being a funeral march. The emphasis of the Symphony is upon rhythm; its themes are shaped so as to stress movement and festive activity or celebration.

Symphony No. 9 in D Minor, Opus 125. Beethoven's last completed symphony. It is called the "Choral Symphony" because for the first time a chorus enters the domain of what had been purely instrumental music. The text for the choral finale is Johann Schiller's *Ode to Joy*. (See translation below.)

Violin Concerto in D Major, Opus 61. Beethoven's only completed concerto for violin and orchestra. It begins with four soft taps on a drum, followed by the lyrical main theme of the movement. The taps set a rhythm that pervades the movement and secures its unity.

PERSONS OF INFLUENCE IN BEETHOVEN'S LIFE*

Beethoven, Johann (1740? – 1792). Beethoven's tipsy father. Johann tried to pass off his son as a child prodigy like Mozart. Johann falsified his son's age by two years. He got into trouble with the police and needed to be rescued by Louis, who often bailed him out. On January 1, 1793, the elector of Bonn wrote Court Marshall von Schall that "the revenues from the liquor excise have suffered a loss" by the death of Johann van Beethoven.

Brentano, Antonie (1780 – 1869). Daughter of Johann Melchior Edler von Birkenstock of Vienna. She married Franz Brentano in 1798 and lived in Frankfurt. She met Beethoven in 1810 when she returned to Vienna to auction her father's estate. In 1811 Beethoven gave her, at her request, an autographed song, *An die Geliebte* ("To the Beloved"), and in 1821 he dedicated his *Diabelli Variations* to her. Scholars never considered Antonie a candidate for the honor of being his "Immortal Beloved" until Maynard Solomon's study of 1977 made it highly probable, if not certain, that she is the intended recipient of his famous love letter of 1812.

Brentano, Clemens (1778 – 1842). A poet. Brother of Bettina Brentano. He visited Teplitz in the summer of 1812, along with Varnhagen.

Brentano, Elizabeth—"Bettina" (1785 – 1859). Flirtatious friend of the poet Goethe and Beethoven. She married the poet Achim von Arnim in 1811. Sister of Clemens Brentano. Bettina wrote a book about Goethe, *Goethe's Correspondence with a Child*, and she published letters written to her by Beethoven—but these letters sound more like Bettina's imagination than Beethoven himself. She claimed that Beethoven was in love with her. She has been seriously considered for the honor of being the "Immortal Beloved."

Brentano, Franz (1765 – 1844). Half-brother of Bettina. He was a successful merchant and politician in Frankfurt. In 1798 he married Antonie von Birkenstock of Vienna and took her to Frankfurt.

Breuning, Helene von (1750 – 1838). Widowed in 1777. Her home in Bonn was a second home to young Beethoven, and a center of artistic expression and intellectual stimulation.

Breuning, Stephan von (1774 – 1827). Stephan was a friend of Beethoven from the Bonn days. He was one of three sons born to Helene von Breuning, and the father to little Gerhard (Hosenknopf) who gave pleasure to Beethoven in his last days. Stephan and Beethoven had an argument over Beethoven's nephew, Karl, but the two friends reconciled.

Fries, Moritz, Count von (1777-1826). One of Beethoven's patrons, and an earnest admirer. He was a wealthy banker, but lost his money through unwise decisions.

Goethe, Johann Wolfgang von (1749 – 1832) .The great poet from Weimar met Beethoven in 1812, in Teplitz. More than a poet, he was a man of science, philosophy, and the arts. He was infatuated with Bettina Brentano. He respected Beethoven, but was repelled by the composer's manners and deportment, calling him "an untamed personality."

Guicciardi, Giulietta (1784 – 1856). Beethoven met her in 1800 and gave her piano lessons. He had a great but fleeting interest for her and dedicated the *"Moonlight Sonata"* to her when his emotions were running high. She married Count Gallenburg. Anton Schindler was convinced that she was Beethoven's "Immortal Beloved." A miniature portrait of her was found among Beethoven's possessions at his death.

Haydn, Franz Joseph (1732 – 1809). Haydn was the most celebrated composer in Vienna when Beethoven arrived as a young man. Haydn brought sonata form to a level of high artistic accomplishment in his chamber music and symphonies. He wrote numerous operas, and was a favorite of many members of the royalty including Marie Antoinette.

"Hosenknopf" The little son of Stephan von Breuning, Gerhard, who liked to visit Beethoven when they lived across the street from each other. The affectionate term means "Trouser button." His memories of Beethoven have entered into the literature.

Kant, Immanuel (1724 – 1804). The great philosopher from Kaliningrad, East Prussia. On the subject of religion, Kant stated that creed and ritual had replaced the good life. And prayer is useless if it aims at a suspension of natural laws that hold for all experience. Worse, it is a great evil when the church becomes the instrument of a reactionary government, when priests become the tools of political repression. This is exactly what happened in Prussia in 1788, when the government of Frederick William II outlawed any teaching inconsistent with Lutheran Protestantism. Kant's political thought railed against the oligarchial powers that ruled Europe and contributed to imperialistic greed. The "Categorical Imperative" is an instance of Kant's moral philosophy: "Act so as to treat humanity whether in your own person or another, as an end, never as a means only," and "Act as if the maxim of our action were to become by our will a universal law of nature." Beethoven read Kant when he was in Bonn, and later in life he quoted the philosopher's famous words about the two wonders of life—"the starry heavens above, the moral law within."

Koch, Barbara "Babette" (dates uncertain). Daughter of the widow Koch, in Bonn. Babette helped her mother run the Zehrgarten, a tavern where many students gathered to drink and discuss political currents of the day. Babette was known as the "belle of Bonn."

Levin, Rahel (1771-1833). Rahel was an idealist and visionary who expressed her ideas of a free society through her many connections and letters. She was close to many philosophers, diplomats, actors, poets, and musicians. She advocated a Jewish-German unity, which was partly honored in 1812 when Jews in Prussia received official emancipation.

Lichnowksy, Prince Karl (1756 – 1814). The first of Beethoven's admirers and patrons in Vienna. Beethoven lived in the Lichnowsky residence for a time. His wife, Maria Christiane, a beautiful woman, one of "The Three Graces of Vienna," was also an admirer of Beethoven.

Lobkowitz, Prince Josef Franz Max (1772 – 1816). One of Beethoven's great patrons, and a guarantor of the annuity. Beethoven made him immortal when he dedicated the *Eroica Symphony* to him.

Malfatti, Therese (1792 – 1851). Niece of Dr. Johann Malfatti, who treated Beethoven for various maladies. Beethoven was infatuated with Therese and thought to ask her to marry him.

Mozart, Wolfgang Amadeus (1756-1791). A child prodigy and genius. His music was supreme in all forms, from instrumental to opera to liturgical. Beethoven may have visited him in Vienna during his first sojourn from Bonn. According to one source, he said of Beethoven that he will "make noise in the world someday."

Napoleon Boneparte (1769-1821). The self-vaunting First Consul of France, who marched all over Europe claming to liberate the masses from oppressive governments, and captured the imagination of Beethoven's humanitarian sympathies. Beethoven denounced him when he had himself crowned Emperor of all the lands he had conquered, which included Beethoven's Austria. Beethoven never met Napoleon, but was almost killed by shell fire from Napoleon's *Grand Armee* during the siege of Vienna.

Rokel, Josef August (1783-1870). A singer who took the role of Florestan in the revised *Leonore,* the title of which was changed to *Fidelio.*

Rudolph, Hapsburg Archduke of Austria (1788-1832). A great supporter of Beethoven who studied music under Beethoven's tutelage. The "*Archduke*" Trio of 1816 was dedicated to him. The *Missa Solemnis* was intended to be performed at a ceremony in 1820 that elevated Rudolph to the status of Archbishop of Olmutz. Beethoven failed to complete the work in time; but he dedicated it to the Archduke in affectionate memory of their friendship.

Salieri, Antonio (1750-1825). Musician, great friend of Haydn. Composer of many operas and instrumental works. Salieri was falsely accused of poisoning Mozart.

Sebald, Amalie. (1787-1846). A fine singer, with whom Beethoven may have had a passing romantic interest. She was one of the candidates among scholars who pondered the identity of Beethoven's "Immortal Beloved."

Schiller, Johann Christoph Friedrich (1759-1805). One of the famous figures of German Romantic literature, along with Lessing and Goethe. Professor of History at the University of Jena, he composed poems and historical dramas to express his idealism. His *Ode to Joy* influenced Beethoven, who set it to music as the choral finale of the *Ninth Symphony*.

Schindler, Anton Felix (1795-1864). Devoted "secretary" of Beethoven, and his first biographer. His biographical sketches of Beethoven are tainted with his personal biases. He was convinced that Giulietta Guicciardi was Beethoven's lover and the recipient of the threefold love letter of 1812.

Varnhagen, von ense, Karl August (1786-1858). A fine poet and diplomat. He joined Beethoven in Teplitz in 1811 and thus began a fine friendship. His wife was Rahel Levin, whom Beethoven met when the engaged couple were in Teplitz in 1812. Rahel was considered by some to be the one Beethoven had in mind when he composed the song cycle "To the Distant Beloved," and thus that she must also be the "Immortal Beloved."

Zmeskall, Nikolaus (1759-1833). Zmeskall formed a friendship with Beethoven soon after Beethoven arrived in Vienna, and the friendship stood up until the end. We must thank him for much biographical material of quality more reliable than that of Schindler.

*This list is limited to those persons who are mentioned in *My Angel Leonora*.

SCHILLER'S ODE TO JOY

Hail to Joy, Immortal beauty from Elysium,
You divinity from Heaven's abode,
We come to your presence inspired
To worship at your shrine.
The magic of your spell will heal
The wounds of evils past.
All men then shall be as brothers,
As you from the beginning ordained.

Joy's great bounty is poured forth
So that friends will be loyal to one another.
And a man who has found a loving wife,
He above all should raise his voice.
If any man calls even one other soul
His own, let him join our chorus.
Else, gnashing his teeth, he weeps
Bitter tears in darkness,
To all the world unknown.

Nature's bosom nurtures with draughts
Of joy full to the brim, and freely given
To the good and the wicked alike.
All living souls are blessed by her largess.
Wine and kisses she bestows to us,
She is our true friend on life's way.
Lowly creatures, even the worm, partake
As do the angels who dwell with God.

Joyful as the suns that blaze
Across the majesty of heaven,
Heros march in file among the stars,
In the holy vault above where surely there
Must dwell a loving Father.

O you millions, I reach out to you
With a kiss for all the world.
Brothers—above in the starry vault
Surely there lives a loving Father.

Why then bow you down, O millions?
Do you feel your Creator near, o world?
Seek Him above, in the starry vault
Where He dwells among the stars.

(Translated from the German by Carter Gregory)

GRILLPARZER'S FUNERAL ORATION
(excerpt)

"He fled the world because in the depths of his loving nature he found no means by which to deal with the world. If he withdrew from men it was because they did not want to climb up to him and he could not descend to them. He dwelt alone, because he found no second Self. Yet to the end his heart beat for all men…

Thus he was, thus he died, thus will he live till the end of time."

March 29, 1827

ABOUT THE AUTHOR

Carter Gregory is a psychotherapist whose work has immersed him in the study of troubled persons whose childhood, like Beethoven's, was distorted by family discord, conflict, and alcoholism. Mr. Gregory is also a priest of the Episcopal Church and a Certified Pastoral Counselor. He has lectured on the subject of spirituality and the arts. He is a member of Phi Beta Kappa and he engages in numerous musical, religious, and cultureal endeavors. The life and music of Beethoven has been the subject of a lifelong study that has lead to the writing of My Angel Leonora, a fictional presentation of the composer's relationship with his father and with women. Mr. Gregory's first book, The Fourth Watch of the Night, explores the mythic dimension of the lives of great men such as Jesus and Paul.

Mr. Gregory's work as a Pastoral Counselor has proved to him the power of the "Monomyth," as Joseph Campbell calls it, in the lives of people who strive for spiritual growth. The mythic journey consists of three stages. The "hero" answers a call to separate from his family and the familiar world of his origins, and seek a new life that is compelling, mysterious, full of wonders and fraught with dangers. He achieves status in this new realm of meaning and elevated purpose. Finally, he is empowered to return to his origins as a transfigured individual with great wisdom and power, from which he confers a gift to his fellows. In My Angel Leonora, Mr. Gregory traces Beethoven's journey from Bonn to Vienna and a second journey from Vienna to the Bohemian mountains where, with the help of a woman's love, he achieves his apotheosis.

Mr. Gregory, at his home in Dutchess County, New York, is currently working on a new book that will be a study in death, rebirth, and newness of life: A dedicated priest discovers that in a former life he was a sociopathic criminal.

Printed in the United States
32993LVS00004B/394-402

9 781420 802337